Criminal litigation

First steps to survival

Anthony Metzer is a barrister practising in both criminal and civil law at Doughty Street Chambers, a common law set with a reputation for civil liberties and human rights work. He has considerable trial and appellate experience in all the criminal courts and has been involved in many of the leading death row cases to the Privy Council from the Caribbean.

Julian Weinberg qualified as a solicitor in 1985 and is now a partner at Clifford Watts Compton in north London. He has considerable experience as a duty solicitor at eight London schemes and as a court duty solicitor at two schemes.

Criminal litigation
First steps to survival

Anthony Metzer and Julian Weinberg

Legal Action Group
1999

First edition published in Great Britain 1999
by LAG Education and Service Trust Limited
242 Pentonville Road, London N1 9UN

British Library Cataloguing in Publication Data
A CIP catalogue record for this book is available from the British Library

ISBN 0 905099 83 4

Typeset by Legal Action Group
Printed in Great Britain by Bell & Bain Ltd, Glasgow

Foreword
by Baroness Helena Kennedy QC

All newly-qualified criminal practitioners have had the experience of receiving a brief and feeling blind panic. The next problem is where to turn. Even more practised lawyers have been in the situation where they ought to know a simple point of law or procedure, but have not got it at their fingertips.

Anthony Metzer and Julian Weinberg have written an excellent book, which is highly readable and easily accessible; it identifies and successfully fills a clear gap in the criminal law. The content ranges from a helpful and up-to-date summary of the law and procedure in all the criminal courts to guidance in areas neglected by formal training, such as client care, professional ethics and how best to succeed in the potentially daunting arena of the courtroom. It is also of considerable help in de-mystifying the whole court set-up and the solicitor/barrister relationship.

I would strongly recommend this book, which will be an invaluable aid both inside and outside court.

Acknowledgments

We should like to thank Sally Hatfield at Doughty Street Chambers with whom the first ideas for writing a guide for criminal practitioners were discussed; David Walsh at Simons, Muirhead and Burton for his assistance in regard to the disclosure legislation; Christine Kings, the Practice Manager at Doughty Street, who provided the initial encouragement and subsequent wise counsel, and all the staff at LAG, who have shown remarkable patience and understanding towards us, coupled with considerable good sense throughout the book's genesis.

On a more personal level, we should like to thank our families, families-in-law, friends, colleagues and numerous other lawyers for their support and advice, and in particular to Louise and Mandy and our children, Jonathan, Anya and Rebecca, and Natasha and Jake, to whom this book is dedicated.

The law in England and Wales is stated as at 1 November 1998.

Contents

Table of cases

Table of statutes

Table of statutory instruments

Abbreviations

CDA 1998   Crime and Disorder Act 1998
CJA 1967   Criminal Justice Act 1967
CJPOA 1994   Criminal Justice and Public Order Act 1994
CPIA 1996   Criminal Procedure and Investigations Act 1996
CYPA 1933   Children and Young Persons Act 1933
MCA 1980   Magistrates' Courts Act 1980
OAPA 1861   Offences Against the Person Act 1861
PCCA 1984   Police and Criminal Evidence Act 1984

CPS   Crown Prosecution Service
DSS   Department of Social Security
PII   public interest immunity
YOI   young offender institution

Introduction

In writing this book, great consideration was given to how such a well-documented area of law, namely criminal litigation, could be approached from a fresh perspective. Any newly-qualified solicitor or barrister will be aware that there are already many sources in which to look up the law. Therefore, there is little purpose in this book repeating that which the newly-qualified practitioner can readily research from such well-established authorities as, for example, *Archbold* or *Blackstones* – which, between them, detail the law covering most substantive offences, together with related areas such as sentencing powers and evidence. In addition, criminal litigation practitioners can keep themselves regularly appraised of developments by keeping abreast of case reports as and when they are published. The intention, therefore, is not to 'tread on the toes' of such publications to which all practitioners will no doubt refer at some time.

In addition, the Law Society's continuing professional development requirements for solicitors now require that all newly-qualified solicitors undertake 48 hours of continuing education over each three-year period. The range of courses available to the practitioner is diverse and covers most aspects of the practitioner's life, from applying to become a duty solicitor to presenting forceful and compelling pleas of mitigation. Each area that is the subject of a continuing education course is a detailed subject in itself, and the sheer physical size and weight of publications such as *Archbold*, *Blackstones* or, for example, Wilkinson's *Road Traffic Offences*, bears witness to the complexity of those areas. For this reason, we thought that a further publication on the subject of criminal litigation should adopt a fresh approach and present the reader with a perspective not found elsewhere.

Every solicitor or barrister, regardless of when s/he qualified, will recall the day s/he passed the final examinations. That euphoria would invariably be coupled with the belief that s/he knew everything on his/her subject. By the time that trainee solicitor had concluded articles, or that pupil had completed a pupillage, s/he will have become aware that qualification was merely a starting point in a process of continuous learning. A solicitor's or barrister's first attendance in the magistrates' court is invariably a nerve-racking experience, no matter how straightforward the hearing may be. Six months on, hearings of the same nature pose less of a worry for a more experienced advocate. Until now, little consideration has been given to providing advocates with essential practical assistance either in preparing cases or in presenting them at court – somehow, it is a skill that a solicitor or barrister is left to acquire at his/her own pace. Coupled with that, newly-qualified solicitors and barristers may feel some embarrassment in asking their more experienced colleagues for advice about handling situations that they may feel they should already know about.

The concept of this book was devised to assist solicitors and barristers in such situations. It aims to provide a source of reference for those recently qualified, to assist in areas that are either neglected or skimmed over by the educational establishments and in order to provide practical down-to-earth advice in areas where little formal training is given. As an example, all solicitors and barristers will anticipate that, in the majority of cases, their client will be legally-aided. But when should the application be made and in what form? How are delays in the granting of legal aid to be avoided? All solicitors will be aware that when instructions are taken from their clients, a proof of evidence should be drawn up and barristers will expect to see the same in their brief. What information should the solicitor be looking for and what areas of the client's case should it cover? Similarly, solicitors and barristers dealing with a client's first appearance in court will be fully aware of the provisions of the Bail Act 1976 and, therefore, this book does not seek to dwell on the minutiae of its provisions. Instead, the bias is geared towards ensuring that the advocate making the bail application has taken adequate instructions and that s/he is sufficiently acquainted with the relevant facts to make as compelling and as forceful an application as possible. Similar thinking has gone into all the chapters of this book. It is hoped that it will provide the reader, who may well wish to read this publication in conjunction with established text books, with sufficient practical advice to ensure that s/he has taken care of the practicalities of that particular stage in the proceedings.

New solicitors and barristers will learn that, if they are to survive in a competitive market and further the best interests of their clients, in what is, after all, a rewarding and satisfying area of the law, then they must master not only the law governing the area in question, but also those areas of client care and professional ethics and, ultimately, receive remuneration for that expertise which in turn requires a detailed knowledge of the workings of the legal aid system.

The aim of this book, therefore, is not to render other text books redundant but, instead, to provide a framework around which solicitors and barristers can apply their knowledge of these other areas to better effect, thereby improving their own performance and, ultimately, improving the service provided to their clients.

The book is structured in a way which takes the reader in chronological order through the criminal process. Thus, the book begins with a chapter about the duty solicitor, where a solicitor or barrister may first encounter the defendant that s/he is to represent. Obviously, there are occasions where the defendant is first encountered at the police station. However, this is a substantial topic in itself and one that is more than adequately covered in Cape with Luqmani, *Defending Suspects at Police Stations* (LAG, 3rd edn, forthcoming). The book then deals with the continuing legal process through the courts, from the application for legal aid, through to sentencing and appeals, covering each topic in the order in which the reader is most likely to encounter that particular area of the criminal process.

The duty solicitor at court

Introduction

1.1   The court duty solicitor scheme was established to make free and independent legal advice available to defendants who attend court at their first hearing who would otherwise be without legal representation. The scheme was designed to enable solicitors to advise and represent defendants at their initial hearing on a non-means-tested basis.

1.2   The current regulations regarding the selection of duty solicitors are covered by the Legal Aid Board *Duty Solicitor Arrangements 1997.*[1] The relevant sections (ie, paras 31 to 48) dealing with the selection of court duty solicitors (as opposed to police station duty solicitors) are set out in Part V (see appendix I).

What is the scope of the scheme?

1.3   Paragraph 25(6) allows the appropriate local committee to limit the number of magistrates' courts at which a solicitor may appear as a duty solicitor – the number is currently set at two. While acting as a duty solicitor, the following services can be offered to any defendant who approaches the duty solicitor, wishing to receive either advice and/or representation from him/her in the following circumstances, namely:[2]

1)   To give advice to any defendant who appears at court in custody. Defendants may appear in custody unrepresented where, for example, they had not requested a solicitor to represent them at the police station, but, when having been charged and having been refused bail, feel that their interests are best served by seeking legal advice or representation once produced at court in custody. It is also not uncommon for defendants to appear at court unrepresented even where they had nominated a firm of solicitors to represent them at the police station. This may occur where, for example, on being charged with an offence for which they may be unlikely to be granted legal aid, they may have been advised that they should seek the advice of the duty solicitor at court who would still be able to represent them free of charge,

---

1   As amended by the *Duty Solicitor (Amendment) Arrangements 1998* paras 22(3)–(6), 38(2) and (4), 48(2)–(6) and 61(2) with effect from 1 May 1998.
2   See Legal Aid Board *Duty Solicitor Arrangements 1997* para 50.

irrespective of whether or not they would be granted legal aid if they were to apply for it.

2) To make a bail application unless the defendant has had a similar application made on his/her behalf on a previous occasion.

3) To represent any defendant who appears in custody on a guilty plea where the defendant wishes the case to be dealt with at that appearance in court. The scheme does not cover representation where the case should be adjourned either in the interests of justice or of the defendant himself.

4) To give advice and representation to any defendant who appears before the court for non-payment of fines or other sums ordered to be paid where s/he has previously been convicted or has failed to comply with any other order of the court in circumstances where failure to pay may lead to the defendant being at risk of imprisonment.

5) To give advice and, if appropriate, representation to any defendant who, although s/he may not be in custody, requires advice or representation.

6) To give help to any defendant to make an application for legal aid in respect of any subsequent appearance of that defendant before the court. In such circumstances, the duty solicitor is under an obligation to enquire whether or not that defendant wishes to instruct another solicitor to represent him/her or whether s/he wishes the duty solicitor to continue acting. The name of the appropriate solicitor should then be inserted in the relevant section on the legal aid application form.

7) To give advice and, if appropriate, representation to the parent/guardian of a child under 16 years old if the court proposes to bind over the parent/guardian under Criminal Justice Act 1991 s58, or where such an order has been breached.

1.4   As a general rule, unless there are exceptional circumstances, a duty solicitor is not entitled to represent defendants in respect of cases where they are charged with a non-imprisonable offence.[3] In addition, the scheme does not cover duty solicitors to represent defendants where they have previously been advised or represented by the duty solicitor in that same case, or where legal aid has previously been refused. Furthermore, a duty solicitor cannot represent a defendant when the duty solicitor or a member of his/her firm is representing the Crown Prosecution Service (CPS) in the same courtroom.[4]

---

3   Ibid para 51.
4   Ibid para 51(3).

1.5   It should be emphasised that in all cases, where a solicitor acts as a duty solicitor at court and the defendant's case is adjourned to another date, the defendant must be notified of his/her right to instruct other solicitors should s/he so wish.

1.6   As a result of those requirements and limitations on a duty solicitor, s/he will usually find him/herself being instructed at the defendant's first hearing or, alternatively, where an otherwise unrepresented defendant appears in custody following his/her previous non-attendance at court on the execution of a 'no bail warrant'.

Practical considerations

1.7   The work of a duty solicitor differs from that of a solicitor attending court to deal with one of his/her own defendant's cases in that, when attending court, s/he will know neither the number of people that will require his/her services nor how complex those cases may be. In addition, not having previously met the defendant, s/he will be unaware of any particular difficulties that may be encountered in taking comprehensive instructions. Therefore, a duty solicitor should always attend court as early as possible to allow sufficient time to take as comprehensive instructions as possible from the greatest number of defendants who may require his/her services before the court sits.

1.8   The duty solicitor's first step should then be to attend the court cells to enquire whether or not there are any defendants in custody who require advice and/or representation. In practice, taking instructions from defendants in custody is likely to take longer than from those on bail, given that the question of bail will have to be discussed as well as any other matters, eg, pleas, sentencing and, where appropriate, mode of trial. Reference should be made to chapter 3 on bail applications for details of instructions that should be taken where a bail application is to be made on behalf of a defendant. Once initial instructions have been taken, the duty solicitor should try to make contact with the CPS representative and establish, at the very least, the following information:

1) The precise details of the charge, although this will be known if the defendant has retained his/her copy of the charge sheet.
2) A summary of the evidence. If possible, a copy of the prosecution statements should be obtained and considered.

3) Details of why the defendant appears in custody.

4) The prosecution's views about whether or not bail is opposed or whether any conditions would be acceptable to the prosecution.

5) Whether, in the case of either-way offences, the prosecution is in a position to deal with plea before venue and, where appropriate, mode of trial and, if so, what its views are (for further information see chapter 5 on mode of trial proceedings).

6) Whether, if appropriate, the prosecution would be prepared to consider accepting guilty pleas to alternative charges. This may be of particular relevance to clients who, for example, would be prepared to plead guilty to 'allowing to be carried', as opposed to taking and driving away, where a defendant is in custody, and may not be granted bail if the case were to be adjourned for trial. By approaching the CPS in such circumstances, the client may be able to enter a guilty plea at the first opportunity, ensure maximum credit for an early guilty plea (pursuant to Criminal Justice and Public Order Act 1994 s48), and possibly secure an early release, if his/her case is concluded at that hearing without the need for a further adjournment, eg, for a pre-sentence report.

1.9 The above information gleaned from the CPS may well differ from the instructions obtained from the defendant. Any inconsistencies should be ironed out with the defendant before his/her case is called into court, so that a coherent case can be presented.

1.10 Where relevant to the defendant's case, all the above factors (unless there appears to be a particular difficulty) should be considered with the CPS representative in respect of all cases, whether or not the defendant appears in custody or on bail from the police station following charge.

What information should be obtained from the defendant?

1.11 The answer will depend primarily upon the nature of the charge the defendant faces, ie, whether or not the charge is summary only, either-way or indictable only, and whether or not the defendant appears at court on bail or in custody. The defendant's first hearing at which the duty solicitor acts may cover a number of different aspects of the defendant's case.

Matters commonly raised at first hearings

1.12   A typical morning at court as a duty solicitor may involve dealing with any permutation of the following hearings, namely:

1) A formal remand, either on bail or in custody. This may be requested for any of the following reasons:
   a) to adjourn the defendant's case to apply for legal aid;
   b) to request or, if already received, to consider a copy of any prosecution statements that the Crown may be under an obligation to serve in accordance with the Magistrates' Courts (Advance Information) Rules 1985;[5]
   c) to approach the CPS formally in writing with a view to agreeing a form of disposal, for example, by inviting the Crown to consider discontinuing proceedings, agreeing for a defendant to be bound over or by inviting the Crown to accept a plea to a lesser charge than the one that the defendant faces. Examples might include where a defendant would be prepared to offer a guilty plea to a charge of common assault as opposed to assault occasioning actual bodily harm, to possession of a bladed point as opposed to possession of an offensive weapon, or to a charge of possession of drugs as opposed to possession with intent to supply drugs. In cases such as these, where the weight of the list may result in the CPS representative having insufficient time to consider those proposals at court, adjournments for the CPS to consider such proposals from defence solicitors is commonplace.

2) Plea before venue and mode of trial proceedings (see chapter 5).
3) Guilty pleas.
4) Bail applications.
5) Hearings in respect of unpaid fines where the defendant is at risk of being committed to prison.

1.13   A duty solicitor may be asked to deal with various aspects of a client's case. S/he should therefore be careful to ensure that the instructions taken are as comprehensive as possible. Where plea before venue and mode of trial proceedings are to be dealt with, or bail applications are to be made, reference should be made to the relevant chapters in this book (chapters 3, 5 and 10) which detail the nature of the instructions that should be taken in those circumstances. However, in all cases, the following details should be

5   SI No 601.

obtained wherever possible for each and every defendant that is represented by the duty solicitor:

1) Name.
2) Address and phone number. Instructions should be taken about how long the defendant has resided at that address and in what capacity s/he lives there. Are the premises privately rented, owner-occupied or is it council or housing association accommodation? Does s/he live there alone or with others?
3) Marital status. Is the defendant cohabiting?
4) Details of financial dependants, if any.
5) Employment status. Is the defendant employed? If so, for how long and in what position? What are his/her income and outgoings? Is s/he in receipt of welfare benefits? What is the likelihood of the defendant finding work?
6) Details of the defendant's previous convictions, if any, and record of offending while on bail, if relevant.
7) Details of the defendant's proposed plea and the basis for that plea.
8) Name of the police station at which the defendant was detained, together with the date. This information is important in the event that a request needs to be made at a later time for a copy of the custody record and tape of any interview given.
9) Details of admissions, if any, made to police while detained in police custody. Was the defendant interviewed and, if so, what was said? Brief instructions on the defendant's version of events should be obtained.
10) Does the defendant suffer from any addiction to either alcohol or any illicit drug? Is the defendant suffering from any mental or physical disorder?
11) In the event that a guilty plea is to be entered, appropriate instructions for mitigation should be taken (see paras 14.17–14.28).

1.14   Once the above instructions have been obtained, the duty solicitor will have a clearer view of whether or not the case can proceed at that hearing or whether it should be adjourned to another date, in which case, if appropriate, an application for legal aid can then be made. A duty solicitor should ensure that the instructions taken are as complete as possible in order to avoid repeated requests throughout the defendant's hearing to take further instructions. It is inevitable that there will be times when, owing to the pressure to take instructions from a large number of defendants, duty solicitors will be unable to take full instructions on all aspects of each defendant's case. However, every effort should be made to ensure that such eventualities are kept to a minimum. Many solicitors find it useful to attend court with pre-prepared checklists to ensure that instructions are taken in a consistent manner. Such checklists should at least cover the above aspects of any client's case.

1.15   Once instructions have been obtained from defendants in custody, those defendants who appear at court on bail ('extended bail' cases) should then be seen and appropriate instructions sought.

1.16   There will always be occasions at busy periods when some defendants will resent having to wait for what they consider to be an inordinately long period of time to see the duty solicitor. How each solicitor deals with such scenarios is a matter of personal style. Solicitors should, however, always try to retain a sense of calm. Failure to do so, at its best, is undignified and, at its worst, will result in the solicitor failing to allocate sufficient time to each defendant so that s/he can fully prepare for that defendant's hearing. A poor performance at the defendant's first hearing will not be the best preparation for protecting the defendant's interests.

Mentally disordered defendants

1.17   Not infrequently, mentally disordered defendants attend court for their first hearing unrepresented (and very often in custody because their lifestyle may be such that they have no fixed address, or because, rightly or wrongly, the custody officer at the police station where they were detained may be of the view that, if released, they may do harm to themselves, or not understand the significance of having to appear at court to answer their bail). The mental disorder itself may well be the reason for the defendant forfeiting his/her right to legal advice at the police station. Taking instructions from mentally disordered defendants can be especially difficult and time-consuming. However, the situation has been eased over recent years because an increasing number of courts now provide access to a duty mental health worker at court. If a solicitor (duty solicitor or otherwise) suspects that it may be appropriate for a psychiatric assessment to be made of the defendant, then a duty mental health worker system should be contacted and asked to make an initial assessment on whether a formal psychiatric assessment should follow.

1.18   A limited number of courts operate a system whereby defendants can be professionally assessed by a team of psychiatrists at court. Where appropriate, cases can be remitted to those courts for an assessment to be made at the earliest possible opportunity. Duty solicitors should also consider asking the CPS whether or not it remains in the public interest to continue with the prosecution in the case of relatively trivial cases where a mentally disordered defendant may have been detained in custody for some time (eg, most of the weekend when a defendant has been arrested on Saturday and appears in court on Monday morning).

CHAPTER 2

Legal aid

Introduction

2.1   Strictly speaking, the question of legal aid has no bearing on court procedure per se, as legal aid only affects the basis on which solicitors or counsel receive their remuneration. However, because legal aid issues are so inextricably linked with criminal proceedings, this chapter discusses its workings. This chapter is not a detailed guide to the Legal Aid Act 1988; it concentrates on the practical issues which arise throughout the course of criminal proceedings. For more detailed analysis of the current legal aid provisions, reference should be made to the Legal Aid Board's *Legal Aid Handbook* (Sweet & Maxwell, annual).

When should legal aid be applied for?

2.2   An application for legal aid should be dealt with at the earliest possible opportunity. At this point it is important to distinguish between those defendants who are charged at the police station and kept in custody to appear in court the following day, and those who are met for the first time while on police bail after charge, or, alternatively, are bailed to appear at court from the police station. Such cases are commonly referred to as 'extended bail' cases (see para 2.4).

Overnight prisoners

2.3   In the case of those defendants who have been remanded in custody by the police to appear at court the following day, it is good practice to complete a legal aid application form (a copy of which is reproduced in appendix J) while at the police station so that the form can be lodged in court at the earliest opportunity (usually first thing the next morning). Very often, the solicitor who attended at the police station may not be the advocate attending court the next day for the defendant's first appearance. This may occur, for example, where a colleague of the solicitor attending court represented the client at the police station. If, for example, counsel is to be briefed to appear at that first hearing, there is little purpose in completing the legal aid application form while at the police station unless that form will be passed to the advocate who will be appearing at court the next day. If that is not possible, the responsibility for completion of the application form should be left to the advocate at court, who should complete the form and ensure that it is signed by the defendant and lodged with the legal aid office before the first hearing.

Extended bail cases

2.4 In cases where defendants are bailed to appear at court, legal aid application forms should, again, be completed and submitted to the court's legal aid office at the earliest opportunity, usually after the defendant has been charged at the police station. If that is not possible, arrangements should be made for the form to be completed as soon as possible thereafter. Many courts, regretfully, take some time to process applications. Furthermore, the length of time that it takes for the results of those applications to be notified to solicitors varies significantly from court to court. It is best to give courts as much time as possible to process applications in case solicitors have to deal with any requisitions raised by the legal aid officer.

2.5 It should be pointed out that the magistrates are generally sympathetic if legal aid applications have not been processed by the first hearing. This is likely to occur in cases where applications have been lodged but there has been a difficulty in complying with a particular query raised by the legal aid officer before an order can be granted. For example, where a delay in submitting an application form results from a defendant having delayed in supplying proof of income or state benefit as required. Where a defendant has failed to take any steps to ensure that s/he is represented, eg, by failing to contact a firm of solicitors and, as such, has not taken any steps to complete an application form, the courts may be less willing (or even unwilling) to grant a further adjournment to allow the defendant to do that. Neither defendants, nor their legal advisers, should assume that a second adjournment will be granted as a matter of course in any event.

2.6 Inevitably, there are times when applications for legal aid have to be made at the time of the first hearing. This may occur, for example, if an advocate is at court and another defendant of the firm also requires representation by that advocate, for example, because s/he regularly uses that firm but until then has made no contact with that firm. In those cases, even though a written application for legal aid will have to be lodged at court, many advocates adopt the practice of making an application for legal aid orally in court. In cases where legal aid is 'granted' in court, advocates should be aware not only that written applications must still be lodged with the legal aid office, but that the effect of 'granting' legal aid is only to state that, in the magistrate's view, the case is one which is suitable for legal aid to be granted. The defendant must still be financially eligible. The fact that the court has considered a case to be suitable for legal aid should be stated on the application form. Again, practice varies between courts about whether they would be prepared to entertain an oral application in court. Stipendiary magistrates generally appear to be more willing to certify in court that a case is suitable for legal aid. Advocates who appear regularly in the same court will soon learn that court's practice. Where magistrates are not prepared to certify the suitability of a case for legal aid in open court, applications should be lodged with the legal aid office of that court. In practice, where applications are made orally in open court, the application would usually be made at the end of the hearing. Advocates should therefore be aware of the potential difficulty that arises if a defendant's case is concluded at that first hearing and legal aid is then refused.

What information should be included in the legal aid application form?

2.7   Legal aid is granted in those cases where two criteria are satisfied:[1]

1) it must be in the interests of justice for legal aid to be granted; and
2) the defendant must be financially eligible.

Legal aid can, therefore, only be refused where it does not appear to the court or the justices' clerk that the above criteria are made out.[2] To assist in deciding whether these preconditions have been met, detailed guidance notes issued jointly by the Lord Chancellor's Department, the Legal Aid Board and the Justices' Clerks Society have been issued and these are reproduced in appendix K .

2.8   Therefore, as much information as possible, to ensure that those conditions can be met, should be included on the form. Solicitors or

---

1   Legal Aid Board *Legal Aid Handbook 1997/8* Part One: Notes for Guidance, 18–06.
2   Legal Aid in Criminal and Care Proceedings (General) Regulations 1989 SI No 344.

counsel should be careful to ensure that all relevant sections of the form are completed and in as much detail as possible.

Completing the form

2.9   Particular care should be taken to complete fully the section of the application form dealing with the reason why legal aid should be granted. Completing the form inadequately or incompletely may result in the processing of the application being delayed. Particular care should be taken to ensure that defendants sign both parts of the legal aid application forms (known as Forms 1 and 5). Form 1 requires the applicant to give personal details and to state the reasons why legal aid should be granted. Form 5, in essence, deals with the applicant's financial situation. In the case of defendants under the age of 16, their parent or guardian should complete the means section of the application form (Form 5), giving details of their own income and, in due course, providing supporting documentation of their income. Defendants over the age of 16 should complete the application form themselves, giving their own income details. Occasionally, defendants refuse to sign the application form (eg, because they may be unusually difficult) and in those circumstances, advocates may sign on their behalf although an explanation should be given about why that has been done. Illiterate defendants should also be carefully guided through the forms and should be asked to leave their mark where appropriate, even if it is only a cross.

Special considerations in multi-defendant cases

2.10   Where a solicitor represents one of two or more defendants, advocates should be aware that the court will only grant legal aid to one firm (usually the firm that lodges the defendant's application form first in time).[3] This will be the case unless, when the form is lodged, reasons are given about why it is appropriate for legal aid to be granted to more than one firm. This may be necessary where there is, for example, a conflict of interest between defendants or some other reason why the same firm of solicitors cannot represent all the defendants. In many cases, the conflict will be quite apparent,

3   Notes for Guidance (see note 1) 18–11.

eg, where both co-defendants deny the allegations but blames their co-defendant for the offence in question). In other cases, a conflict may be more difficult to establish. For example, when dealing with a large multi-party conspiracy, it may simply be impracticable to know whether or not a conflict exists between any or all defendants because each solicitor may only have dealt with one of the suspects at the police station and, until full instructions are taken from each defendant and/or other defendants, it may not be known whether a conflict exists. In those circumstances, if there is likely to be a conflict, reference should be made to the likelihood of this at the appropriate section of the legal aid application form.

What supporting documentation should also be lodged?

2.11   Legal Aid in Criminal and Care Proceedings (General) Regulations 1989[4] reg 24(1) states that:

> The court or the proper officer may at any time require the applicant, the legally assisted person or the appropriate contributor to provide further evidence of any information given in a statement of means or of any change in his financial circumstances together with such additional information as the court or the proper officer may require.

Regulation 24(2) goes on to state the position where an applicant is unable to provide such supporting documentation. It states:

> Where representation is granted to an applicant who provided a reasonable explanation of why, at the time of submission of the statement of means, it was not reasonably practicable to provide supporting documentary evidence, the court or proper officer may subsequently require the assisted person to provide documentary evidence where it appears that it has become reasonably practicable to do so.

2.12   Such circumstances may arise, for example, where a defendant initially appears in custody, and as such is unable to provide documentation to confirm his financial position, but is subsequently granted bail. While there is no authority for a time limit for supplying such documentation, the courts will, as a matter of policy, require the documentation to be provided within 14 days after a defendant's release from custody.

---

4   SI No 344 as amended.

2.13   Such documentation may be in the form of, for example, proof of receipt of state benefits, be it income support or jobseekers' allowance or payslips if defendants are in employment. In the case of those defendants in receipt of state benefits, the courts will accept a letter from the Benefits Agency confirming that the defendant receives a particular benefit and giving details of the amount payable. A copy of the giro-cheque that a defendant receives is also acceptable. Solicitors should take care to ensure that whatever documentary evidence is provided, it refers to the type of state benefit received and the amount of it. Proof that a defendant is out of work will not suffice. The Lord Chancellor's Department has now directed that the courts should not accept a copy of the UB40 form as appropriate proof that a defendant is in receipt of income support. To avoid difficulties, in cases where the defendant receives state benefits, solicitors should ensure that a signed letter of authority is obtained from the defendant to approach the Department of Social Security (DSS) directly to receive written confirmation from it about his/her financial position. Confirmatory letters received from the DSS are invariably accepted by the courts as satisfactory evidence of receipt of state benefits. Defendants in employment should lodge payslips or a letter from their employers confirming their income. If a defendant has no income but is supported by his/her family, for example, in the case of younger defendants living at home, a letter from the defendant's parents confirming that fact will be required, together with documentary evidence to confirm his/her own income.

2.14   If defendants do not personally receive any income but their spouse or partner with whom they live does, then an accompanying letter from the spouse or partner should be provided with the legal aid application form, confirming that they live together and that that individual supports the defendant. The spouse's resources will be aggregated with the defendant's in deciding on the defendant's financial eligibility,[5] unless they are living separately or the spouse's interests are at odds with the defendant's,[6] for example, where a husband is alleged to have assaulted his wife.

2.15   Solicitors should be aware that the assets of persons other than the applicant for legal aid may be taken into account following the introduction of a discretionary power that affects applications made

5   Civil Legal Aid (Assessment of Resources) Regulations 1989 SI No 338 reg 7(1).
6   Ibid reg 7(2).

on or after 1 June 1996.[7] The regulation applies where the defendant has transferred resources to another or where a third party has been maintaining the defendant, or where that third party's resources have been made available to the defendant. In such circumstances, those resources may be treated as the applicant's resources, and documentary proof confirming that person's finances will have to be produced to the court.

2.16   Delay in submitting acceptable documentation will result in a delay in the application being processed. Application forms lodged without appropriate supporting documentation will be returned to solicitors who will be asked to resubmit them as and when the necessary documentation becomes available.

2.17   Similarly, where a legal aid applicant wishes any of his/her expenses to be taken into account in determining his/her financial eligibility, documentary evidence to support those expenses should be lodged with the application form. By way of example, a copy of a client's tenancy agreement will satisfy the court of the amount of rent payable, or a letter from a client's mortgagee confirming the amount of any mortgage repayments will suffice to verify those payments. While the courts tend to disregard everyday living expenses, such as food, lighting and heating, the following non-exhaustive list gives an indication of those expenses which the courts will take into account (subject to production of supporting documentation to confirm those payments):

1) rent
2) mortgage payments
3) council tax payments
4) travel costs to and from work
5) debt repayments to a bank or other financial institution
6) hire purchase payments
7) loan repayments, for example, on credit card or store card debts
8) maintenance payments for children/estranged spouses.

2.18   Where defendants are remanded in custody, documentary evidence confirming their financial position would not usually be required while they remain in custody. If the defendant is granted bail subsequently, documentary evidence will have to be submitted to the court within 14 days of his/her release from custody, otherwise the courts may withdraw legal aid. The courts take the view that, once a

7   1989 SI No 338 (see note 5) reg 7A, as added by Civil Legal Aid (Assessment of Resources) (Amendment) Regulations 1996 SI No 434.

defendant has been released from custody, it then becomes reasonable for him/her to provide documentary evidence to confirm his/her financial position.[8] Solicitors and their defendants would be informed in writing by the court of such an intention so that appropriate steps can be taken to provide the outstanding documentation. Solicitors' and counsel's fees would, of course, be covered up to the date of withdrawal but solicitors should be careful to warn defendants that, if their legal aid is withdrawn, the firm cannot continue to represent them under the legal aid scheme, which may result in the defendant appearing at court unrepresented at the next hearing.

2.19   As a matter of good practice, unless impracticable to do so (eg, because the form is completed and lodged at court at the same time), copies of legal aid applications should always be kept on file, in case reference to the application is made by the court at a later date (or even in the event that the court loses the application form).

What if legal aid is refused?

2.20   If legal aid is refused, a notice stating the reasons for refusal will be sent to the defendant and to his/her nominated solicitors. Legal aid may be refused because the court does not consider it to be in the interests of justice to grant legal aid, by which it means that the case is not so serious that a community disposal or custody are likely case dispositions, or, alternatively, based on the defendant's means as disclosed on the application form, it calculates that the defendant is not financially eligible for legal aid.

2.21   In such circumstances it is, of course, possible for defendants to instruct solicitors privately. However, solicitors should always consider whether there are grounds for reapplying to the court or, unless the case relates to a summary only offence, appealing against the refusal to grant legal aid to the legal aid area committee. Solicitors should always advise defendants about their rights of appeal and about the likely success or failure of any appeal. In any event, a new application can always be submitted if there is a change of circumstances, financial or otherwise.

8   Ibid reg 23(5).

What if the defendant's circumstances change?

2.22   Defendants should always be advised that if their financial circumstances change then that information should be given to the court. A further statement of means may need to be submitted. The court will advise the solicitor if this is the case or whether a covering letter dealing with the change will suffice. This may result in defendants become financially eligible when they were previously not, any contribution order being revoked or a contribution being required towards the costs of their legal aid.

What does the legal aid order cover?

2.23   Where legal aid is granted, care should be taken to ensure that the order covers the charges that the defendant faces. It may sound obvious, but solicitors and counsel should be aware that throughout the course of proceedings, charges may be added or substituted and for solicitors' and defendants' own protection, care should be taken to ensure that the appropriate amendment of any legal aid order is forthcoming. Following the confirmed point of principle,[9] a separate fee can be claimed for offences of failure to appear and solicitors and counsel should take care to ensure that when charges under the Bail Act are put to defendants, an application is made in court to extend the legal aid order to cover that further charge. Such an application can be made orally in court and, if granted, a 'follow-up' letter to the court should be written to ensure that the amending order is forwarded to solicitors.

2.24   Practitioners should also be aware that unless what is known as a 'through order' is received', ie, an order granted in the magistrates' court which covers representation for both the magistrates' court and Crown Court proceedings, an application would have to be made at the end of any committal hearing (whether it is a Magistrates' Courts Act 1980 s6(2) committal or an 'old style' committal – see chapter 7) for legal aid to be extended to cover the Crown Court proceedings. Do not take it for granted that the court will automatically extend legal aid to cover the Crown Court proceedings – it will not do so unless an application is made. When that application is made, the court should be notified, where appropriate,

9   Legal Aid Board reference CRIMLA 42 and Notes for Guidance (see note 1) 18–65.

that there is no change in the defendant's financial circumstances. If his/her financial position has altered, a new statement of means should be lodged with the legal aid office.

Who is covered under a legal aid order?

2.25   In the magistrates' court, legal aid orders generally only cover representation by solicitors. Of course, on many occasions, where a solicitor is personally unable to attend court, counsel may have to be instructed. This is commonplace, but fees should be agreed with counsel's clerk before any hearing. Any fee agreed with counsel will in due course need to be deducted from the solicitor's fixed fee when submitting the claim for costs on the appropriate claim form to the Legal Aid Board. There is an exception where a certificate for counsel is granted pursuant to Legal Aid and Criminal Care Proceedings (General) Regulations 1989 reg 44(3)(a). A certificate covering representation by counsel in the magistrates' court will only be granted where the case is unusually grave or difficult and thereby justifies the assignment of counsel. Applications must be made in writing to the 'proper officer', namely the legal aid clerk.[10] A certificate for counsel cannot be granted by magistrates on an oral application in court. Where legal aid is extended at committal (or where a through order is initially granted), legal aid will cover the services of junior counsel to conduct proceedings at the Crown Court and also to advise on any appeal following conviction. In serious cases, where the services of Queen's Counsel are sought, junior counsel should prepare the necessary advice which solicitors should submit to the Crown Court legal aid officer for his/her decision. However, both solicitors and counsel should take care to check the scope of any order authorising the instruction of second counsel. A Queen's Counsel can only be instructed where the order specifically refers to Queen's Counsel as opposed to a leading junior counsel. Should it not do so, and a Queen's Counsel is briefed, that Queen's Counsel's fees will not be covered under that order.

2.26   Where cases proceed beyond the Crown Court to the Court of Appeal, generally speaking, both solicitors and counsel will be covered to deal with the drafting of initial grounds and advice on appeal, and for submitting papers to the Court of Appeal. However,

10 Legal Aid in Criminal and Care Proceedings (General) Regulations 1989 reg 53.

orders will only cover the instruction of counsel in respect of Court of Appeal hearings. In exceptional circumstances, the scope of the legal aid order may also cover solicitors.

What should be done with the legal aid orders at the end of a case?

2.27   When either magistrates' courts or Crown Court proceedings are concluded, care should be taken to ensure that legal aid claim forms are submitted within three months, in the case of magistrates' court proceedings, to the relevant legal aid area office and, in the case of Crown Court proceedings, to the taxing officer at the relevant Crown Court. Counsel's Crown Court fees will be dealt with by their clerks but, in the case of magistrates' court proceedings, solicitors should ensure that counsel's clerk submits to their instructing solicitors the appropriate counsel's fee note (form CLAIM 9) so that solicitors can submit their claim for costs form (either on form CLAIM 7 where a lower standard is being claimed, or on form CLAIM 8 where a higher, or non-standard fee is being claimed) within the three-month time limit.

CHAPTER 3

Bail in the lower courts

For complete chapter contents, see overleaf

Introduction

3.1 It is often said that a barrister is only as good as his/her last case. Perhaps, if the expression were more accurately written, it would read, 'a barrister is only as good as his/her last bail application' for if there is one thing closer to a defendant's heart than an acquittal, it is being granted bail pending his trial. Like it or not, solicitors and barristers will be largely judged by defendants on the question of whether they are granted bail and, therefore, on the quality of their bail applications. This chapter deals with the practical considerations in making a successful bail application and considers the steps to be taken towards achieving that end that are rarely touched on in formal textbooks.

Legal framework of bail

3.2 The provision of bail is governed by the Bail Act 1976. Subject to para 3.30 below, any person in criminal proceedings is entitled to bail.[1] The right to bail applies to:

1) a defendant appearing before a magistrates' or youth court and the Crown Court;[2] or
2) a convicted person before any of the above courts but only if the court is adjourning the case for the purposes of enabling reports to be prepared before sentencing;[3] or
3) an offender appearing before the court for alleged breach of a requirement of a probation, community service, combination or curfew order.[4]

Courts must consider bail at every hearing; this obligation exists even if the defendant does not apply for bail.

When to apply for bail

3.3 Most defendants, having been detained by police in custody overnight following charge, will expect a bail application to be made

1 Bail Act 1976 s4(1).
2 Ibid s4(2).
3 Ibid s4(4).
4 Ibid s4(3).

the following morning when they are brought before court. Perhaps not surprisingly, it is in the early stages of detention that defendants feel most aggrieved about the denial of their liberty. Strictly speaking, a defendant is entitled to two bail applications which should be made at the first two hearings.[5] In practice, most courts will allow two applications at any time throughout the magistrates' court proceedings. Once two bail applications have been made and refused, a defence advocate will have to argue that there is a 'change of circumstances' such that the court is entitled to hear a further bail application. An example of a change of circumstances would exist where, for example, bail is refused for a defendant charged with causing grievous bodily harm contrary to Offences Against the Person Act (OAPA) 1861 s18 and, following a review of the file by the CPS, a lesser charge of assault occasioning actual bodily harm contrary to OAPA 1861 s47 were substituted. There is some doubt about whether the mere fact of committal will in itself amount to a change of circumstances, in the light of the conflicting authorities of *R v Reading Crown Court ex p Malik*[6] and *R v Slough Justices ex p Duncan.*[7] It would, however, seem that, while it cannot be argued that a committal hearing per se amounts to a change of circumstances, the raising of, for example, evidential issues that become apparent when the committal bundle is received, may amount to a change of circumstances. Advocates should of course be aware that a successful argument that there is a change in circumstances merely allows him/her to make a further bail application, which may or may not be successful.

3.4   Solicitors should always bear in mind that many defendants will wish to have an application made on their behalf, no matter how unlikely it is to succeed. While, in many cases, it will be entirely appropriate for a bail application to be made on a defendant's first appearance at court, and perhaps a second application if the first one is not successful, a week later, there may be many circumstances in which it may be more prudent to delay the making of an application. Such circumstances may exist, for example, in the following situations:

1) Where, because of a history of absconding, a surety will be required by the court as a bail condition and a surety has yet to be found. However, in many cases, defendants will give clear instructions that a surety is unlikely to be found no matter how

5   Ibid Sch 1 Part IIA para 2.
6   [1981] QB 451, DC.
7   (1982) 75 Cr App R 384, DC.

extensive enquiries to find one may be and, in those circumstances, an application should be made at the earliest opportunity. It should always be borne in mind that even if, for proper reasons, an advocate feels that a bail application is more likely to succeed if time were allowed for further enquiries to be made (eg, to locate a surety or to find an address), defendants often consider that by giving such advice, their solicitor or barrister is not pursuing the bail application forcefully enough and, in such circumstances, a request to change solicitors may follow. Advocates should be aware that, while they should advise defendants fully, not only about the chances of a bail application being successful, but about the tactical wisdom in making an application at any point in time, it is the defendant that must make the final decision regarding the timing of an application, and advocates must abide by that decision. As in all cases where a defendant wishes a step in his/her case to be taken that his/her legal adviser considers to be inappropriate, the client should be asked to confirm those instructions in writing by, for example, endorsing counsel's backsheet so as to avoid any possible misunderstanding between the client and his/her legal advisers.

2) Where the defendant has no suitable address to reside at and enquiries need to be made of family and friends to find an address where s/he can live, this being on the basis that the defendant cannot be found a placement at a bail hostel (see para 3.9 below).

Preparation for a bail application

3.5   As with all advocacy, thorough preparation is vitally important. Often, defence advocates will not have had the opportunity to acquaint themselves fully with the full facts of the case prior to the hearing. They may not have been the lawyer who attended the defendant at the police station. In addition, a copy of the prosecution statements may not have been seen. This should not, however, be seen as a justification for lack of preparation.

3.6   Advocates need to keep in mind the basis on which bail can be withheld under the Bail Act 1976 (a copy of which appears as appendix D). It is the defence advocate's objective to overcome the prosecution's objections to bail under that Act in order to secure the defendant's liberty.

3.7   Advocates will be aware of the general proposition that the defendant has a right to bail[8] (see para 3.2 above). There are exceptions to that right if the prosecution can establish that there are substantial grounds for believing that the defendant would:

1) fail to surrender to custody;
2) commit an offence while on bail;
3) interfere with witnesses or otherwise obstruct the course of justice, whether in relation to him/herself or any other person.

While there are other exceptions to the right to bail as laid out in Bail Act 1976 Sch 1 Part I (see appendix D), these three grounds are those most commonly relied on by the prosecution.

What information should the advocate have about the defendant before making a bail application?

3.8   Solicitors should ensure that the following information is available to the advocate at court, namely:

1) the defendant's permanent address or proposed bail address if s/he does not have an appropriate long-term address;
2) details of ownership of that property;
3) the capacity in which the defendant lives there;
4) details of any proposed surety (see para 3.17 below for further explanation);
5) details of the defendant's community ties, which should include his/her date of birth, where s/he was raised, whether s/he is single, married or cohabiting, whether s/he has any children, where his/her family may live, employment status and, if s/he is unemployed, what prospects s/he has of finding work;
6) if relevant, details of the defendant's previous criminal convictions, with particular attention being paid to whether the defendant has been convicted of an offence of failing to appear in the past;
7) if relevant, details of the defendant's previous convictions and record of offending while on bail.

Issues relating to the suitability of a bail address

3.9   As indicated earlier at para 3.4, if bail is to be granted, the court will always require that the defendant is able to reside at a permanent

8   Ibid s4.

address. Checks carried out at the police station during detention may conclude that the defendant does not live at the address given to police or otherwise have sufficient ties to that address. Advocates should be aware that it is not uncommon for family or friends to feel that they are in some way helping the defendant by saying that they either do not know him/her or that s/he does not live at that address, whereas in practice the opposite is true. Advocates should contact relatives if phone numbers are available to try to substantiate the defendant's instructions.

3.10 If no suitable address is forthcoming, enquiries should be made of the Probation Service to see whether or not it can assist in finding a placement at one of the many bail hostels available. Frequently, the duty probation officer will wish to wait until the magistrate has specifically asked the Probation Service to make the appropriate enquiries before taking any steps to find a suitable placement. Any such placement is unlikely to be forthcoming if the defendant has a severe alcohol or drug problem or has previous convictions, for example, for arson or where the defendant is charged with an offence of a sexual nature.

The importance of liaising with the CPS

3.11 Once instructions regarding bail have been taken from the defendant, the advocate should, where time allows, speak informally to the CPS representative at court to ascertain the prosecution's view regarding the following aspects of the defendant's bail position:

1) Is s/he objecting to bail outright?
2) If so, on what grounds?
3) Would s/he be prepared for conditional bail to be granted and, if so, what conditions would be acceptable?
4) A list of the defendant's previous convictions should be obtained from the CPS representative – it is not unknown for this to differ materially from the information given by the defendant.

The effect of previous convictions

3.12 If the defendant has previous convictions, then careful attention should be paid to the following issues:

1) frequency of committing offences;
2) when the last offence was committed;
3) whether the previous convictions are of a similar nature to the charge currently before the court;

4) whether those offences were committed at a time when the defendant was on either court or police bail for other offences;

5) whether those offences were committed while the defendant was on licence following a recent release from prison or while subject to any court orders, eg, while on probation or subject to a conditional discharge;

6) whether the defendant was on bail or remanded in custody before being sentenced for an earlier offence. This may be particularly important where a client remained on bail throughout the duration of a case, only to receive a custodial sentence at disposal. Such conduct may support an argument that, in spite of the real risk of a custodial sentence being imposed, the client still answered his/her bail, and is therefore likely to answer his/her bail in the current proceedings.

The effect of previous convictions for Bail Act offences

3.13   If the defendant has previous convictions for Bail Act offences, an explanation should be sought from the defendant about the circumstances giving rise to each such conviction. Was the defendant simply late for court? Did s/he surrender voluntarily, albeit late? Was s/he arrested a substantial period of time after the hearing at which s/he failed to appear? In consultation with the defendant, a decision should be taken about what conditions the advocate feels the court is likely to impose and whether s/he is willing and able to abide by those conditions. For example, if the defendant is in regular employment, daily reporting to the local police station in the middle of the day may prove to be impractical.

Events arising out of the defendant's detention at the police station before charge

3.14   A matter which is often overlooked by advocates but is of crucial significance is to be aware that there may be several issues raised during the prosecution's observations on bail which relate to matters that occurred when the defendant was detained at the police station. In such cases, if the advocate making the bail application was the solicitor who attended the defendant at the police station, s/he will be at an advantage, in that s/he will be familiar with those events. If that solicitor is not the advocate, s/he should ensure that the solicitor or barrister who does attend court has been fully appraised of all relevant facts. Examples of the more commonplace issues that the prosecution might raise in objecting to a defendant's bail include:

1) that the defendant's identity has not been established because s/he was in possession of documentation in other names;

2) that the defendant was in possession of a flight ticket or that s/he had stated that s/he might leave the country if given the opportunity to do so;

3) that the defendant gave a false name on arrest or while detained at the police station or tried to evade arrest by running away or by assaulting the arresting police officer;

4) that the defendant had stated an intention to return to a particular address (where the offence is alleged to have taken place) or to contact a particular individual, eg, the victim or a prosecution witness.

3.15 This list is, of course, not exhaustive but consideration must be given to how those objections to bail can be overcome. Matters to consider are, for example, the fact that the defendant initially gave a false name but as soon as s/he arrived at the police station or received legal advice, s/he gave his/her correct name or allowed his/her fingerprints to be taken, which would thereby establish his/her identity (provided s/he has previous convictions). Only a thorough knowledge of, and familiarity with, events at the police station will adequately equip the advocate with the necessary information required to counter prosecution objections to bail successfully.

Further factors for the court to consider

3.16 Consideration should also be given to the strength of the evidence against the defendant. Defendants are often mistakenly of the view that, if they deny the charge, they should be given bail. Magistrates, whether lay or stipendiary, will consider the weight of evidence of the prosecution's case together with the objections that the prosecution puts forward. That will then be weighed up against defence submissions. The question of the defendant's innocence or guilt will be decided on a different occasion. However, if the prosecution case should suffer from serious evidential flaws, then that fact will no doubt be brought to the court's attention by the defence advocate.

Sureties

3.17   If it is either known or likely that one of the issues to be considered in deciding whether the defendant is granted bail is the question of whether s/he is likely to fail to appear (which can be gleaned from the seriousness of the charge or from the defendant's antecedents) a surety may need to be found to stand on the defendant's behalf. A surety is an individual, preferably with no previous convictions, who is well known to the defendant and who is prepared to guarantee with a sum of money that the defendant will attend as and when required.

Suitability of sureties

3.18   Advocates should always take steps to satisfy themselves that a surety put forward is likely to be suitable to the court. The personal connection with the defendant will be easy to establish. It is the financial commitment that frequently causes most difficulty. The court will need to satisfy itself that the surety does indeed have the money that s/he is guaranteeing.

3.19   Sureties should be advised to bring along documentary proof that they do own the savings that they are guaranteeing to ensure the defendant's attendance at court, commonly in the form of a bank statement or the surety's building society passbook or some other recognised documentation. Savings should preferably consist of liquid assets, ie, savings in a bank, building society or other financial institution. That documentation should be carefully checked prior to the hearing to satisfy the advocate that:

1) the surety does indeed own the money put forward;
2) the money is in the surety's own name (if assets are in joint names, both individuals should offer themselves as sureties); and, most importantly,
3) the money really does belong to the surety and has not been placed there by a third party. The fact that funds have recently been transferred into the surety's account may be evidence of that fact and the surety should be asked to account for recent receipts of those monies. The court may be concerned if, for example, a defendant has limited savings and yet, shortly before the court hearing at which the surety proposes putting him/herself forward, there has been a large cash injection into that surety's account. Advocates will no doubt be aware that indemnifying a surety is an offence. If the court concludes that the proposed surety has been indemnified, the surety will invariably not be accepted by the court.

Matters to bring to the surety's attention before the hearing

3.20 The surety should be made aware that if s/he is guaranteeing, for example, £1,000, which is contained in a bank account, that that money cannot be used and should be kept available in the event that the defendant fails to appear. If the surety is called on to part with that money, and if it is not available, the surety could risk being sent to prison. Advocates should be aware that the prosecution and the court have the right to cross-examine any proposed surety. Such questions may well be designed to discredit him/her or in some other way to suggest that s/he is not suitable to stand as a surety, for example, because the proposed surety is not able to exert sufficient control over the defendant to ensure his/her attendance at court. This may occur, for example, when the proposed surety lives far away from the defendant or where s/he has not seen or had contact with the defendant for many years. All possible steps should be taken, therefore, to pre-empt problems over ownership of funds arising once the hearing has started – if problems should arise, it will do little to enhance the defendant's chances of securing bail. If the defendant does have previous convictions for failure to appear, the surety should be made aware of that fact before the hearing so that s/he is not taken by surprise during the hearing. Similarly, the proposed surety should also be made aware of the seriousness of the charges that the defendant faces so that the surety can satisfy the court that s/he is prepared to stand as a surety in the full knowledge of the facts of the case.

Non-attendance of sureties at court

3.21 Sometimes, it is not possible for a surety to attend court because, for example, s/he is working. In these circumstances, a bail application may have to be made in that surety's absence. If that is the case, and the court decides that bail can be granted subject to a surety being taken, the court may order that the surety can be taken in one of the following circumstances:

1) at a police station;
2) at the court (which means that the duty court clerk can 'take the surety' in his/her office); or
3) in court, ie, in open court before the magistrate.

Duration of the surety – continuous or not?

3.22 When a surety is taken, advocates should note carefully whether or not the surety's obligations last until the next hearing or until the matter has been finally dealt with at that court (either by way of trial or committal/transfer). For more serious charges, magistrates, even if they take sureties in court, may prefer sureties to attend on each and every occasion that the defendant appears in court. Advocates must be aware that, if a surety is taken at a police station, that surety must attend the magistrates' court at the next occasion so that s/he can be retaken as a surety. A surety cannot be made continuous beyond the next hearing when taken by the police, and failure to ensure that the surety attends court will result in the defendant remaining in custody until such time as the surety is taken – again, a situation that any solicitor should wish to avoid, or at least advise the defendant about before the hearing. Sureties cannot be made continuous for summary only charges. In addition, if bail is granted at the Crown Court when appealing against the magistrates' court's decision to refuse bail, the surety should be retaken at the magistrates' court at the next hearing and the surety should be notified to that effect in writing. Failure to do so will result in a defendant remaining in custody until the surety is taken.

Remands on bail subject to surety, where sureties cannot be found

3.23   If bail is granted subject to one or more sureties standing on behalf of the defendant, but those sureties are not forthcoming, the defendant will find him/herself in the unfortunate position where s/he will remain in custody until those sureties are taken but, given that s/he has technically been granted bail, time spent in custody will not count towards any custodial sentence that may subsequently be imposed. Furthermore, the defendant will be produced every seven days at court until such time as the surety is taken and the client can be released from custody. Solicitors should make the appropriate checks with the prison or young offender institution where the client is being held, to check whether the client has or has not been released from custody. If s/he has not, the client will be produced at court and will no doubt be expecting representation.

The hearing

3.24   The question of bail is always for the court to determine. It is a matter that is dealt with (often most inconveniently from the defendant's point of view) at the conclusion of the hearing. This prohibits the defence deciding on its course of action in a particular case once it knows whether or not bail is to be granted.

3.25 The usual procedure in a bail application is as follows:

1) the defence is asked if it is making a bail application;
2) the court clerk reads the defendant's previous history relating to bail;
3) the prosecution makes its observations and hands up a list of any previous convictions to the magistrate;
4) the defence puts forward its reasons for granting the defendant bail, dealing specifically with each of the prosecution's objections;
5) reference is made to any relevant law by the defence, prosecution or the court clerk;
6) if it is suggested by the defence advocate that conditional bail be granted, those conditions are then put forward concisely.

3.26 Either party is entitled to adduce evidence in support of its representations, although in practice this is likely only to amount to the officer in the case being called to substantiate the prosecution's objections. That evidence is given on oath and witnesses can be cross-examined.

Possible bail conditions

3.27 There is no exhaustive list of conditions that can be offered by the defence, but those commonly imposed are that the defendant:

1) resides at a particular address;
2) abides by a curfew (usually covering the night hours);
3) does not contact either the victim or prosecution witnesses directly or indirectly (which means that s/he must not ask anybody else to contact them on his/her behalf);
4) does not go to a particular address or area or keeps a certain distance away;
5) surrenders his/her passport;
6) reports to his/her local police station at appropriate intervals;
7) provides a surety/sureties and/or a security/securities.

3.28 Each case will, of course, turn on its own facts and, on occasions, more lateral thinking may be required to suggest conditions appropriate to individual cases – for example, that a defendant reports to his/her local police station sober, or that s/he does not leave an address except for the purpose of attending court or seeing his/her legal advisers on prior written appointment.

Points to remember if bail is not granted

3.29   If bail is refused or granted subject to conditions, careful note should be made about the reasons given. If bail is refused, and if it is intended that an application should be made on appeal to the Crown Court, a certificate of full argument should be requested. Practice differs between courts, although usually the court clerk will make the certificate available to the defence advocate before leaving court. Occasionally it may have to be requested in writing. The procedure for appealing to the higher courts is dealt with more fully later in this book (see chapter 10).

Bail granted for murder, manslaughter or rape offences

3.30   People charged with offences in these categories come within special provisions. Criminal Justice and Public Order Act 1994 s25 states:

> (1) A person who in any proceedings has been charged with or convicted of an offence to which this section applies in circumstances to which it applies shall not be granted bail in those proceedings.
> (2) This section applies, subject to subsection (3) below, to the following offences, that is to say –
> (a) murder;
> (b) attempted murder;
> (c) manslaughter;
> (d) rape; or
> (e) attempted rape.
> (3) This section applies to a person charged with or convicted of any such offence only if he has been previously convicted by or before a court in any part of the United Kingdom of any such offence or of culpable homicide and, in the case of a previous conviction of manslaughter or of culpable homicide, if he was then sentenced to imprisonment or, if he was then a child or young person to long term detention under any of the relevant enactments.

Even where the above does not apply, where bail is granted to a defendant who is charged with murder, attempted murder, manslaughter, rape or attempted rape, the court must state its reasons for granting bail and, again, a note of the reasons should be made.[9] Furthermore, where a defendant is granted bail when charged

---

9   Bail Act 1976 Sch 1 Part 1 para 9A.

with murder, the court must impose a condition of his/her bail that s/he be examined by two medical practitioners, one of whom must be an approved Home Office psychiatrist, and attend for appointments to be examined, unless the court is satisfied that satisfactory reports on his/her mental wellbeing have already been obtained.[10]

What if bail is granted against all the odds?

3.31   First, congratulate yourself. Second, be aware of the provisions of the Bail (Amendment) Act 1993, as a result of which the prosecution is entitled to appeal to the Crown Court against a decision by the magistrates' court to grant bail. The procedure for doing so is complicated and it is not the intention of this book to deal with that Act in detail here. It is limited to the following cases:

1) where a defendant is charged or convicted of an offence punishable by a term of imprisonment of five or more years or of an offence of taking a conveyance without authority or of aggravating vehicle taking; and
2) the prosecution has objected to bail before the hearing; and
3) the prosecution has given oral notice of its intention to appeal at the conclusion of the hearing.

Should all the above conditions be satisfied, the defendant will remain in custody until the appeal has been heard or, as occasionally happens, until the prosecution decides not to pursue its application further.

Further practical considerations

3.32   There may, of course, be justifiable reasons for advising a defendant that no bail application should be made (and the more experienced defendant may well be aware of them). If a defendant is to enter a guilty plea in due course for an offence for which s/he will inevitably receive a custodial sentence, although there are occasions when the defendant will wish to secure his/her bail 'in order to get his affairs in order', many may wish simply to spend as much time on remand as possible. To do so will allow them certain freedoms that will not be available to them once their status changes to being that of a convicted prisoner. In addition, advocates should be aware that,

10   Bail Act 1976 s3(6A) and (6B).

where a defendant is in custody on other matters, whether as a serving prisoner or on remand for more serious cases, again, to apply for bail in those cases would merely result in a defendant continuing to spend time in custody without that period of time counting towards any overall sentence that may in due course be imposed.

Youth court provisions

3.33   The Bail Act 1976 in its entirety also applies to children and young persons. The court must decide the same considerations as for an adult. Only if bail is refused will the law be substantially different. Ironically, even though defendants aged between 17 and 18 will have their cases dealt with in the youth court, they are subject to the same provisions as adults in the magistrates' court in relation to bail and remands. For those defendants aged 16 or under, different rules apply. The guidance in Home Office Circular 30/1992 *Criminal Justice Act 1991: Young People and the Youth Court* para 49 should always be borne in mind:

> Removing children and young persons from home should be a course of last resort, and the government believes that as many defendants under 17 as possible should be granted bail.

3.34   As a result of that guidance, where bail is withheld to a defendant in the youth court, the remand of that defendant is always to local authority accommodation, unless any of the conditions set out in Children and Young Persons Act 1969 s23(5) are satisfied. (A copy of that section appears at appendix C. See also Defending Young People in the Criminal Justice System (LAG, 1997) p179.)

3.35   To come within the ambit of that section, the following conditions must be satisfied:

1) the defendant must be male;[11]
2) the defendant must be aged 15 or 16;[12]
3) the defendant must be legally represented;[13] and
4) the court must have consulted with a probation officer or a social worker of a local authority social services department.[14]

If the above conditions are satisfied, s23(5) states that a defendant can only be remanded to secure accommodation where either:

11   Children and Young Persons Act 1969 s23(5).
12   Ibid.
13   Ibid s23(4A).
14   Ibid s23(1).

(a) he is charged with or has been convicted of a violent or sexual offence, or an offence punishable in the case of an adult with imprisonment for a term of fourteen years or more; or

(b) he has a recent history of absconding while remanded to local authority accommodation and he is charged with or has been convicted of an imprisonable offence alleged or found to have been committed while he was so remanded.

Where a defendant falls within the above categories, the remand can only be to custody where the court believes that only remanding him to a remand centre or prison would be adequate to protect the public from serious harm from him.

Preparation for the hearing

3.36   As with adult defendants, adequate preparation for a bail application is essential. Advocates should take advantage of the benefit of any additional information that the youth justice social worker may have. S/he invariably has a detailed knowledge of the personal history of the defendant, which in many cases is more thorough than the advocate's. Furthermore, the social worker may offer assistance in suggesting suitable arrangements that could be made for the defendant, should bail be granted. The importance of that assistance should not be underestimated, where the prosecution opposes bail. Magistrates are often persuaded by representations made by youth justice social workers during a bail application because the courts will routinely be concerned that adequate arrangements are made for the defendant's welfare, and that procedures are in place to ensure that the young defendant's behaviour can be controlled. Indeed, they are obliged to consider the defendant's welfare pursuant to the provisions of Children and Young Persons Act 1933 s44.

3.37   Advocates should further ensure that sufficiently detailed instructions are taken from the defendant, with any assistance that can be offered by family members who may be at court, on the following additional matters:

1) the family circumstances;

2) any history that the defendant may have of being in care, foster homes, etc;

3) details of schooling and, if appropriate, history of truancy.

CHAPTER 4

The proof of evidence

Introduction

4.1   The taking of a proof of evidence from a defendant is perhaps one of the more straightforward aspects of case preparation. That being the case, it is not the intention to complicate the situation unduly. However, newly qualified solicitors should be aware that, in preparing a proof of evidence for a defendant, they will need to consider the case more laterally than simply stating that a defendant denies the allegation and, in broad terms, setting out the nature of his/her defence. Set out below, therefore, are guidelines for areas to be considered as part of the proof-taking process.

Content of the proof

4.2   It will come as no surprise to any solicitor that there are certain prerequisite details that a proof should contain. It should always at its outset state the defendant's name, address and telephone number, age, marital status, details of any financial dependants and recent employment history. Not unexpectedly, the contents of each proof will be dictated by the nature of the allegations against any individual defendant. Having said that, the following areas should be considered.

Youths and mentally disordered defendants

4.3   In respect of both these categories of defendants, details of the name and address of an appropriate adult should be obtained. In the case of mentally disordered defendants, a full medical history should be detailed. In such cases, as well as in the case of defendants who suffer from physical illness, it will undoubtedly be appropriate for an authority form to be signed by the defendant so that disclosure of medical records can be obtained.

The defendant's offending history

4.4   The defendant should be shown a list of his/her previous convictions, if any, and the proof should confirm whether or not that list is agreed. If the defendant is in breach of any court orders or is the subject of other criminal proceedings, again, that fact should be clearly stated in his/her proof of evidence. If the defendant is subject to a probation/combination order or if the defendant is in care, the identity of the defendant's probation officer/social worker should, again, be given.

The defendant's version of events

4.5 Solicitors should ensure that the defendant clearly understands the nature of the charge(s) against him/her. Once that has been done, the defendant should be asked to give his/her version of events and comment on any prosecution statements that have been served. In practice, most defendants want to give their version of events before ploughing through a list of lengthy prosecution statements that may well not read in chronological order. Furthermore, by taking instructions in this way, it will undoubtedly speed up the process of going through the prosecution statements when that is done. In taking instructions, defendants should not be 'led' in giving their version of events. They should be asked as many 'open' questions as possible, ie, questions which invite the defendant to recount events rather than 'closed' questions which merely demand a yes or no answer in reply. Questions such as 'what happened then?' will be more constructive in eliciting a comprehensive version of events from the defendant rather than 'Did you then hit the victim?'. The defendant's reply should be as detailed as possible. Inevitably, defendants, in giving instructions, tend initially to skim over issues that they may not consider to be of importance. Solicitors should be on their guard to ensure that they persevere in obtaining as detailed a response to questions as possible. Defendants who may well not understand the significance of the element of dishonesty in a theft charge will not understand why solicitors ask the question, 'What were you thinking at the time?'. However, it is naturally an essential element of the offence that must be considered and the defendant's comments obtained. This should be explained clearly to defendants.

4.6 The proof of evidence, once taken, will form the basis not only of cross-examination at trial, but also of the defence statement that in Crown Court cases will have to be served on the prosecution. The defendant's comments should therefore be sufficiently detailed to enable his/her solicitor or barrister to draft that statement. As such, the defendant's proof should deal with all those areas of the prosecution's case that are in dispute, and the reasons why.

Events at the police station

4.7   In the event that the defendant was either unrepresented when detained, interviewed and charged at the police station or, alternatively, represented by another firm of solicitors, it is essential that the defendant's full instructions be taken about anything relevant that took place while detained. At this point, cross-reference should be made to chapter 6 on summary trials, for the specific relevance that this area has. Full instructions should be taken on events as recorded in the custody record and, if necessary, the defendant should be asked to explain any comments made during the interview. This may require listening to the interview tape in the presence of the defendant. Clearly, in giving his/her proof the defendant should be asked to explain any inconsistencies that may arise either during the course of his/her police interview or between instructions given at the time of his/her proof and the earlier version of events as given to police during interview. This will be of particular relevance, for example, if the defendant has made admissions or confessed to the offence to police in situations where the allegation is subsequently denied. The proof of evidence should deal comprehensively with reasons for the apparent inconsistencies.

Multi-defendant cases

4.8   The defendant should be asked in giving his proof to comment on the role played not only by him/herself but also for his/her view of any part played by any co-accused, irrespective of whether or not that firm of solicitors is also acting for those co-accused.

Medical history

4.9   If the defendant is suffering from a medical condition, again, full details should be taken, and as previously indicated, a medical authority consent form signed. Instructions should be taken from the defendant about the nature of that condition, its relevance to the offence and details of the defendant's doctor and of any medication that the defendant is taking. If relevant, instructions should be taken regarding any hospitalisation to which the defendant has been subject.

Mitigating factors

4.10   Regretfully, there are always occasions when, following a contested trial, a defendant is convicted. Irrespective of how hopeful either the defendant or his/her solicitor may be of obtaining an acquittal, instructions should always be taken and the defendant fully proofed regarding information which may be useful for the defendant's plea in mitigation. Reference should be made at this point to chapter 14 on sentencing. It is, however, appropriate to say at this stage that where relevant, instructions should be taken in the following areas.

Addiction

4.11 If the defendant has a drink/drug, psychiatric or gambling problem, the defendant should be fully proofed about the extent and nature of his/her problems, and instructions obtained about the steps that the defendant may have taken in dealing with those problems. If the defendant, for example, voluntarily attends a drug advisory centre or has approached a rehabilitation unit, the relevant instructions should be sought.

Multi-defendant cases

4.12 If the defendant is one of a number of defendants, s/he should be asked to give instructions regarding the influence that either his/her co-defendants or others may have had in the defendant committing the offence in question.

Offences of violence

4.13 In cases of violence, if the defendant had been subject to provocation, the defendant should be asked to provide full details.

Remorse/contrition

4.14 If the defendant has expressed remorse following the commission of the offence (rather than distress at having been arrested for it), the appropriate instructions should again be sought from the defendant and details stated in his/her proof of evidence. Have any letters of apology been written? Has the victim been financially compensated on a voluntary basis either before charge or before entering a plea? In cases of theft, burglary or other similar offences, has assistance been given to the police in recovering stolen property? Again, if that is the case, details should be fully stated in the defendant's proof.

Effect on employment

4.15   If convicted, the effect that a custodial sentence may have on his/her employment should be fully stated.

Completing the proof

4.16   Once the proof has been taken, the defendant should carefully read through it to ensure that it entirely matches his/her instructions. Any amendments or alterations can be added, as appropriate. Two copies should then be sent to the defendant as soon as possible. The defendant should be asked to retain one copy for his/her own reference, and to return the other copy after checking it thoroughly and signing every page at the bottom. The importance of sending a copy of the statement to the defendant cannot be over-stated. In supplying a copy, the defendant is being asked to confirm his/her instructions, thereby ensuring that the solicitor who took the proof has fully and accurately understood all that the defendant has said.

Witness statements

4.17   So far as the preparation of witness statements is concerned, where relevant, the above information (in paras 4.11 to 4.15) should be obtained in any statements taken from the defendant. Solicitors should ensure that the statements are typed in an admissible form as required by Criminal Justice Act 1967 s9 (appendix C). Similarly, once a statement has been taken, two copies of that witness statement should be supplied to the proposed witness who should be asked to sign each page where indicated and have his/her signature witnessed by a third party. This is an element in the preparation of the defendant's case that should not be overlooked. Solicitors should always bear in mind that evidence given at trial must be in an admissible form. That being the case, solicitors should be aware of the provisions of Criminal Justice Act 1988 s23, which provides:

> ... a statement made by a person in a document shall be admissible in criminal proceedings as evidence of any fact of which direct oral evidence by him would be admissible ... [in certain prescribed circumstances].

That will, of course, depend on whether the statement has been prepared for the purpose of current or pending criminal proceedings (which will usually be the case) but, more importantly, if the statement was so prepared, that statement can only be tendered where the conditions set out in Criminal Justice Act 1988 s23(2) and (3) are satisfied, namely where:

1) the maker of the statement is dead or unfit to attend;
2) the maker of the statement is outside the UK and it is not reasonably practicable to secure that witness's attendance;
3) the maker of the statement cannot be found; or
4) the statement was made to a police officer and the maker does not give oral evidence through fear or because s/he is kept out of the way.

4.18 So far as defence witness statements are concerned, the last of those conditions is unlikely to cause defence solicitors difficulties. However, solicitors can no doubt envisage situations where one of the other conditions may be relevant to a defendant's case. If they are, leave of the court, pursuant to Criminal Justice Act 1988 s26, will have to be sought. In granting leave, the court will not admit that statement to be given in evidence unless it is in the interests of justice to do so. Circumstances that the court will have to consider when deciding whether to admit the evidence are:

1) the contents of the statement;
2) the risk (bearing in mind the chances of being able to dispute that statement) of its admission or exclusion resulting in unfairness to the defendant; or
3) any other relevant circumstances.

4.19 Solicitors should be particularly wary in situations, therefore, where witness statements are taken on behalf of the defendant from elderly or ill witnesses or from witnesses who do not intend to remain within the jurisdiction of the court until the trial date.

Changes to statements

4.20 In practice, the preparation of a defendant's proof of evidence will become second nature and relevant issues on which instructions should be sought will become readily apparent to solicitors. In the event that substantial changes are made to the proof of evidence, or to any witness statement, another copy incorporating the amendments should be typed and the defendant/witness asked to sign the amended statement, and in the case of witness statements prepared on behalf of the defendant, have that statement witnessed as previously instructed in para 4.17.

CHAPTER 5

Plea before venue and mode of trial

Introduction

5.1   Before the provisions of the Criminal Procedure and Investigations Act (CPIA) 1996 came into force on 1 April 1997, in particular, s49 (see appendix F), mode of trial proceedings would take place for all either way charges that came before the courts. This would be the case even if, for example, in the case of criminal damage charges, it was just for the purpose of clarifying the value of the damage involved with a view to establishing whether that value was within or outside the magistrates' court's limits. The concepts involved in the mode of trial process were perhaps the easiest to grasp and the hearing rarely provided an opportunity for acrimony between defence and prosecution.

Which courts are affected by CPIA 1996 s49?

5.2   CPIA 1996 s49 amends Magistrates' Courts Act (MCA) 1980 s17 by inserting a new s17A. It only applies where a defendant has attained the age of 18 and appears before a magistrates' court charged with an offence triable either way. These new provisions therefore have no relevance for proceedings before the youth court, where the mode of trial provisions remain unchanged and are detailed later in this chapter.

When is the question of venue decided?

5.3   This chapter aims to consider, in those cases where such a hearing takes place, the factors that will determine the outcome of the hearing, together with other practical considerations, in deciding whether to elect for the case to be tried in the Crown Court. The decision is not one that should be taken lightly, particularly when considering the Crown Court's greater sentencing powers. Indictable only offences, by their nature, must be dealt with at the Crown Court and, conversely, summary only charges must always be dealt with by a magistrates' court. The election of court can be made as early as the first hearing, if parties possess sufficient information to enable that decision to be made. That, in itself, requires that the prosecution has all relevant facts to enable both sides to make appropriate representations to the court. Clearly, in a case of assault occasioning actual bodily harm, for example, no decision on mode of trial would be made until a statement had been received by the CPS from a doctor who had examined the victim, thereby setting out in detail the full extent of the injuries that the victim had allegedly suffered. Without such a statement, the prosecution would have difficulty establishing that the victim had in fact suffered injury. Alternatively, for straightforward shoplifting matters where there are no unusual features, a decision could be made at the first hearing where a defendant is before the court.

When does a mode of trial hearing take place?

5.4   The effect of the new MCA 1980 s17A is that, instead of entering into a mode of trial hearing, the court clerk will explain to the defendant that s/he may indicate, if the offence were to proceed to a trial, that s/he would plead guilty or not guilty. The defendant will then be told that if s/he indicates that s/he will be pleading guilty, the magistrates' court will proceed to sentencing him/her. The court can reserve its right to commit him/her for sentence to the Crown Court pursuant to MCA 1980 s38 if it is of the opinion that its sentencing powers are insufficient, as mentioned in s38(2). The defendant will then be asked whether s/he would plead guilty or not guilty. If the defendant then indicated that s/he would enter a guilty plea, the above would apply, the defendant would be treated as if s/he had entered a guilty plea and the court would then proceed to sentence/commit for sentence. In effect, therefore, mode of trial proceedings do not take place when a defendant indicates that s/he would enter a guilty plea.

Tactical decisions

5.5   Advocates should be aware of the dilemma facing their defendants. If they wish to take advantage of the credit that the court gives for entering a guilty plea at an early stage in the proceedings, pursuant to Criminal Justice and Public Order Act (CJPOA) 1994 s48, and therefore do so, they risk being remanded in custody until such time as they are sentenced by the Crown Court, if the court seeks to apply MCA 1980 s38. The court may consider that, if the defendant's case needs to be committed to the Crown Court for sentencing (because its own sentencing powers are insufficient), any interim remand period should be spent in custody. Defendants on bail should be advised that, if there is a strong likelihood that their case would be committed for sentence, then there is the risk that their bail may be taken away. Many defendants may prefer to give no indication of plea, to allow their cases to be dealt with at the Crown Court (for example, because the magistrates' court declines jurisdiction of the case) and enter a guilty plea after committal has taken place. That decision may be made, for example, because they are aware that custody is likely following conviction, but they would prefer to delay imprisonment for as long as possible, either to get their affairs in order or for any other reason. Furthermore, defendants who are at risk of having their bail stopped, or those defendants who are remanded in custody, should be advised (although many 'experienced' defendants will be aware) that, if committed to the Crown Court in custody for sentence pursuant to MCA 1980 s38, having stated that they would enter a guilty plea, they will be treated as convicted, as opposed to being on remand, while awaiting sentence. That decision may be significant to many defendants who lose various 'privileges' once their status changes to that of a serving prisoner, most notably the right to unlimited visits while on remand.

5.6   Defendants will, therefore, have to balance the likely benefits on sentencing that follow from applying CJPOA 1994 s48, against the risk of early custody.

The hearing

5.7   Where a defendant indicates that s/he would plead not guilty, the court would then proceed to decide on the venue, and mode of trial would take place. Where a defendant does not indicate a plea, for the purpose of mode of trial proceedings, s/he is deemed to have indicated that s/he would plead not guilty and mode of trial proceedings would follow.

5.8   No decision will be made about mode of trial until both the defence and the prosecution are in a position to make their representations. When that is the case, the prosecution will be invited to summarise the facts of the case and to make appropriate representations. In serious cases, an officer in the case may be called to deal with facts that may be relevant to that hearing. Defence advocates would be entitled to cross-examine that officer. The defence would then be given the opportunity to make its representations should it so wish. At this point, it should be pointed out that, if the case is clearly suitable for the magistrates' court to deal with, defence advocates may feel that no representations need be made. Generally, proceedings would only become protracted where the prosecution would be inviting the court to decline jurisdiction and the defence would be asking for the court to accept jurisdiction, presumably so that a guilty plea could be entered. Subject to the defendant being committed for sentence under MCA 1980 s38, the court would then be bound by its lower sentencing powers.

5.9   If the magistrates' court declines jurisdiction of the case then the defendant would not be able to choose the venue of his/her trial and the case would be adjourned for a committal date at a future time. However, if jurisdiction is accepted, the court clerk would then inform the defendant that s/he has the right to be tried at the Crown Court before a judge and jury, notwithstanding the fact that the court feels that it could be properly dealt with in that court. S/he will then be invited to state in which court s/he wishes the case to be dealt with. S/he would be advised that if s/he either pleads guilty or is found guilty in the magistrates' court, the court may commit him/her for sentence to the Crown Court in any event, if it felt that the offence was so serious or if the defendant proved such a risk to the public, that its powers to sentence him/her were inadequate.[1] The defendant would then make his/her choice about where s/he wished the case to be dealt with. If s/he elects the magistrates' court, then the case will proceed to the charge being read out and the plea being entered. If s/he elects the Crown Court, then the case would be adjourned and an anticipated committal date set.

Factors determining mode of trial

5.10   Determining mode of trial will only occur when the defendant has indicated that s/he will be pleading not guilty or has not given any indication as to his/her plea (see para 5.7, above). Only then does the court have to decide whether or not it is prepared to accept jurisdiction of the case.

5.11   There are two possible outcomes that can result from the mode of trial hearing:

1   By virtue of MCA 1980 s38.

1) the court accepts jurisdiction of the case – the defendant would then be given the option to have his case dealt with in either the magistrates' court or the Crown Court; or

2) the court declines jurisdiction of the case – regardless of the defendant's wishes, the case would then be prepared for committal to the Crown Court.

5.12   For the court to reach that decision, it should be told of all relevant facts by the prosecution, whereupon the court must decide whether it has sufficient sentencing powers to deal with the defendant. If the magistrates' court decides that it does have jurisdiction, the defendant would then be allowed to choose whether the case is to be dealt with in that court or the Crown Court. If the defendant elects to have his/her case dealt with in the Crown Court, then it *must* be dealt with there.

5.13   While the question of the court's sentencing powers will be uppermost in its mind in reaching this decision, it is not the only factor that determines the eventual outcome of the hearing. The court will consider the overall gravity of the case. To assist magistrates in reaching a decision, reference should be made to MCA 1980 s19, which sets out the following general principles to be considered when deciding whether or not a case should be dealt with summarily or on indictment:

1) the nature of the case, ie, whether the case is unusually complex or difficult;

2) whether the circumstances make the offence one of a serious nature;

3) whether the magistrates' court's sentencing powers are adequate;

4) any other circumstances which appear to the court to make it more suitable for the offence to be dealt with in one way rather than another; and

5) any representations made by the prosecution or defence.

5.14   The *National Mode Of Trial Guidelines* (1995), endorsed by the Lord Chief Justice, state that in making that decision neither the court nor the prosecution or defence should base their decision on convenience. In addition, the court should not draw conclusions that the prosecution version of events is the correct one. The fact that a defendant proposes having further offences taken into consideration should be disregarded. If the case is unusually complex either on its facts or in respect of questions of law, consideration should usually be given to the case being committed to the Crown Court and jurisdiction should be declined. As a general rule, the court should accept jurisdiction of the case unless any of the aggravating factors contained in the *Magistrates' Court Association Guidelines* are present. In addition, the court must, of course, have sufficient sentencing powers.

5.15   This chapter does not intend to repeat the *National Mode of Trial Guidelines*. The relevant sections do appear, however, in appendix M of this book. It is sufficient to say that solicitors and counsel should become fully familiar with them and, in respect of each category of offence, should acquaint themselves with those 'aggravating' or 'mitigating' factors that may be relevant to the case in question. It is sufficient for the purpose of this chapter to state that the guidelines deal with the following charges:

1) burglary of both residential and non-residential premises;
2) theft and fraud;
3) handling stolen goods;
4) social security frauds;
5) violent offences (more specifically, Offences against the Person Act 1861 ss20 and 47);
6) public order offences;
7) violence to and neglect of children;
8) indecent assault;
9) unlawful sexual intercourse;
10) drugs offences;
11) dangerous driving;
12) criminal damage.

5.16   In preparation for mode of trial proceedings, defence advocates should acquaint themselves with all relevant facts so far as they may have a bearing on the mode of trial decision, so that appropriate representations can be made in court. This, on most occasions, will involve defence solicitors requiring sight and consideration of prosecution statements served in accordance with the Magistrates' Court (Advance Information) Rules 1985 SI No 601 which, in turn, will need to be considered with the defendant. Defence representatives at court, whether solicitors or barristers, should ensure that their defendant is fully appraised of the procedure in court and the basis on which a defendant is to make any decision.

5.17   From the defence perspective, the decision about whether or not a defendant elects to be dealt with in either a magistrates' court or a Crown Court will largely depend on whether or not s/he proposes entering a guilty or a not guilty plea. It is prudent to advise a defendant to have his/her case dealt with in a magistrates' court if s/he intends pleading guilty, because the magistrates' court has lesser sentencing powers. In addition, the defendant's decision to have his/her case heard in the magistrates' court will prevent an unnecessary delay in dealing with the case when it could have been disposed of to the defendant's advantage at an early stage. Alternatively, if a defendant proposes contesting the charges, unless there is good reason why s/he should not wish to have his case dealt with at the Crown Court, for example, because s/he wishes to have his/her case heard as soon as possible (and many clients do express the need to get their case 'over and done with'), s/he should generally elect to have his/her case dealt with there and, therefore, tried before a judge and jury. The basis for this advice is straightforward. Most defence lawyers still consider that a defendant has a greater prospect of being acquitted at the Crown Court than before a magistrates' court, which many lawyers consider, cynically or not, to be prosecution-minded. A defendant should always be advised of the Crown Court's greater sentencing powers and the different nature of the trial, namely that it will be before a judge and jury. The defendant should, furthermore, be informed of the longer time scale for his/her trial date to come round as many defendants simply do not want the stress of prolonged proceedings.

5.18   Defence advocates should be aware of an anomaly. Even though certain offences may, strictly speaking, be either way offences, in certain circumstances the court is bound to accept or decline jurisdiction. The most notable cases are as follows:

1) residential burglaries – jurisdiction cannot be accepted by magistrates where any individual in the premises in question was subjected to violence or the threat of violence;[2]

2) unlawful sexual intercourse – if the victim is a girl under the age of 13, the case is triable only on indictment;[3]

3) criminal damage – cases must be tried summarily unless the value of the damage in question is £5,000 or more.[4]

5.19   Advocates should be reminded that, where two or more defendants are jointly charged, each defendant has an individual right of election.[5] Following conflicting elections from two or more defendants, a decision

---

2   MCA 1980 Sch 1 para 28(c).

3   Sexual Offences Act 1956 s5.

4   MCA 1980 s22(1).

5   R *v Brentwood Justices ex p Nicholls* [1991] 3 All ER 359, HL; [1990] 2 QB 598; [1990] 3 All ER 516; [1990] 3 WLR 534, DC.

would then have to be made about whether or not the defendants' cases are to be severed or, alternatively, whether they are so inexorably linked that they should be dealt with together. Should that be the case, where one or more defendant elects to have his case dealt with at the Crown Court, the others would follow. However, an election to have one's case dealt with in a magistrates' court can be advanced by way of mitigation at any Crown Court sentencing hearing, where a defendant has his/her case committed to the Crown Court to be heard with a co-defendant.

5.20   In addition, where a defendant is charged with one or more indictable-only charges as well as an either-way offence, notwithstanding the fact that it may be appropriate for a defendant to have that charge dealt with in the magistrates' court if s/he were charged with that matter alone, the magistrates may feel, again, that if the facts of those charges are so closely linked, jurisdiction should be declined and the either-way charge be dealt with at the Crown Court with the indictable-only matters.

Youth court provisions

5.21   The general rule for defendants who are children or young persons is that their cases should be heard in the youth court, ie, tried summarily.[6] However, the following exceptions apply:

1) Where the youth is charged jointly with an adult, his/her case must be heard in the adult court.[7]
2) Where the youth is charged with an offence with an adult charged at the same time with aiding and abetting, causing, procuring, allowing or permitting that offence, the youth may be tried by the magistrates' court.[8]
3) Where the youth has been charged with aiding and abetting, causing, procuring, allowing or permitting an offence with which an adult is charged at the same time, his/her case may be heard in the magistrates' court.[9]
4) Where the youth is charged with an offence relating to the same facts as those giving rise to proceedings against an adult charged at the same time, his/her case may be heard in the magistrates' court.[10]

6   Children and Young Persons Act (CYPA) 1933 s46(1).
7   Ibid s46(1)(a).
8   Ibid s46(1)(b).
9   CYPA 1963 s18(a).
10 Ibid s18(b).

5.22   The magistrates' court may remit a youth to the youth court for trial where:[11]

1) the adult elects to have his case dealt with summarily (where s/he is charged with an either way offence) and the youth pleads not guilty, or

2) the court proceeds to enquire into the information as examining magistrates and either commits the adult for trial or discharges him/her, and in the case of the child or young person, proceeds to the summary trial of the information.

5.23   However, there are exceptions to the general rule that may result in a child or young person being committed for trial to the Crown Court. MCA 1980 s24(1) sets these out as follows:

1) a young person between the ages of 10 and 17 is charged with a 'grave crime' as defined in CYPA 1933 s53(2), ie, with an offence punishable by 14 years' imprisonment or more in the case of an adult, or where s/he is charged with indecent assault on another person;

2) a young person aged 14 or over who is charged with causing death by dangerous driving or with causing death by careless driving while under the influence of drink or drugs;

3) a young person is jointly charged with an adult and the court considers that it is necessary in the interests of justice for the youth to be committed to the Crown Court with the adult.

This list is not exhaustive and a full list of offences defined as grave crimes appears at appendix N.

5.24   The effect of the definition of 'grave crimes' is that the issue of jurisdiction must be addressed in cases of, for example, robbery, rape, and residential burglary. Unlike in the adult court, the issue of mode of trial need not be considered in cases of, for example, non-residential burglary, where the maximum sentence for an adult is ten years' imprisonment.

5.25   It is not surprising, therefore, that the guidelines for deciding mode of trial in the youth court differ from those guidelines referred to earlier in this chapter. Instead of relying on the *National Mode of Trial Guidelines*, the court has to consider not only the age of the defendant charged but also the desirability of disposing of the case expeditiously. However, the court must also have due regard to the proper sentence that should be imposed for that particular offence.

11   MCA 1980 s29(2).

Following *R v Inner London Youth Court ex p DPP*,[12] the position has been clarified. The court should consider, for defendants aged between ten and 14, whether the offence is so serious that a custodial sentence can be justified. In the case of 15- to 17- year-olds, the court must decide whether the case is so serious that, if the court were sentencing offenders aged between 18 and 20 years old, a sentence substantially more than two years would be justified.[13] A distinction can be drawn between these provisions and those that apply in the magistrates' court in that the court should be asked to consider the particular circumstances of each defendant. However, from what limited guidance has been forthcoming from the Court of Appeal, the following issues have been determined:

1) A youth court should not accept jurisdiction of rape cases.[14]
2) Jurisdiction should have been declined in the case of a youth charged with two robberies, 13 charges of burglary, various other offences and where he was asking for 52 other offences to be taken into consideration.[15]
3) Jurisdiction should be declined where a defendant was charged with assault with intent to rob, where a victim had been assaulted in the dark and a dog chain pulled around her neck.[16]

The procedure to be adopted at the mode of trial hearing is, however, the same as that adopted in the magistrates' court where mode of trial proceedings take place. Again, both prosecution and defence advocates will be permitted to make their representations, although the court will take into account the prosecution's version of events. As in the adult court, the court should not consider the defendant's previous convictions when deciding mode of trial issues.[17]

---

12 [1986] 1 WLR 1374, CA.
13 CYPA 1933 s53(2).
14 *R v Billam* [1986] 1 WLR 349, CA
15 *R v Corcoran* (1986) 8 Cr App R (S) 118, CA.
16 *R v Learmouth* (1988) 10 Cr App R 229, CA.
17 *R v Hammersmith Juvenile Court ex p O (a minor)* (1987) 151 JP 740, DC.

CHAPTER 6

Summary trials

Introduction

6.1   The summary trial before magistrates arguably places the most difficult demands on criminal lawyers in their early years. Its difficulty is often under-estimated and, as a result, it tends to be regarded as a prelude and a stepping stone to the Crown Court trial. However, the whole procedure is extremely speedy, requiring a versatile and agile approach. One minute the advocate may be tearing into a police officer, the next minute, assuming a moderate and academic tone in making a submission of no case to answer. Aside from the speed of the whole procedure, the tribunal itself should not be under-estimated. Many magistrates are notoriously pro-prosecution and simply will not be persuaded not to accept the evidence of police officers whom they see appearing before them regularly, even when there is overwhelming evidence to suggest that the officers were lying. This can, at times, be a depriving and demoralising experience and contrasts markedly with any likely experiences with juries in the Crown Court.

The forum

6.2   The quality of justice administered in the magistrates' court does not always meet the standards that one expects. The all too common failure of magistrates (particularly a lay bench) to apply properly the requisite burden and standard of proof can be particularly disappointing. There can be a tendency (although of course never expressed) to believe that all defendants are guilty unless a very strong case for the defence can be made out, particularly if magistrates are not told that a defendant is of good character. In addition, as mentioned above, there can be a reluctance to accept that police officers are lying, particularly in less cosmopolitan areas of the country where the same police officers appear in court regularly and where an arguably unhealthy degree of respect for the law enforcement officers exists. It is particularly difficult to win cases where the charges consist of, or include, assaulting police officers and it is perhaps partly for this reason that some offences, originally triable either way are converted by the CPS to offences triable in the magistrates' court only. Offences which may be prosecuted in the magistrates' court only include assaulting a police constable in the execution of his/her duty, contrary to Police Act 1964 s51(3) (as opposed to assault occasioning actual bodily harm to a police officer which is triable either way) and the lesser public order offences, contrary to Public Order Act 1986 s4 or s5 (as opposed to s3, affray, where the defendant has a right to trial by a jury).

Before the trial

6.3   Usually, there will be no other legal adviser representing the defendant's interests at court. It is, therefore, particularly important to have a pre-trial conference with the defendant, taking him/her through the proof of evidence, addressing potential evidential difficulties and other issues, such as whether or not s/he should be called to give evidence and which, if any, defence witnesses should be called. If the defendant has not co-operated with solicitors before the trial, it may be necessary to obtain a full proof of evidence outside the courtroom.

6.4   In addition, if proofs of evidence have been obtained from defence witnesses, the defence should ensure that those witnesses are at court and give them copies of their proofs of evidence to refresh their memories. Usually, the rules of court do not permit any discussion concerning the evidence they propose to give and those witnesses should be reminded that, assuming they are not character witnesses, they must remain outside court until they are called. Exceptionally, if proofs of evidence have not been obtained from witnesses who have arrived at court and whose evidence may support that of the defendant, it is permitted to take full instructions from those witnesses on matters of fact and thereafter to make a decision with the defendant whether to call them. It is obviously not ideal to have to take instructions from potential witnesses at the last minute, but the relaxation of the rules has removed the previous rigid requirement which forbade advocates at court to speak to any of the defence witnesses (except for character witnesses) before they were to give evidence. In those circumstances, when a witness attended unexpectedly or had not previously provided instructions, the advocate was forced either to apply for an adjournment, call a witness unprepared, or discard that witness, whose evidence may have been of assistance to the defendant.

6.5   Before the trial commences, it is also useful to speak to the prosecution advocate to ensure that all the witnesses which the prosecution proposes to adduce are at court. In addition, it may be possible to agree certain evidence, thereby releasing some witnesses (for the prosecution and/or the defence) or to obtain admissions pursuant to Criminal Justice Act 1967 s10 (where, for example, there are statements from witnesses not at court, not in the requisite s9 form, but whose evidence is unchallenged).

6.6   If some or all of the prosecution witnesses are not at court and their evidence cannot be agreed or dispensed with, the prosecution advocate is likely to apply for an adjournment. A decision then needs to be taken on whether to oppose that application. Usually, if the defendant is ready to proceed it should be opposed. If the application is not granted, the prosecution may be forced to offer no evidence and the charge or charges will be dismissed. However, there may be good reasons why an adjournment is appropriate and, in the authors' experience, the prosecution will often be granted at least a second bite at the cherry before being ordered to proceed, in the absence of all or a significant part of the prosecution's evidence.

Composition of the court

6.7   The make-up of the tribunal in the magistrates' court is of particular significance. In the majority of courts in England and Wales, the tribunal comprises three lay members (known as 'the lay bench') who are advised on legal matters by a clerk, who potentially has significant power and influence over the magistrates and over the whole court procedure. When addressing a lay bench, the chair should be addressed as 'Sir' or 'Madam' and the two wing members referred to as 'your colleagues'. It is only police officers and a few old-fashioned advocates who, for some peculiar historical reason, choose to refer to a lay bench as 'Your Worships'.

6.8   In some magistrates' courts (particularly in large urban areas) stipendiary magistrates sit (although such magistrates also have a clerk working with them). Stipendiary magistrates (loosely referred to as 'stipes') are legally qualified and, where matters of law arise, it is generally considered preferable to have a stipendiary magistrate. A stipendiary magistrate is referred to as 'Sir' or 'Madam'.

Disclosure

6.9   Once the trial is ready to proceed, witnesses (except for character witnesses) will be required to remain outside the courtroom and the defendant will need to surrender him/herself to the dock and be formally identified. The prosecution advocate will then open the case in summary form. It is obviously helpful to have advance disclosure of the witness statements and that happens automatically for an offence triable either-way.[1] However, the prosecution is not under a duty to disclose statements for offences which are summary only and unhelpful prosecutors do not necessarily provide copies of the statements as a matter of course. Instead, it may only be possible to obtain a summary of the statements, just before the hearing, which results in the particularly laborious exercise of having to write down everything put to the prosecution witnesses in chief, as opposed to merely perusing the statement and adding additional evidence, if adduced.

6.10   Unlike the situation now in the Crown Court, there is still no duty on the defendant to disclose a defence statement in advance of the trial in the magistrates' court. However, it is open to the defendant to provide a statement.[2] Careful consideration needs to be given to whether it is in the defendant's best interest to provide voluntary disclosure of his/her defence before the trial, which would give the prosecution the opportunity of knowing the defence case in advance, but which, in appropriate cases, may result in the prosecution deciding not to proceed with the trial. The prosecution still has a duty of primary disclosure[3] (see further para 9.2) and if the defendant provides a voluntary defence statement within 14 days of primary disclosure, the prosecution will have the duty of secondary disclosure.[4] The issues relating to whether the defendant should provide a disclosure of his/her defence statement[5] are discussed in more detail in chapter 9.

Admissibility of evidence

6.11   If there are any matters of law concerning, for example, the potential admissibility of evidence which would require a voir dire, or non-agreement concerning the editing of potentially prejudicial or irrelevant evidence, those matters should be dealt with at the outset

---

1   Pursuant to Magistrates' Courts (Advance Information) Rules 1985 SI No 601.
2   Under Criminal Procedure and Investigations Act 1996 s6.
3   Ibid s3.
4   Ibid s3.
5   Ibid s6.

and should not be referred to in opening. One of the particular handicaps of the magistrates' court system is that the tribunal of law is the same as the tribunal of fact and there is an obvious artificiality in the same tribunal having first to consider whether to admit evidence and, if ruling it inadmissible, then, second, putting it outside their minds in determining the issues of guilt on the basis of evidence properly adduced at the conclusion of the hearing or at the end of the prosecution case where a submission of no case to answer is made. That does not mean that arguments about admissibility are necessarily a waste of time as they may focus the magistrates' minds on some of the important and contentious issues between the parties, which may be of benefit to the defendant, even if the challenged evidence is ruled admissible.

The prosecution case

6.12   Once there has been a determination of any issues of law, the prosecution will call its evidence. Usually, lay witnesses are called before police officers. Usually, witnesses will have seen copies of their statements before entering court to refresh their memories. Note that police officers are trained in cross-examination techniques and are unlikely to 'crack' in the way that some lay witnesses may. Nonetheless, cross-examination may disclose areas of factual conflict between witnesses which can later be exploited by the defence advocate when making his/her address to the court.

Cross-examination

6.13   The whole process of cross-examining prosecution witnesses is a difficult one. As there will be usually be no other legal representative on behalf of the defendant at court, there will be no other person taking notes and where important points of evidence emerge in cross-examination, it will be up to the defence advocate to note those parts of the evidence without losing the flow of cross-examination. The balance of timing is not easy.

6.14   Generally, police officers make their notes together with other officers and, if the prosecution is satisfied that it has the evidence it wishes to adduce before the court, some police officers may be tendered solely for cross-examination. Sometimes, therefore, cross-examination of one witness after another can occur rapidly. It is obviously a matter of tactics about the degree of cross-examination of each witness. If helpful answers are obtained from one police officer then, in general, it is not an area worth exploring with a further witness in case an unhelpful response is obtained. If it is clear that all police officers will deny the same allegations, for example, that they assaulted the defendant, it may be worth while, once the case has been put to one or two police officers, for the defence to inform the court that the same case is made against each witness, without necessarily going through the time-consuming and fruitless exercise of formally putting the same points a number of times in cross-examination to each witness.

No case to answer

6.15 At the conclusion of the prosecution case (which would be read), it is open to the defence advocate to make a submission of no case to answer.

6.16 There has been academic debate about whether the test in the magistrates' court pursuant to the Practice Note[6] sets out a different test from that in the leading case relevant to the Crown Court, namely, *R v Galbraith*.[7] The test is considered to be the same one, although adapted as appropriate for the magistrates' court where, as noted above, the magistrates are judges both of fact and law. The test set out in *Galbraith* per Lord Lane LCJ[8] is as follows:

> (1) If there is no evidence that the crime alleged has been committed by the defendant there is no difficulty. The judge will of course stop the case. (2) The difficulty arises where there is some evidence but it is of a tenuous character, for example because of inherent weakness or vagueness or because it is inconsistent with other evidence. (a) Where the judge comes to the conclusion that the Crown's evidence, taken at its highest, is such that a jury properly directed could not properly convict on it, it is his duty, on submission being made, to stop the case. (b) Where however the prosecution evidence is such that its strength or weakness depends on the view to be taken of a witness's reliability, or other matters which are generally speaking within the province of the jury and

6 Sub nom *Practice Direction (Submission of no case)* [1962] 1 All ER 448, DC.
7 [1981] 1 WLR 1039; [1981] 2 All ER at 1060; (1981) 73 Cr App R 124; [1981] Crim LR 648, CA.
8 [1981] 2 All ER at 1062.

where on one possible view of the facts there is evidence on which a jury could properly come to the conclusion that the defendant is guilty, then the judge should allow the matter to be tried by the jury.

6.17   Applying the Practice Note, it would be open to the magistrates to stop the case, even where at the close of prosecution case there is some evidence which, if accepted, would entitle a reasonable tribunal to convict or to acquit if it does not accept the evidence, whether because it is conflicting, or has been contradicted or for any other reason.

6.18   In a submission of no case to answer, reliance has regularly been placed by defence advocates on *R v Shippey*,[9] sometimes referred to as the 'plums and duff' case. Turner J held that:

> ... the requirement to take the prosecution case at its highest did not mean 'picking out the plums and leaving the duff behind'. The judge should assess the evidence and if the evidence of the witness upon whom the prosecution case depended was self-contradictory and out of reason and all common sense, such evidence was tenuous and suffered from inherent weakness. It was necessary to make an assessment of the evidence as a whole and it was not simply a matter of the credibility of individual witnesses or of evidential inconsistencies between witnesses, although those matters might play a subordinate role.

6.19   However, many magistrates, in the authors' experience, take an unsympathetic approach to *Shippey*-type submissions and, while the judgment has not been disapproved in a higher court, a submission based on inconsistencies where there is some evidence to support a prima facie case would be unlikely to succeed.

6.20   It is of course open to the defence advocate to make a submission of no case on one or a number of charges the defendant is facing, while accepting that there is a prima facie case in respect of other charges. Should the submission prove successful, the relevant charge or charges will be dismissed. If that represents the totality of the charges, the defendant will be discharged and an application for the defendant's costs out of central funds can be made. In general, assuming the defendant was legally aided (see further, chapter 18), the only costs likely to be awarded are the relatively modest ones involving his/her travel to court.

9   [1988] Crim LR 767, DC.

The defendant as witness

6.21 If it is held that there is a prima facie case on at least one charge against the defendant, or no submission is made, the next important decision is whether or not to call the defendant to give evidence in his/her own case. The defendant will need to be reminded that if s/he does not give evidence, it is open to the magistrates to draw an adverse inference in accordance with the caution under Criminal Justice and Public Order Act 1994 s35. The effect of s35 has been that more defendants have chosen to go into the witness box. However, if cross-examination of prosecution witnesses has gone well and/or the defendant has previous convictions which it will be necessary to protect following an attack of the witnesses' credibility and the defendant is potentially vulnerable to losing his/her 'shield' pursuant to Criminal Evidence Act 1898 s1(f), and/or where the defendant has given a full explanation of his/her defence in interview which is unlikely to be improved on by him/her giving evidence, it may nonetheless be preferable not to call the defendant.

Other defence witnesses

6.22 Once the defendant has given evidence, or if s/he is not giving evidence, then the remaining defence evidence may be called. There may be a number of defence witnesses in support of the defendant and another decision will need to be made about who to call. It is not always the best decision to call all witnesses. In general, one good witness may be preferable to a number of witnesses of varying quality. The potential for the prosecution advocate to exploit inconsistencies between defence witnesses and between those witnesses and the defendant should be borne in mind and it is worth the advocate assessing the potential quality of the witnesses when introducing him/herself to them before the hearing and, where appropriate, relying on the views of the solicitor's representative who obtained the witness statements in the first place.

Closing speeches

6.23 At the conclusion of the defence case (including agreed evidence read by the defence advocate) it is the time for the closing address to the court. This is the one opportunity the defence advocate will have to submit that the prosecution has failed to prove its case beyond reasonable doubt. Advocates will have the opportunity to take the magistrates through parts of the evidence and to exploit areas of conflict between the prosecution witnesses, referring to defence evidence if it assists the defendant's case and to make submissions of law about whether the prosecution has proved its case to the requisite standard. The prosecution advocate does not have the right to make a closing address in response and s/he is limited to correcting any matters of evidence which the defence advocate has got wrong and making submissions of pure law. It is impossible to estimate how many cases are won or lost on a closing address but it is the opportunity for the last words that are said about the case before the magistrates retire to consider their decision on whether the charges have been proved.

The decision

6.24   If the court is a lay bench, the court clerk is often called into the magistrates' room to assist them on matters of law. What passes between the clerk and the magistrates is not revealed, although on occasion some clerks tell the advocate afterwards what advice was given to the magistrates. Practice varies between courts, but sometimes the degree of influence of the clerk appears to be fairly substantial. This can lead to clashes during the trial if the defence advocate perceives that the clerk is overstepping his/her role.

6.25   Once the magistrates have reached a decision, the court reassembles. The decision is announced by the chair and the court is not informed about whether it was a unanimous decision or not. If the charge or charges are dismissed, the defendant is discharged and an application for costs out of central funds may be made as well as an application to revoke the legal aid contribution, if there was such a contribution, and for remittance of all contributions already paid by the defendant. If the defendant has been instructing the defence advocate privately, then an application for all of his/her legal costs to be met by central funds should be made. The award of costs is ultimately a matter of discretion for the magistrates.

6.26   If the court finds that one or a number of charges have been proved against the defendant the first matter for consideration will be sentencing (see chapters 13 to 15).

Checklist for summary trial

1) Have a full proof of evidence from the defendant and his/her comments on the prosecution witnesses. It may be necessary to take a proof before the court sits.
2) Find out the composition of the tribunal. Court clerks may be able to give advocates useful information about their views/prejudices/personalities.
3) Are there any legal submissions? If so, consider the appropriate stage to raise them.
4) Can a submission of no case to answer in respect of at least one charge be made at the end of the prosecution case?
5) Ensure that defence witnesses are at court and remain outside the courtroom (unless they are only character witnesses).
6) Prepare points for the closing submissions in advance, because that submission must be made immediately on completion of the defence case.
7) If the defendant is convicted, is it an appropriate case for an adjournment for a pre-sentence report to be obtained, or for a committal for sentence to the Crown Court? Be prepared to make a bail application on conviction.
8) If the defendant is acquitted, make an application for a defence costs order out of central funds.

CHAPTER 7

Committal proceedings and committals for sentence

Committal proceedings

7.1   Criminal cases which are proceeding to the Crown Court require committal proceedings, except serious fraud cases and certain cases involving children, for which transfer proceedings take place under Criminal Justice Act 1987 ss4 and 5 and Criminal Justice Act 1991 s53 respectively. Magistrates must be satisfied on the evidence placed before them that they should commit the defendant for trial by jury for an indictable offence, by Magistrates' Courts Act (MCA) 1980 s6, as amended by Criminal Procedure and Investigation Act (CPIA) 1996 s47.

7.2   Mode of committal can take place in two ways:

1) 'short-form' committal,[1] whereby the defendant accepts that s/he has a prima facie case to answer which hearing would usually only take five to ten minutes; or

2) committal whereby the defendant challenges the prosecution to establish that there is a case to answer (somewhat misleadingly referred to as an 'old-style committal').[2]

Section 6(2) hearings

7.3   The majority of cases proceed by a committal hearing under s6(2). In those circumstances, the examining justices commit the defendant for trial in the Crown Court without considering the prosecution evidence, unless the defendant is unrepresented or the defence advocate requests them to consider a submission that there is insufficient evidence to commit the defendant for trial on at least a committal charge.

Section 6(1) hearings

7.4   Alternatively, the examining justices will be requested to consider written evidence produced by the prosecution, comprising statements, depositions, copies of exhibits and other documents.

7.5   It is no longer possible to request the attendance of 'live' prosecution witnesses to give oral evidence, which subsequently becomes their deposition. It is important for the defence advocate to advise the defendant of that change in the law, introduced from April 1997 by CPIA 1996 s47, because some 'experienced' defendants may

1   By way of MCA 1980 s6(2).
2   Ibid s6(1).

be familiar with 'old style' committals, in their earlier form, which they see as offering 'two bites of the cherry', and will, therefore, be insistent to have a particular witness brought to the magistrates' court.

7.6   Other changes introduced by the CPIA 1996 include the abolition of any witness orders at committal and the requirement to give an alibi warning (in an appropriate case). Instead, these matters are incorporated into pleas and directions hearings and defence statements.

7.7   Under MCA 1980 s6(1), it is open for the defence advocate to make a submission of law that there is insufficient evidence produced by the prosecution advocate to support the charge on which the defendant is sought to be committed. This can only be done when all the written evidence has been adduced and summarised orally by the prosecution advocate. The basis for the submission is likely to be that a necessary element of the offence has not been made out or there is a gap in the evidence which the prosecution has been unable to plug. No defence evidence may be adduced at the committal hearing and the examining justices will know nothing at that stage about the defendant's antecedents. It is perhaps trite to state that the prospects of a successful submission, where the prosecution has considered that there is sufficient evidence to commit the defendant, will be very low.

7.8   If, however, a submission is successful, the defendant will be discharged on that charge(s) and, if there are no other charges on which s/he has been committed, the defendant will be discharged and the defence advocate would be entitled to apply for costs out of central funds in the same way as if the defendant had been acquitted after a trial. It is worth informing the defendant that if s/he has been discharged, this is not the same as an acquittal and it would be open to the CPS, if further evidence became available, to re-charge the defendant or even voluntarily bill him/her directly via the High Court, by which committal proceedings are by-passed. Fortunately, re-charging a defendant rarely happens in practice.

Magistrates' Courts Act 1980 s41

7.9   If the defendant is committed for trial for offences either triable only on indictment, or triable either way, the magistrates may also commit him/her on summary trial for offences allegedly committed at the same time; provided that the offences are either imprisonable or endorsable under the provisions of MCA 1980 s41 (see para 7.1).

Bail applications at the committal hearing

7.10   If the defendant has been on bail, and has attended a reasonable number of times at court without any suggestion of a breach of conditions, bail will usually be continued to trial on the same, if any, conditions. The defendant may wish to have conditions removed or varied. If so, instructions would need to be obtained by the defence advocate about the reasons why and whether the defendant is able to offer alternative conditions if required by the court. It will be helpful for the defence advocate to obtain the prosecution advocate's view before making an application to vary or remove bail conditions, to see if there is likely to be objection and, if so, whether that objection can be met by the imposition of alternative conditions. If the defendant has had sureties, it is important to clarify whether they have been made continuous to disposal of the case in the Crown Court. If the sureties were only taken as far as committal, they would need to be re-taken either at court or at a local police station. If the sureties are not at court, the defendant should be warned of the risk that s/he may temporarily be remanded in custody until the sureties have been taken. If the defendant has been in custody until his/her appearance in the Crown Court and there is a proper basis for making a renewed bail application, for example, the availability of new and/or further sureties, where the defendant has not been committed on all the charges, or where further evidence has come to light strengthening the defendant's case, then the court would require at least 24 hours' written notice if such an application is to be made.

After the committal hearing

7.11   Once it has been determined that the defendant will be committed to the Crown Court and the question of bail has been resolved, the chair of the examining justices will announce that the defendant will be committed to stand his/her trial at a nearby Crown Court (except for certain serious offences, which may be heard at another court, for example, the Central Criminal Court) and s/he will be told of the first date to appear at the Crown Court. It is worth checking with the clerk beforehand when that date will be, which is usually about six weeks after committal. The next appearance will be the pleas and directions hearing.

7.12   As far as legal aid is concerned, the defence advocate should check whether a through order covering the Crown Court has been obtained. If not, s/he should apply for an extension of legal aid (subject to means) to cover the Crown Court hearing. Only in a murder case will a legal aid order allow for representation of two advocates, including a QC, from the first hearing in the Crown Court and the order will therefore usually be extended to allow for representation by one advocate and instructing solicitor in the Crown Court.

7.13   The defence advocate should have a short discussion with the defendant, reminding him/her that the committal hearing took place without any defence evidence being adduced and should not, therefore, be considered as anything more than the magistrates considering that there was sufficient evidence to commit the defendant on one or a number of charges.

Checklist for committal hearing

1) Determine mode of committal.
2) Explain to defendant what the committal hearing means in practice.
3) Ensure that legal aid is extended through to the Crown Court.
4) Establish from the clerk what the place and date will be for the pleas and directions hearing in the Crown Court.
5) Consider whether there is any need for a bail application or variation.

Committal for sentence

7.14   Where the magistrates' court takes the view, that having heard about the defendant's previous convictions and antecedents, its own sentencing powers are too limited, or where it becomes apparent that the defendant has been in breach of an order of the Crown Court, the defendant will be committed to the relevant Crown Court for sentence. If the defendant has been on bail up until then, it is likely that bail will be withdrawn at this stage as a custodial sentence of reasonable length is the most likely outcome once the matter comes before a judge at the Crown Court.

The effect of Crime (Sentences) Act 1997 s51

7.15   Crime (Sentences) Act 1997 s51 came into effect at the same time as the implementation of CPIA 1996 s49[3] which implemented the provisions affecting plea before venue (see paras 5.1 to 5.6), by inserting a new s38A into the MCA 1980. Its effect is to extend the circumstances in which a magistrates' court may commit to the Crown Court a person convicted of an either way offence. Where a person who has indicated a guilty plea, following the plea before venue procedure, is convicted by a magistrates' court, and where s/he is also being committed for trial to the Crown Court for a related offence(s), s/he may be committed to the Crown Court for sentence for the offence for which s/he has pleaded guilty, to avoid the possibility of being sentenced for related offences by different courts. For the purposes of s38A, two offences will be treated as being related to one another if those charges (were they both to be prosecuted) could be joined on the same indictment.[4]

What if the defendant is acquitted following trial at the Crown Court?

7.16   If a defendant is convicted following his/her trial at the Crown Court, that court may then sentence the defendant pursuant to its powers under Powers of Criminal Courts Act (PCCA) 1973 s42. However, where a defendant is acquitted of a related offence following a not guilty plea and committal to the Crown Court, the Crown Court may not sentence for the offence for which s/he pleaded guilty, pursuant to that provision, unless the magistrates' court had previously stated that one of the conditions set out in MCA 1980 s38(2) is satisfied and that it could have committed him/her for sentence for that offence. In such circumstances, where the Crown Court cannot exercise its powers under PCCA 1973 s42, the Crown Court will have to sentence the defendant for the offence in such a way that the magistrates' court might have sentenced him/her.

7.17   By way of example, where a defendant:

3   1 October 1997.
4   MCA 1980 s38A(6).

1) indicates a guilty plea to possession of an offensive weapon, but
2) elects a Crown Court trial for theft following the plea before venue procedure, and
3) both cases are committed to the Crown Court, and
4) s/he is subsequently acquitted of that offence,

the Crown Court may only sentence him/her for the offensive weapon charge as if s/he was being sentenced in the magistrates' court.

Multi-defendant cases

7.18   Where two or more defendants are jointly charged with an offence, and one defendant indicates a guilty plea in accordance with the plea before venue procedure, and another defendant elects to have his/her case dealt with at the Crown Court, the position remains as it was before MCA 1980 s38A came into force, and those defendants will be dealt with separately.

How to prepare a brief

Introduction

8.1   Any solicitor's objective in preparing his/her brief should be to provide his/her chosen barrister with all relevant documentation, as well as details of all further relevant issues that may arise throughout the course of the trial. This is to ensure that counsel will be able to prepare fully for trial on the strength of that document. In many cases, except for any conferences that may be held with counsel, the brief and its enclosures will amount to the only knowledge of a case that a barrister may have. Style naturally varies between solicitors, regarding the depth to which the case should be explained in the brief. However, notwithstanding the importance of that document, the preparation of it is a skill that, in practice, newly-qualified solicitors are left to 'pick up' by following the examples of others in their practice. The aim of this chapter is, therefore, to shed some light on those required skills.

8.2   This chapter will, in general, deal with the preparation of a Crown Court brief for counsel, although, of course, there will be occasions when barristers are briefed to appear in the magistrates' court (see para 8.43).

The layout of a brief

8.3   Most solicitors will be aware that a brief has a backsheet. The backsheet contains a summary of the main details of the case. The backsheet should be typed up with the printing on the right hand side of the paper commencing with the heading of the case and case number (if known) at the top. Underneath, the name of the case should be stated, eg, 'R v Smith' and underneath that, the brief should be endorsed stating whether or not it is a legal aid case. If it is, the words 'legal aid' should simply appear at this part of the backsheet.

8.4   Below that, in the centre of the backsheet, the nature of the document should be stated. In its simplest form, a brief may simply state 'Brief to counsel'. However, there may be many occasions where a solicitor has to be more specific about the nature of the document. Counsel should readily be able to ascertain whether the brief requires counsel to attend, for example, a plea and directions hearing in addition to the trial. The document may also require counsel to deal with the following aspects of a case:

1) to advise on evidence including expert evidence,
2) to advise in conference,
3) to settle, for example, a defence statement.

8.5   If these aspects of a case are to be specifically considered by counsel, the backsheet should specifically refer to the fact that counsel is instructed to deal with those issues. The purpose of detailing the issues to be addressed in the document are so that a barrister will be aware from simply looking at the backsheet, even before s/he reads the papers, that s/he will be expected to advise in some respects on the case. An example of such an endorsement on the backsheet would read:

> Instructions to counsel to Advise on Evidence and to settle a defence Statement, Brief to appear on behalf of the defendant at a Plea and Directions Hearing on [date] and at any subsequent hearing.

8.6   Counsel's details should then be placed underneath that section of the brief, followed by the solicitor's details, which should be placed at the bottom of the backsheet. Those details should include the name of the solicitor with conduct, his/her practice address, telephone number, fax number (and e-mail address if appropriate) together with the file reference number.

8.7   Special mention should be made at this point of a difference in layout if both leading and junior counsel are to be briefed. That part of the brief dealing with counsel's details would appear as follows:

> Leading counsel
> John Smith QC
> Middle Chambers, Temple EC4
>
> With You
> Junior counsel
> David Brown
> 1 Temple Chambers, Temple EC4

8.8   In those circumstances, where leading counsel is to be briefed, two identical sets of papers should be sent, to both leading and junior counsel. In the event that, for example, only one copy of a particular enclosure is available (for example, an audio tape of interview or video tape, or set of photographs), the brief should make it clear to both counsel that that is the case.

8.9   The inside of the brief should commence on the front page with the same heading as the case, as appears on the backsheet. Beneath the heading at the commencement of the brief, the solicitor should set out by way of a list, the enclosures which are being sent to the barrister. A brief would usually therefore start with the words 'counsel has herewith:' followed by a list in numerical order of all the enclosures being sent.

What enclosures should be sent?

8.10 The list of enclosures will vary from case to case. Depending on their relevance to the case in question, consideration should be given to the following enclosures (paras 8.12 to 8.29, below) being included in the brief.

Papers previously before counsel

8.11 In some cases, barristers may well have been briefed throughout the magistrates' court proceedings and papers sent to them at that stage. Papers previously received should still be enclosed with the brief. In many cases, this may only amount to a backsheet, but in the event that there is further documentation than has previously been included in an earlier brief, that documentation should be enclosed.

Committal bundle

8.12 It is not anticipated that anybody reading will fail to understand why a copy of the prosecution papers should be enclosed with the brief to counsel and no doubt this paragraph is self-explanatory. The full committal bundle should be sent to counsel so that counsel is aware of the totality of the evidence that has been disclosed. Furthermore, if, before the brief is sent to the barrister, any notice of further evidence has been received from the CPS, those documents should be enclosed and placed in chronological order. If such notices are not received until after the brief has been delivered to counsel, once received, they should be sent to him/her as soon as possible for consideration with the brief at that stage.

Defendant's proof of evidence

8.13 Irrespective of whether or not the case is contested, the defendant's version of events will always be needed by counsel. In the case of a contested trial, it will provide the basis of cross-examination because the areas of dispute will be known. In the event of a guilty plea being tendered in due course, it will provide the basis for any mitigation.

Defence statement

8.14   Following the coming into effect of the provisions of the Criminal Procedure and Investigations Act 1996, in the case of defended cases committed to the Crown Court (where the defendant is actively defending his case as opposed to putting the prosecution to proof), the defence will be under an obligation to serve the CPS with a defence statement. Failure to do so may result in an adverse inference being drawn. The statement should set out the nature of the defendant's defence in general terms, ie, self defence or consent in a rape trial, and in it, s/he must set out those matters on which s/he takes issue with the prosecution case. In addition, s/he is under an obligation to set out in respect of each and every matter, the reason why s/he does take issue. In many cases solicitors may abrogate that task to counsel (in which case the defendant's proof of evidence must be sufficiently complete to enable counsel to draft that statement). Where solicitors have drafted the defendant's defence statement, a copy of the defence statement signed by the defendant should be included in the brief to counsel so that s/he is aware of the basis on which the case is to be defended. If counsel is to settle the defence statement, the brief should clearly state on the backsheet that counsel is instructed to do that. The details concerning the preparation and service of the defence statement are dealt with more in chapter 9.

Witness statements taken on behalf of the defence

8.15   If corroborating or supporting statements have been taken on behalf of the defendant, these should be sent to counsel with the brief. In cases where a defendant is of good character and character statements have been taken, again, those should be included.

Copy indictment

8.16   This should always be included in a brief, together with any amended indictments that may be received.

Miscellaneous documentation

8.17   This heading refers to any additional documentation in the solicitor's possession that may be of relevance to a defendant's case and its scope is really limitless. A common example of such additional miscellaneous documentation may include diaries, court papers used in civil proceedings, miscellaneous correspondence to and from the defendant or to any third party. Solicitors should be aware that defendants often consider certain documentation to be of more relevance than in fact it is. Many solicitors feel that for the sake of completeness, all documentation should be sent to counsel with the brief, but if such documentation remains of limited evidential use, then that should be clearly stated in the brief.

Copy of the custody record and interview tapes

8.18   As a general rule, a copy of the custody record and tape of interview should always be requested by solicitors from the police station where the defendant was detained and those items, once received, should always be sent to counsel. Of course, solicitors will be aware that not all cases will turn on events at the police station. Many cases will of course be decided simply on the credibility of the defendant's version of events as opposed to that of the victim. However, that being said, a copy of the custody record will be of particular use to counsel if the issue of admissions made in interview or other breaches of the Police and Criminal Evidence Act 1984 (PACE) and/or the Codes of Practice are in issue. If the prosecution will be relying heavily on admissions made by the defendant in interview, counsel must be able to peruse the custody record which, in conjunction with any interview tape, may disclose breaches of PACE or the Codes of Practice giving rise to the exclusion of admissions made in interview pursuant to PACE s78. The custody record will disclose whether or not, for example, a defendant was reminded of his/her right to free independent legal advice (even by way of a telephone call) when s/he is initially detained at the police station, when reviews take place, when the question of intimate samples is dealt with and the time of his/her interview. In addition, the custody record should deal with the following issues, for example:

   1) whether or not the appropriate authority was obtained when the question of intimate samples was dealt with;

2) whether a forensic medical examiner was called to the police station to consider whether the defendant was fit to be detained and interviewed in circumstances where the defendant may have been suffering from any illness, the effects of medication, or even lack of sleep, at the time of his/her interview.

By perusing the custody record, a decision can be made about whether or not the custody sergeant will be required to attend court to give evidence. Decisions of this nature could simply not be considered unless the custody record is seen by counsel.

8.19   With regard to the tape of the interview(s), by sending it to counsel, a decision can be made about whether or not counsel feels that the summary supplied by the CPS in the committal bundle is accurate (or indeed for that matter, whether or not any transcript of the interview is required). There will of course be occasions when the tape needs to be listened to so that a decision can be made about whether or not questioning in an interview was oppressive or whether there are other grounds to argue that admissions should be excluded from the trial.

8.20   Furthermore, since the Criminal Justice and Public Order Act (CJPOA) 1994 came into effect, it has become increasingly important to listen to the taped interview. The issue of whether or not a defendant has failed to mention in his interview something on which s/he then relies at his/her trial will depend largely on the questions asked of him/her during interview. In addition, in deciding whether an inference can be drawn following a defendant's failure to answer questions during his/her interview, counsel will no doubt wish to satisfy him/herself that the caution and, where appropriate, the 'special warnings' pursuant to CJPOA 1994 ss36 and 37 were given to the defendant.

Video tapes

8.21   These will often be exhibited to statements contained in the committal bundle. Video tapes take many forms, for example, videos of interview (although still relatively rare), observation evidence, for example, in Customs and Excise/drugs cases or videos from security cameras, for example, at Post Offices, petrol forecourts, etc. Their relevance is obvious and, as such, counsel should have the opportunity of viewing them.

Photographs

8.22   These will, as with video tapes, be exhibited to prosecution statements. They may deal with, for example, injuries in assault cases or show the locus in quo. Their relevance is self-explanatory. Photographs may also be prepared on behalf of the defendant and, again, these should be included with the brief, together with any Criminal Justice Act 1967 s9 statement exhibiting them.

Bail record decision form

8.23   Irrespective of whether or not bail is in issue in any particular case, it is good practice to submit this form with the brief to counsel, so that written confirmation from the court about the defendant's bail position is known to counsel. However, the depth into which solicitors will need to consider the bail aspect of a defendant's case will, of course, depend on whether or not the defendant is on bail or in custody, whether or not previous bail applications have been made and if the defendant is in custody, whether it is anticipated that a bail application will be made, for example, at the pleas and directions hearing or at any subsequent hearing. It may be sufficient if the defendant is on unconditional bail, simply to state that fact in the brief. However, if the situation is more complex and a defendant has been remanded on conditional bail, or in custody and it is anticipated that a bail application will be made, then all relevant documentation should be sent to counsel. This should include not only a copy of the bail record decision form but a copy of any notice of application made to the Crown Court in respect of any appeal to the Crown Court from a magistrates' court's refusal to grant bail (see further, chapter 10), together with any other relevant documentation.

8.24   Counsel should always be fully appraised of their defendant's bail position because, when the issue of bail is first considered either at the pleas and directions hearing or at the trial itself, the question of that defendant's continued bail can be quickly disposed with. In particular, if a defendant has been granted bail subject to a surety, counsel must be aware of that fact so that the appropriate application can be made to court for that surety to be retaken, usually at the commencement of the trial.

Expert's reports

8.25   The question of experts will usually be an issue considered in the brief itself (see para 8.38, below). In most cases, it is unlikely that experts' reports will have been prepared before committal and hence, before counsel is instructed. This may not be the case where the scope of the client's legal aid order was extended at the magistrates' court stage of the proceedings to authorise the instruction of counsel. In such situations, counsel may well have previously advised that an expert should be instructed to deal with a particular aspect of the case and, if those reports are available, they should be included with the brief.

Miscellaneous correspondence/attendance notes

8.26   The relevance of documents under this heading will depend on the nature of the case in question. This heading is intended to cover primarily correspondence between solicitors and the CPS and may be relevant in the following situations (although this list is not exhaustive):

1) where statements or exhibits have been requested and not received;
2) where the crime support group at the police station where the defendant was detained has not supplied either the custody record or tape of interview, having previously been requested to do so;
3) where a request of some other nature has been made to the CPS that has either not been replied to or complied with in its entirety.

8.27   Since the introduction of the CJPOA 1994, and the widespread changes that were made to the rules regarding the right to silence, the question of advice given by solicitors to defendants to remain silent during an interview is one that has become a focal point for lawyers' attentions. This issue is dealt with later in this chapter at para 8.37. However, if the question of solicitors' advice to defendants to remain silent is likely to be an issue, a copy of the solicitor's note of attendance at the police station (or that of a colleague if the solicitor drafting the brief is not the same solicitor who attended at the police station) should be enclosed.

Plea and directions hearing questionnaire and copy practice rules

8.28   Most courts will, following committal, give the advocate at court a copy of the above documents so that the questionnaire can be completed in time for the plea and directions hearing (see chapter

11). If those documents are supplied, they should be enclosed with the brief for completion by counsel.

A copy of the legal aid order

8.29 This is not always strictly needed by counsel. However, an exception would exist where leading and junior counsel are to be briefed where legal aid is extended to cover the services of leading counsel. The legal aid order should specify whether or not Queen's Counsel is to be briefed or simply a leading counsel. Counsel's clerks will no doubt wish to be satisfied that, if a brief is sent to a Queen's Counsel in their chambers, the legal aid order does indeed cover the services of the counsel chosen.

The narrative

8.30 Once the exhibits have been listed, the solicitor should then set out a narrative dealing with all relevant aspects of his/her defendant's case. Style will of course vary considerably from solicitor to solicitor and it is a style that develops over the years. However, there is a common element that runs through all briefs in that, as stated at the outset of this chapter, once completed, they should provide all relevant information to enable counsel to prepare fully for the hearing(s) for which s/he has been briefed and to be able to advise where instructed to do so.

8.31 As a matter of style, solicitors should always refer to themselves as 'Instructing solicitors' as opposed to 'I' or 'we' and barristers should always be referred to as 'counsel' or, if appropriate 'leading counsel' and 'junior counsel'. The narrative should initially begin by stating for whom the solicitor acts. While this is obvious in the case of single defendants, where there are multiple defendants, solicitors should clearly state for which defendant they are acting, and who acts for the other defendants. If the solicitor acts for more than one defendant, the brief should clearly state which defendant that barrister is to represent, and who has been briefed on behalf of his/her other defendants. For example, a brief may start in the following way:

> Instructing solicitors act for John Smith and David Brown, the third defendant, Simon Green, being represented by Messrs White & Co. Counsel is briefed to appear on behalf of John Smith, Henry Sharpe of counsel being briefed on behalf of David Brown.

8.32   A section should then follow dealing with certain essential details about the case, namely:

1) what the defendant is charged with,
2) his/her proposed plea,
3) whether s/he is on bail or in custody, and if on bail setting out any conditions,
4) from which court s/he was committed and when,
5) whether or not it was a s6(2) committal or an 'old style committal',
6) details of witness orders given at committal should then be given.

8.33   It is at this point in setting out the facts of the case that practice differs substantially between individual solicitors. Many solicitors adopt the practice of setting out the prosecution case in substantial detail while others will simply summarise the salient points, referring counsel to specific statements and pages as appropriate. Similarly, many solicitors will effectively repeat what is contained in their defendant's proof while others will summarise the nature of the defendant's defence and refer counsel to the appropriate part of that proof. The method any solicitor adopts is a matter of personal choice. In setting out the nature of the defendant's defence, reference should be made to appropriate witness statements that have been taken on behalf of the defendant.

Reference to witness statements prepared on behalf of the defendant

8.34   It is not uncommon to find that while there are potential witnesses that need to be proofed, by the time that the brief is dictated, those witnesses may not have come forward. If there is an intention to see witnesses or an appointment has been made for them to attend solicitors' offices, then that should also be stated in the brief. Additional paperwork, for example, further evidence received from the CPS or, alternatively, further statements taken on behalf of defence witnesses can always be forwarded to counsel at a later stage.

Notice of witness requirements

8.35 Within 14 days of the committal hearing, the defendant (through his/her solicitors) is required to notify the Crown Court and the CPS of those prosecution witnesses which s/he shall require to attend the trial to give live evidence. Failure to notify both parties may result in the defendant forfeiting his/her right to cross-examine those witnesses at the trial as a result of not being able to compel the prosecution to call them. Cautious solicitors should inform the court and the CPS that, unless it is obvious that any prosecution witnesses' evidence can be accepted, all witnesses will be required to attend the trial. Counsel should therefore be specifically instructed to notify his/her instructing solicitor should s/he feel that any witness can be de-warned or to deal with that aspect of the case at the plea and directions hearing. Solicitors should be careful to ensure that prosecution witnesses are not needlessly required to attend the trial, yet at the same time, they should ensure that they retain their defendant's right to have them called if it proves necessary, by serving the appropriate notice within the requisite time limits.

Relevant law

8.36 At this stage it would be appropriate to deal with the law relating to the relevant issues of the particular case, for example, about admissibility of evidence and any case-law that may be appropriate to the case. Solicitors should then deal with any material issues that arose during the defendant's detention at the police station and at any interview. Any breaches of PACE should specifically be brought to counsel's attention. If the interview was one where the solicitor intervened and objected to questioning, then this fact should also be brought to the attention of counsel, who should be specifically instructed to listen to the interview tape(s). At that juncture, counsel should also be instructed to consider whether or not the tape summary, if provided to solicitors, can be agreed.

Events at the police station and the 'no comment' interview

8.37 Perhaps one of the lengthier, more complex issues that solicitors will now be required to deal with in their brief to counsel is the question of defendants giving no comment interviews. Solicitors should fully set out all relevant events as they occurred at the police station and should specifically bring to counsel's attention all issues that may be relevant in justifying advice given not to answer questions. While the right to silence provisions changed in April 1995, guidance to assist practitioners has not been forthcoming from the higher courts in great numbers, especially about those issues that will be considered as bona fide reasons for defendants refusing to answer questions. The purpose of this chapter is not to deal with the change in the right to silence provisions but to advise solicitors, who may well have to give evidence on the defendant's behalf about the reason why such advice was given, to set out fully to counsel the reasons for that advice. Issues to be considered in the brief, in particular, should include, for example, vulnerability of the defendant, his/her mental well-being, whether s/he was on medication, suffered from depression or simply did not wish to answer questions for fear of implicating others. This list is not of course exhaustive and should be dealt with thoroughly in the brief.

Expert evidence

8.38   If the question of expert evidence is in issue in the case then, again, this aspect of a defence should be set out fully in the brief. The issues in dispute should be set out fully and the areas in which it is felt that an expert could usefully be instructed should also be clearly stated. If solicitors propose instructing a particular expert, those details should be given, with counsel being given the opportunity to comment on that solicitor's choice of expert. On many occasions, solicitors may require assistance from counsel in selecting appropriate experts to be instructed in any particular case. If such advice is required, the brief should specifically detail the nature of the advice sought.

Outstanding evidential issues

8.39   The brief should further instruct counsel to consider the evidence generally against the defendant. Solicitors should refer counsel to the evidence against the defendant, dealing with any issues of admissibility and about the law generally. Counsel should then be directed towards those parts of statements prepared on behalf of the defendant that counsel may rely on in his/her defendant's defence. It should be pointed out that while these aspects of the brief can easily be summarised in this way, this section of the brief is perhaps the most demanding for solicitors. The facts of every case will be different and the issues, whether legal or evidential, that follow on from that will also, therefore, vary from case to case.

Bail

8.40   If bail is in issue (for example, if the defendant wishes a bail application to be made at some stage), then a full history of this aspect of the defendant's case should be set out dealing with previous applications, any objections to bail, and all information that may be required for counsel to prepare fully for a bail application.

Should a conference be held?

8.41   Of particular concern to defendants may be the issue of whether or not they will see their barrister before the trial and as such, solicitors should always, in their brief, consider whether or not a conference is necessary. In most cases, it will be, if nothing else, to clarify issues that may be raised in a defendant's proof and to give the opportunity to counsel and the defendant to meet each other. Defendants unfamiliar with court procedure will undoubtedly require reassurance from counsel and if solicitors are of the view that a conference should be held, this should be specifically stated in the brief. If that is the case, the issues to be considered at the conference should also be given. The question of the timing of any conference can be decided between solicitors and counsel's clerk at a later time.

Who is the 'instructing solicitor'?

8.42   Finally, counsel should be told the name of the solicitor with conduct of the case so that if there are any further outstanding matters that have not been dealt with in the brief or if there are any further matters on which counsel requires assistance, then counsel will be able to contact him/her to discuss those outstanding matters.

Briefs in the magistrates' court

8.43   In a perfect world, even in the magistrates' court, counsel would no doubt benefit from a comprehensive brief dealing with all those matters referred to in the above paragraphs. However, owing to the nature of magistrates' court proceedings, counsel is often briefed at the last moment, for example, where when a solicitor leaves the police station late at night following the charging of his/her defendant who is to appear in court the next morning as an overnight prisoner. In such circumstances, it will simply be impracticable to prepare a full brief.

8.44   Whatever the scenario, a solicitor should make every effort to ensure that counsel is aware of all relevant facts. Where time allows, solicitors should endeavour to send relevant documentation to counsel although there will be occasions (for example, in the above scenario) where that cannot be done. In such circumstances, solicitors should still make every effort to ensure that the barrister appearing at court has been as fully appraised of the facts of the case as possible. This may require a barrister being 'briefed' over the telephone, with counsel's clerk subsequently preparing a backsheet at a later stage. The essential issue is that counsel attends court having been made aware of all relevant issues. It used to be a common complaint from barristers (although to solicitors' credit this is rapidly becoming a thing of the past), that they would often be sent to court with a backsheet merely giving details of the defendant's name and the court and not having any further information than that. There can be little justification for solicitors dealing with matters in this way and solicitors should make every effort, albeit even by phone, to ensure that counsel will be adequately prepared for the hearing. Failure to do so will not only antagonise barristers but will do little to inspire confidence in their defendants if a barrister has to ask a defendant when s/he meets him/her what s/he is charged with.

The defence statement

Introduction

9.1 Before the provisions of the Criminal Procedure and Investigations Act (CPIA) 1996 came into force (ss3–12 are reproduced at appendix F), except for those cases where a defendant was raising an alibi defence, a defendant was under no obligation to disclose to the prosecution the nature of the defence that would be raised at the trial. The above provisions apply to those cases where the criminal investigation was commenced after 1 April 1997, even if the offence was committed before that date. The principal effect of s5 is to make the service of a written defence statement compulsory in all contested Crown Court cases, if the sanctions set out below (para 9.3) are to be avoided. There is no requirement to serve a defence statement in magistrates' court trials, whether contested or not, or in Crown Court cases where the defence is simply putting the prosecution to proof without putting forward a defence. However, consideration should still be given to whether a statement should be served in contested magistrates' court matters. The issues to consider are dealt with later in this chapter.

9.2 Under CPIA 1996 s3, the prosecution is under a duty to disclose any further material which has not previously been disclosed to the defendant which, in the prosecution's opinion, might undermine the prosecution case against the defendant, or provide written confirmation to the defendant that there is no such further material. Providing such further disclosure or the written statement is referred to as the prosecution completing 'primary disclosure', which would generally be done at or before the pleas and directions hearing. The statement is often served together with the schedule of unused material.

The implications of failing to serve a defence statement

9.3 The court, or any other party, once leave has been granted, may comment on, and the jury may draw proper inferences to determine whether a defendant is guilty of the offence in question, where a defendant:[1]

1) fails to serve on the prosecutor a defence statement, or

---

1 CPIA 1996 s11.

2) gives the statement late, ie, after 14 days has elapsed from the date the prosecutor made 'primary disclosure', or
3) sets out inconsistent defences in the statement, or
4) puts forward any defence which differs from the defence set out in the statement – the court will however have to consider the extent of those differences and whether there is any justification for those differences before any inference could be drawn, or
5) adduces evidence in support of an alibi, or calls an alibi witness at his/her trial where s/he has failed to give details of that alibi in his/her defence statement.

Time limits for service of the defence statement

9.4 As stated above, the statement should be served within 14 days of the prosecution complying with its obligations under CPIA s3.[2] Solicitors should be careful to check when that time limit starts running. Particular care should be taken to check, in those cases where, for example, counsel appears at a committal hearing, that if the CPS purports to make primary disclosure at that time, the committal bundle of statements is returned to the solicitors as a matter of urgency so that, if necessary, instructions can be taken from the defendant and the defence statement prepared at the earliest opportunity. This may be of particular relevance in cases where a defendant is charged with indictable only matters, and the solicitor has not previously had sight of any prosecution statements, and yet the case has proceeded to committal because the papers, once served, disclosed a prima facie case against the defendant.

Applications to extend the time limit for service of the defence statement

9.5 The 14-day time limit can only be extended by the court.[3] The application must:
1) be made in writing,
2) be served on the court and the prosecutor at the same time,
3) state that the defendant believes, on reasonable grounds, that it will not be possible to serve the statement within the 14-day

2 Criminal Procedure and Investigations Act 1996 (Defence Disclosure Time Limits) Regulations 1997 SI No 684 reg 2.
3 Ibid reg 3(1).

period, and

4) set out the grounds for that belief and, further, specify the number of days by which the time limit is requested to be extended.[4]

It is current practice for the Crown Courts to extend the time for service of a defence statement until the date of the plea and directions hearing, but the length of time is a matter for the court's discretion.[5] If the defendant should require further time, an application will have to be made at that hearing. Solicitors should be aware that the courts have no power to grant an extension of time retrospectively and care should therefore be taken to ensure that this time limit is rigidly adhered to.[6]

9.6   It is open to the prosecutor to make such representations as s/he feels may be appropriate to the court. The application may be heard without the need for a formal hearing. However, when such a hearing does take place, both parties may attend and make representations.[7]

Other practical considerations that may affect the time of service of the defence statement

9.7   If the purpose in serving the defence statement is solely to avoid an inference being drawn against the defendant at the trial, solicitors may feel that service should be left as long as possible, remembering to keep within the 14-day time limit which can be extended. By doing so, the police would have less time in which to re-interview prosecution witnesses in the light of issues raised in the statement, or to discuss with them the line that may be taken in cross-examination at the trial. This may be of less significance in cases where the nature of the defence was disclosed by the defendant answering questions when initially interviewed at the police station and where the defence statement merely repeats what is already known by the prosecution.

9.8   In cases where there is concern that secondary disclosure should be made to reveal matters that may benefit the defendant, it may be more appropriate to serve the defence statement at an early stage,

---

4   Criminal Procedure and Investigations Act 1996 (Defence Disclosure Time Limits) Regulations 1997 reg 3(3).

5   Ibid reg 2(5).

6   Ibid reg 3(2).

7   CPIA 1996 s16.

subject to the defendant having given adequate instructions. This may enable the defence to raise the question of either non-compliance or inadequate disclosure on the part of the prosecution at the plea and directions hearing.

Contents of the defence statement

9.9 The requirements are set out in CPIA 1996 s5. The statement should:[8]

1) set out, in general terms, the nature of the accused's defence – this may include, for example, self defence, duress, lack of relevant mens rea, mistaken identity, etc,
2) indicate those matters on which s/he takes issue with the prosecution, and
3) set out in respect of each such matter, the reason why s/he takes issue with the prosecution.

9.10 In those cases where the defendant is relying on an alibi defence, the statement should include the following:[9]

1) the name and address of any witness the defendant believes is able to give evidence in support of the alibi, if such details are known to the defendant when the statement is given, and
2) any information in the defendant's possession which might be of material assistance in finding such witnesses, if his/her name or address is not known to the defendant when the statement is given.

Advantages in giving a defence statement

9.11 Apart from the fact that it avoids the risk of the defendant having adverse inferences drawn against him/her, the fact of service of a defence statement imposes on the prosecutor an obligation to make secondary disclosure of unused material.[10] Such material would include all that unused material which might reasonably be expected to assist the defence as set out in the defence statement. If there is none, the prosecutor must give a further written statement that there is no such further material. The prosecutor is obliged to comply with that

8 Ibid s5(6).
9 Ibid s5(7).
10 Ibid s7.

obligation as soon as reasonably practicable after the defence statement has been served.[11] Where the prosecutor fails to comply with these further obligations, the defence may apply to the court for an order that secondary disclosure is made within a specified time limit, commonly seven or 14 days.[12]

9.12   If a defence statement is served late (which, while not desirable, is preferable to not serving a statement at all and thereby risking the possibility of any of the resulting consequences of CPIA 1996 s11), there is no duty imposed on the prosecution of secondary disclosure, but, in practice, most prosecutors would still consider themselves bound by wider duties of fairness to disclose material relating to the defence which it is considered would be expected to assist the defendant.

How widely should the defence statement be drawn?

9.13   Much will depend on the nature of instructions received from the defendant, for example, whether the defendant's recollection of the incident in question is clear or faded or, for example, where the defence rests solely on the issue of mistaken identity. However, it would seem that the more general the statement, the wider the scope of documents that can be requested by way of secondary disclosure. However, it may be more appropriate to draft a detailed statement in the following circumstances:

1) where the defendant legitimately has a good defence and the statement serves to undermine the strength of the prosecution case with a view to inviting the prosecution to discontinue with the proceedings, or
2) where the defence relies on an alibi and the prosecution is invited to verify the details given to corroborate that alibi, or
3) where the statement is used as a method of inviting the prosecutor to accept a guilty plea to a lesser charge.

Care should be taken to ensure that, while complying with the provisions of CPIA 1996 s1(6), unless the defendant has a very solid defence, the defence statement is not so detailed that it gives the prosecution enough information to enable it to build a case around the defence.

11 CPIA 1996 s7(7).
12 Ibid s11.

Who should draft the defence statement – solicitor or counsel?

9.14 Solicitors should not routinely instruct counsel to draft the defence statement, although this may be the preferred option where the case is complex or unusually difficult. Solicitors should, however, be aware that different counsel may, and often do, have differing approaches to cases. Where a brief has to be returned at a late stage and the case is picked up by another barrister who has a different view about how the case should be presented at trial, the risk of inconsistent defences being raised is increased.

Bail applications in the higher courts

When should the application be made?

10.1   There is no time limit for appealing to the Crown Court against the magistrates' court's refusal to grant bail. However, as a matter of practice, if the defendant has a reasonable prospect of being granted bail on appeal, solicitors will usually wish to make their application as soon as possible after the application in the magistrates' court. Most defendants will expect that to be the case.

What is the procedure?

10.2   Applications to the Crown Court are made on 24 hours' clear notice being given to the court in question and to the CPS.[1] It should be ensured that the application is submitted to the correct Crown Court. For example, in London, certain categories of case (very serious offences, including homicide, technical cases and those within the jurisdiction of the City of London) will be committed to the Central Criminal Court and not to the Crown Court to which more everyday cases are committed. In those cases, the appeal should be lodged with the Central Criminal Court and not to the 'local' Crown Court.

10.3   The application is made by completing the appropriate notice of application. The sections for completion are self-explanatory but should be completed as comprehensively as possible. Crown Court Rules 1982 r20(1) requires the court to be informed of any earlier application to the Crown Court or to the High Court in the course of the same proceedings.

10.4   In advance of the hearing, solicitors should telephone the Crown Court list office to find out when the application will be listed. Preferred dates should be notified to the list officer at that time. Solicitors should be aware that any listing times given will be provisional and a confirmation of the listing will need to be given. The written notice of application should then be forwarded to the Crown Court, together with a copy of the certificate of full argument that must be requested from the magistrates' court. The accompanying letter should make reference to agreed proposed listing times. A copy of the application should also be sent to the CPS. It is not necessary to send a copy certificate of full argument to the CPS.

1   Crown Court Rules 1982 rr11A and 19–21.

Importance of notifying sureties and other interested parties of the listing

10.5 When the listing is known, proposed sureties should be notified to ensure their attendance at court. While such applications for bail are heard in chambers (and may, on occasions, be heard in the judge's private room) proposed sureties will be allowed into court for the hearing. That may not always be the case for applications made in the judge's private room. Proposed sureties or, for example, concerned family members should be encouraged to enter the courtroom to listen to the hearing – the defendant will not be produced from custody for the hearing – under Crown Court Rules 1982 r19(5) an applicant for bail is not entitled to be present on the hearing of his/her application unless the Crown Court gives him/her leave. Furthermore, if the defendant is not granted bail, it is useful for family members or sureties to be able to inform the defendant that everything that could be said for the defendant was indeed put forward at the hearing. Many defendants will undoubtedly feel that their solicitor's failure to secure bail on their behalf is a reflection on the advocate's ability rather than because, for example, the defendant had numerous previous convictions for failing to appear in the past. In such circumstances, it is important for defendants to be informed from a third party that the application for bail was made as forcefully as possible.

Rights of audience

10.6 Such applications can be made by either solicitors or counsel. Solicitors have a right of audience to appeal against a magistrates' court's refusal to grant bail. However, they should be aware that the defendant's legal aid order will not cover the cost of sending a solicitor's clerk to court to accompany counsel, even if the defendant's legal aid order has been extended to cover the services of counsel. This is irrespective of whether the application for bail to the Crown Court is made by way of appealing against the magistrates' court's decision or by way of an application post committal.

What will the Crown Court consider?

10.7   The principles governing the right to bail under the Bail Act 1976 (see appendix D) apply equally in the Crown Court as in the magistrates' court. Bail must be granted by a court if none of the exceptions specified in Schedule 1 applies. The court must consider whether bail should be granted on each occasion that the defendant is brought before it, whether or not the defendant makes an application. When the Crown Court refuses bail to a person to whom s4 applies, or imposes conditions on the grant of bail to such a person, the court is required to give reasons for its decision. However, under s5(5), the Crown Court need not give the defendant a copy of the note of the reasons for its decision where that person is represented by an advocate unless there is a specific request to do so.

10.8   The importance of bail applications should not be underestimated. Aside from the ultimate verdict in the case, the question of bail or custody is foremost in the defendant's mind and a successful application for bail will naturally be very well received by the defendant. It is therefore necessary to prepare bail applications with care, considering the likely objections to bail put forward by the prosecution. The principles set out earlier in chapter 3 regarding preparation for bail applications apply equally to applications on appeal to the Crown Court as they do to applications before the magistrates' court.

10.9   Although this is an application made on behalf of the defendant, procedurally the application commences with the prosecution objections to bail, which must be in accordance with the criteria for objecting to bail as set out in the Bail Act 1976. The exceptions are contained in Bail Act 1976 Sch 1 Part I para 2 and there are only three grounds: where the court is satisfied that there are substantial grounds for believing that the defendant, if released on bail (whether subject to conditions or not) would either:

> ... fail to surrender to custody, or commit an offence whilst on bail, or interfere with witnesses or otherwise obstruct the course of justice, whether in relation to himself or any other person.

Thus, for example, the mere fact that the defendant faces a serious charge is not of itself an exception to the right of bail, although that would be a relevant factor to whether any of the defined exceptions may apply.

10.10   Bail applications do not usually take very long in the Crown Court and the judge will usually announce a decision immediately. If bail is refused s/he would cite which of the exceptions under Sch 1 para 2 apply. If the judge grants bail, s/he would announce any conditions to be attached to bail.

Further considerations after the hearing

10.11   On leaving the courtroom, it is important to explain fully the position to the defendant's supporters at court and, if bail is granted, it is vital that the solicitors are informed immediately so that the prison authorities can be notified to ensure the defendant's immediate release. Sometimes, sureties are to be taken at a local police station and that would need to take place before the defendant can be released. The quicker the sureties are notified of the position, the quicker the defendant will be released.

The High Court

10.12   Under Criminal Justice Act 1967 s22, the High Court has jurisdiction to grant bail or to vary bail conditions. An application is made by summons to a judge in chambers under Rules of the Supreme Court Order 79 r9.

10.13   It is not easy to obtain legal aid to make an application to a judge in chambers, but if instructed, the defendant's solicitors will seek to obtain civil legal aid for that purpose. If legal aid is not granted, an application to a judge in chambers would usually be paid for privately.

10.14   The procedure is for the defence advocate and the prosecution advocate to argue the application before a High Court judge, who will have before him/her a copy of the summons and an affidavit, usually from the solicitor about the full nature and background of the defendant's application, including suggested proposals for appropriate conditions of bail.

10.15   The application is usually speedy, because the High Court judge will have read the papers in advance and, in particular, the prosecution advocate is usually only asked to state the prosecution's objections to bail and to assist the judge on any particular matter if requested. It is then for the defence advocate to seek to persuade the High Court judge to grant bail to the defendant, who may well have had bail refused at both the magistrates' court and the Crown Court already.

10.16 Applications for bail in the High Court are not easy and it is, therefore, rare for bail to be granted. An example of where bail may be granted could be where the evidence against the defendant has become weakened or where a co-defendant of similar previous character has already been granted bail.

10.17 An application to the High Court is usually a last resort for a bail application because, under Supreme Court Act 1981 s18(1)(a), an appeal from the refusal of bail in criminal proceedings by a judge in chambers or from an order varying or refusing to vary conditions of bail is not permitted.

10.18 The defendant is never present for a bail application in the High Court and the advocates are not robed. Bail applications are usually listed first in the morning session or at two o'clock in the afternoon. However, it is possible in certain cases to make emergency applications for bail which can take place outside usual court hours and even over the weekend or by telephone, which both involve a duty judge, although in a criminal case such emergency applications are rare.

The Court of Appeal

10.19 The Court of Appeal has powers to grant bail under the Criminal Appeal Act 1968. Those powers comprise bail pending: (a) appeal to the Court of Appeal; (b) re-trial where a conviction has been quashed; (c) re-trial where a conviction is likely to be quashed or a sentence substantially reduced; and (d) appeal to the House of Lords.

10.20 Usually, bail is only granted by the Court of Appeal where the Court of Appeal has already formed a view that either the defendant's conviction is unsafe and is likely to be quashed or the sentence already served by the defendant far exceeds the sentence which ought to have been imposed. In essence, the Court of Appeal would seek to redress, at the earliest stage, a perceived injustice to the defendant of being held in custody when it is clear that either his/her conviction or sentence appeal will be allowed in due course. Bail would therefore usually only be granted in the Court of Appeal where an application for leave to appeal has been granted and there is clearly a strong appeal on its merits or where the case has been listed by the court itself in order to allow the defendant bail immediately.

Checklist for bail

1) Establish what is/are the objection(s) to bail.
2) Find out whether sureties are available and if so, in what sums.
3) Consider the defendant's community ties (family; fixed address; job; period of time s/he has lived in the UK).
4) Ascertain whether there are any factual inaccuracies in, or material change since, the draft of the written application for bail (Crown Court) or affidavit (High Court).

Preliminary hearings

Pleas and directions hearing

11.1   Usually, the most important preliminary hearing in Crown Court cases is the pleas and directions hearing (PDH). This hearing usually takes place about six weeks after the defendant has been committed from the magistrates' court. These hearings were established to improve the administration of the Crown Court and are treated seriously by Crown Court judges, who require a completed PDH form to be presented by both advocates at the hearing.

11.2   The most important matter to clarify is the defendant's plea. The defence advocate needs to be sure that the defendant has been advised that a plea of guilty would receive maximum credit at the first available opportunity, ie, at that hearing.[1] If the defendant wishes to plead guilty to some or all of the counts on the indictment, s/he should do so at the outset of the hearing on arraignment, ie, when s/he enters his/her plea to the counts on the indictment. The pleas offered by the defendant may not be acceptable to the prosecution at that stage (see para 14.5), in which case not guilty pleas are entered to the other counts and the rest of the PDH continues in the same manner as if the defendant had pleaded not guilty to all counts. If, however, the defendant has pleaded guilty to all counts or the pleas which have been offered to some counts are accepted by the prosecution, the PDH is converted to a potentially effective sentencing hearing, although if the defence advocate wishes the judge to have a pre-sentence report available, s/he would apply for one and if the application is granted, the case will be remanded for sentence.

11.3   If there is a likelihood that the case will be adjourned for pre-sentence (or any other) reports, the prosecution advocate will not usually open the case and the case will be adjourned for about four weeks (usually to a Friday, for the convenience of the court and often the judges and advocates) for the preparation of pre-sentence reports and the case will not be reserved for that Judge. There are usually fairly lengthy lists of PDH hearings and the judge would probably be anxious not to be delayed by lengthy full-sentence hearings. Bail will need to be applied for if the defendant has been on bail previously, but there is a risk that if the offence(s) that the defendant has pleaded guilty to are serious and/or the defendant has a lengthy list of previous convictions for similar offences, bail will now be revoked by the judge.

1   Criminal Justice and Public Order Act 1994 s48.

11.4   Assuming that the defendant has indicated pleas of not guilty or that the pleas of guilty to some counts are not deemed acceptable by the prosecution, the defendant is arraigned and enters his/her pleas to the counts and the PDH proceeds by the judge taking the advocates through the contents of the PDH form.

11.5   Usually before the hearing the defence advocate would complete as much of the form as possible, before showing it to the prosecution advocate for any amendments or further insertions concerning matters of which only the prosecution would have knowledge. As mentioned above, the form tends to be treated seriously by the judge so, despite the grumblings of most criminal advocates, it needs to be completed as comprehensively and seriously as possible.

11.6   Most of the questions on the form are fairly self-explanatory. However, there are issues that require careful consideration, in particular what the issues are in the case and which witnesses are required to attend court. Other matters concern possible directions about the service of further prosecution evidence, whether there are matters of law or admissibility to be resolved during the trial, whether the taped summary of the defendant's interview is agreed, whether there is any further work to be done by the prosecution or defence, and whether the case is likely to require experts, interpreters, the use of video tape or audio tape recording facilities and about a fixed date for trial. Unused material (for example, custody records, incident report books, crime report sheets, computer aided despatch (CAD) messages) may be requested, although some courts insist that such material can only be seen by solicitors inspecting the items at the relevant police station.

11.7   A schedule of unused material would usually be served at or before the PDH. If Criminal Procedure and Investigations Act (CPIA) 1996 s3 has been complied with within 14 days of the PDH, it is often an appropriate time to serve the defence statement, in which case either defence advocate or solicitor would need to have it drafted, for the agreement and signature of the defendant before service. The importance of serving the defence statement and its service within the time limits cannot be overstated. This important aspect of the defendant's case is considered in more detail in chapter 9.

11.8   Although many PDHs are quite routine in form, because of their importance, if the defence advocate is attending on behalf of a more senior advocate, it is worthwhile discussing the contents of the form and the case generally with him/her before the hearing, because sometimes the judge may ask quite detailed and precise questions.

11.9   The defendant will be required to attend at the PDH and it will often be necessary to discuss the contents of the form with the defendant at least in outline. It is sensible to go through the procedure of the hearing with the defendant. Sometimes defendants are under the mistaken apprehension that the PDH hearing is the date of their actual trial. Usually, when not guilty pleas have been entered, the defendant will continue on bail on the same terms, although if the defendant had been on unconditional bail, the judge may place a condition of residence on the defendant's bail. The defendant should be asked before the hearing whether s/he has any difficulties with the present bail conditions. If so, it will be necessary to make an application to vary the bail conditions.

Mentions

11.10   This is a peculiar description of a hearing which essentially covers a whole range of miscellaneous matters for which the case has been listed. Examples of mentions include where the prosecution has been asked to indicate whether it intends to proceed against a defendant or to offer no evidence; where the defendant has not kept in touch with his/her solicitors and the case has been listed because of non-co-operation (which may result in a warrant being issued if the defendant fails to attend court) or where there is some other matter of which the court should be aware which may affect whether there will be an effective trial. For example, where witnesses have disappeared, where a decision has been reached about whether there will be a re-trial of a defendant where a previous jury could not agree, or where there is a belief that one or a number of prosecution witnesses may be unco-operative.

11.11   This is by no means an exhaustive list of the reasons why a case might be listed for mention. Sometimes, a case may be listed for mention as a follow-up to a PDH, for example, where an order of the court relating to disclosure of material has not taken place or where the court simply wants to monitor the progress of a case. Before any mention hearing, it is essential that the defence advocate is fully aware why the case has been listed and whether that was by the court itself or on the request of one of the parties.

Trial (no witnesses)

11.12   A case is listed for 'Trial (no witnesses)' when the prosecution has decided to offer no evidence against a defendant. The position used to be that the defendant had to attend, before a judge could enter a formal not guilty verdict where no evidence was offered against a defendant. However, the practice is now that the court will indicate whether the defendant is required to attend, or whether his/her legal representative would be sufficient, for the purposes of the verdict being entered.

11.13   The prosecution advocate will (which is explained in summary form) tell the judge that the case has been considered and that for whatever reason, the CPS has decided to offer no evidence against the defendant and a formal verdict of not guilty is entered by the judge under Criminal Justice Act 1967 s17. As where a defendant has been acquitted by a jury, an application can be made for the defendant's costs order out of central funds, which would usually cover travel expenditure, a revocation of the defendant's contribution to be made by his/her legal aid order and remission of any payments made already under that order.

Directions/preparatory hearings

11.14   In more complex cases, usually frauds, the case management is more complex and the case cannot be conveniently dealt with at one PDH. As a result, there are several directions hearings which relate to directions concerning the service of skeleton arguments, a case summary and other preliminary matters which will assist in shortening the trial. The most serious fraud cases are dealt with by a formal preparatory hearing pursuant to Criminal Justice Act 1987 ss7–10. Sections 9, 9A and 10 set out very strict criteria about what takes place at such a preparatory hearing but, clearly, if an advocate is required to attend at such a hearing, it would almost certainly be on behalf of a more senior advocate and s/he would be well-advised to discuss the hearing with that person and the directions about the further management and progress of the case to be requested or considered at the hearing.

Public interest immunity hearing

11.15   Public interest immunity (PII) is a vast subject in its own right relating to relevant material which the prosecution does not wish to disclose. For example, to protect an informant or where the material is otherwise highly sensitive. Usually, if there is such material, the prosecution will apply ex parte to the judge and the defence is not present. However, depending on the category of PII hearing, the defendant may be invited to make written submissions in advance of that hearing to be placed before the judge or may be asked to attend court to make oral submissions before the judge considers the material. Sometimes, therefore, defence advocates are required or at least entitled to be present at PII hearings. The judge who makes the decision on whether material is to be disclosed to the defence need not be the trial judge, who is bound by the ruling of his/her colleague.

Severance/abuse of process arguments

11.16   An argument based under either of these two headings usually takes place before the trial judge, just before the beginning of the trial. Usually, the defence advocate will have drafted a skeleton argument which is to be handed up to the judge at or before the hearing. A severance argument is usually based on either there having been misjoinder of a number of offences in the same indictment under Indictment Rules 1971 r9 or for a separate trial for a defendant or different counts for the same defendant under Indictments Act 1915 s5(3). Often, at the earlier PDH, it is indicated that there would be a severance argument and that it would commence before the jury is sworn. However, sometimes the case will be listed for severance a few days before the trial is due to commence.

11.17   Similar procedures happen when making an application to stay the trial as being an abuse of the process of the court under the principles laid down in *Connelly v Director of Public Prosecutions* [1964] AC 1254, HL. There are a variety of reasons why an application may be made, but commonly it will relate to whether a defendant should be re-tried (a previous jury or juries having been discharged), where there has been a substantial time lapse between the alleged offence(s) and the date of trial, or where there is a real risk of prejudice on the basis that the prosecution has not or will not serve relevant material on the defence, or original exhibits have been lost, or where there is any other reason to believe that the defendant may not get a fair trial.

Application for two advocates

11.18   If the case is a serious one or where the trial is to be lengthy, it is open to defence advocates to make an application to extend legal aid to cover two advocates, usually Queen's Counsel and junior advocate or two junior advocates, under Legal Aid in Criminal and Care Proceedings (General) Regulations 1989[2] reg 48. On a murder charge, legal aid automatically covers the instruction of two advocates, including Queen's Counsel, but in all other cases an application would need to be made.

11.19   It is generally advisable that a written application is drafted and presented to the determining judge (who is often the senior judge of the court) before the hearing for a determination and it is rare that the case is listed simply for that purpose. Sometimes, a determination of the extension of legal aid is dealt with on the papers or, alternatively, it may be raised and considered at a directions or mention hearing.

Checklist for preliminary hearings

1) Ensure that the defendant has been advised at or before the PDH on the verdict s/he will receive for a guilty plea.
2) Advise the defendant that on a guilty plea, s/he may lose – and be prepared to make a bail application.
3) Check that the prosecution has properly complied with its obligations of primary disclosure and that you are in time to serve a defence statement, if that has not already been done.
4) Make sure that you fully understand why a case has been listed. If necessary, speak to your solicitor, the advocate whose case it is (if not yours) and/or the prosecution advocate at court.
5) At a PII hearing, try to establish the reason for the hearing so that you are properly in a position to make submissions on disclosure. Ensure that any written applications/skeleton arguments are placed before the judge, before the hearing commences.

---

2   SI No 344.

The Crown Court trial

For complete chapter contents, see overleaf

Introduction

12.1 The Crown Court trial, before a judge and jury, represents the most glamorous aspect of the work of a criminal lawyer. Whether one has been brought up on memoirs of great advocates, a diet of legal sitcoms or glitzy Hollywood films, the image of the gladiatorial fighter arguing against the odds to triumph is a strong one. Inevitably, the majority of Crown Court trials are considerably more pedestrian, low-key, and often do not run smoothly. Nevertheless, there is a special feeling when a difficult witness is broken down or when a powerful speech to a jury is made, and there will be a strong feeling of satisfaction when a case is won, particularly where the justice of the case merits an acquittal. Inevitably, to achieve a good performance requires preparation, both by achieving a full understanding of the factual and legal matters of relevance in the case, and by careful consideration of how tactically to run the case (for example, how to cross-examine a witness and whether to call defence witnesses).

Practical preparation

12.2 Practice varies as to the extent of preparation of questions for cross-examination of prosecution witnesses. Advocates may wish to prepare many questions in advance of the trial, or else may prefer to consider the defendant's comments on the prosecution witnesses and rely more on how the witness proceeds in examination-in-chief. Certainly, it is essential to have a full proof of evidence from the defendant and his/her comments on all prosecution witnesses and interviews before the trial or, if that has not been possible to obtain, to take instructions with the defendant before the trial commences.

12.3 Once the defence advocate has seen the defendant and had an opportunity to discuss the case and for further points and tactics to be clarified, it is then generally useful to speak to the prosecution advocate to see if there are areas of evidence which both sides can agree, and to ascertain precisely how the prosecution puts the case against the defendant. It is often useful to inform him/her that there may be legal arguments about admissibility of some of the evidence and to establish whether some of the evidence which the defence considers to be irrelevant or prejudicial matters can be edited out by agreement, or else will require legal argument and a ruling by the judge.

12.4   In addition, the defendant may be prepared to plead guilty to lesser or a limited number of the charges and it would thereafter be necessary to approach the prosecution advocate to see if there is a possibility of acceptable pleas being entered on behalf of the defendant.

Preliminary matters

12.5   Once the preliminary matters have been completed, the defendant will be asked to surrender into the dock if s/he is on bail or will be brought up, if s/he is in custody. Usually, the judge will sit before a jury is sworn in so that the question of bail until the jury retires can be resolved and, if necessary, for the defendant to be arraigned if (unusually) that has not already taken place. There may also be other matters concerning the timing of witnesses or other procedural matters requiring the assistance of the judge. If there are areas of legal argument, the advocate can canvass those with the judge before the hearing, for example, if it is necessary to have a voir dire with live witnesses, which may need to take place immediately after a jury is sworn. Remember that at the Central Criminal Court, the judge is referred to as 'Your Lordship' and not 'Your Honour' as in all other Crown Courts.

The jury

12.6   After preliminary matters have been resolved, a jury panel will be brought in and 12 of their numbers will be empanelled. Usually, there is no right to challenge any potential jurors except if the defendant knows any of them, or has knowledge that they may be prejudiced against him/her. Occasionally, a question may be asked of them where there would be a reason to suspect that they might be biased against the defendant or would have a particular expertise or knowledge about this offence, victim, etc.

12.7   Once the jurors have been empanelled, the remaining jurors-in-waiting will be released and the jurors will be asked to swear an oath or affirm. It will be useful for the advocate to hear the jurors make their declaration as this is often the only time that it is possible to hear each juror speak and to get some (fairly basic) idea of his/her intelligence. Some advocates are pleased if a number of jurors affirms suggesting an independent mind.

The prosecution case

Opening speech

12.8   Once the jury has been sworn, the trial judge will generally invite the prosecution advocate to open the case, unless there are other preliminary matters still to be resolved. The prosecution advocate will open the case against the defendant, highlighting matters in which s/he anticipates the evidence to be called will support the charge(s) against the defendant. There will probably be reference in outline both to witness statements and to various documentary exhibits, including the defendant's interviews. Usually, the opening will also refer in passing to matters of law, in particular, the burden and standard of proof and the indictment. The length of opening address will generally be determined by the complexity and anticipated length of the trial.

Prosecution witnesses

12.9   Once the case has been opened, the prosecution will call its witnesses, usually lay witnesses first and then police officers. Not all witnesses will necessarily be called, because the contents of some witness statements may be agreed and therefore read under Criminal Justice Act 1967 s9. Before the first read statement the judge will give a direction to the jury to treat it with equal importance as evidence heard from the witness box.

12.10   If, in the course of any of the evidence given, there is an objection taken to the question asked or the area of evidence sought to be put before the jury, or for any other reason there is a matter for concern, for example, if the prosecution advocate appears to be leading the witness without the defence's prior agreement, it may be necessary for the defence advocate to rise, stating 'I object to this line/manner of questioning', or 'There is a matter of law which I wish to raise before Your Honour', and the judge, possibly after a brief enquiry, will ask the jury to retire, often asking both advocates how long the jury should be kept in their room. Once the matter of law has been resolved, the jury returns and, depending on the ruling, the line of questioning presently being asked is continued, abandoned or rephrased.

Cross-examination

12.11   This aspect of the criminal trial has been mentioned in chapter 6. It is difficult to give advice on techniques of cross-examination as advocates will develop their own style. Many defence advocates prepare areas of cross-examination or even a list of questions in advance. Others prefer to mark in the margin of their notebooks areas to cross-examine after hearing evidence-in-chief.

12.12   To ensure that relevant areas of cross-examination are not overlooked, it is very helpful, even almost essential, to have the comments of the defendant on the prosecution witness statements in advance (as well as a proof of evidence). This ensures that, assuming a witness comes 'up to proof', ie, gives oral evidence only in accordance with his/her written statement, the defence advocate is in a position to put the defendant's case adequately. Obviously, substantial variations from the statement may need to be cross-examined, although advocates need to consider whether the evidence given at court is more helpful to the defendant, in which case it might be decided not to cross-examine on what is contained in the statements.

12.13   Although the most exciting part of cross-examination is being able to persuade or force an unhelpful witness to admit points in the defendant's favour, the majority of the time witnesses, particularly police officers, will stick as far as possible to 'their story'. Thus, the purpose of cross-examination becomes two-fold: first, to ensure that the defendant's case is properly put to a witness (so that there can be no criticism later if the defendant disagrees with something said by the witness) and, second, to test the credibility of the witness, ie, how the answers are given.

12.14   Advocates may need to note important tactical decisions about which witnesses to put the defendant's case to, because it will usually be repetitive and unnecessary to do so to every witness, and how to treat different witnesses, ie, whether to pressurise them, cajole them or even accept their evidence in large part in order to further the defendant's case. Cross-examining expert witnesses can be particularly difficult. To cross-examine an expert effectively, advocates need to prepare carefully, relying on the comments of the defendant and, if possible, the expert's report and further comments of the defence's expert witness.

No case to answer

12.15   At the close of the prosecution case, the defence advocate may make a submission of law that there is no case to answer on one or any number of the charges on the indictment, on one or other of the limits set out in *R v Galbraith* (1981) 73 Cr App R 124, CA. This will take place in the absence of the jury. The judge will ask the jury to retire and will ask the defence advocate to commence the submission before calling on the prosecution advocate to respond to the submission, but giving the defence advocate the final bite of the cherry in reply. It is usually clear before the submission is complete whether the judge is likely to accede to the defendant's application and therefore the final points in reply should generally be concise.

12.16   If the submission of law is upheld, the judge, through his/her clerk, will direct a juror (usually the juror nearest to the clerk) to find the defendant not guilty of that count. This procedure appears bizarre and artificial as the jury has not even appointed a foreperson yet, but as the defendant is in the charge of the jury, it is for them to bring in a verdict, even if it is on the direction of a judge.

The defence case

12.17   If there is no submission of no case or where, following a submission, there remains at least one charge that the defendant is still facing, the defence case will commence. If there is more than one defendant, the order of defendants is that contained in the indictment. Each defendant's case is completed, including his/her witnesses before the case for the next defendant on the indictment commences.

Cut-throat defence

12.18   Sometimes, co-defendants seek to blame each other in what is known as a 'cut-throat defence'. This should be avoided wherever possible because it damages the prospects of a successful defence. In particular, the rules limiting the prosecution from cross-examining the defendant about his/her character under the Criminal Evidence Act 1898 s1(f), do not apply to a co-defendant. S/he can cross-examine on any matters relevant to his/her own case, even if that harms and prejudices another defendant's case, provided that that defendant has given evidence against the co-defendant.[1] Effectively, therefore, that defendant is doubly cross-examined and often much more effectively, given the absence of restrictions, by a co-

---

1   *R v Varley* (1982) 75 Cr App R 241, CA.

defendant's advocate. The effect is, very often, that all of the defendants running a cut-throat defence are ultimately convicted, unless the whole trial exposes a much stronger case against one defendant (or a number of them) than other defendant(s).

Calling the defendant?

12.19   One of the most important tactical decisions which the defence advocate will need to decide with the defendant is whether to call him/her. Following the enactment of Criminal Justice and Public Order Act 1994 ss34–37, inferences can be, in certain circumstances, drawn from the defendant's silence. Under s35, inferences may be drawn from failure to give evidence.[2] In practice, the effect is that many more defendants now choose to give evidence, having been advised of the risks and dangers of not doing so. However, there may still be cases where the defendant does not wish to or would be advised not to give evidence, particularly where his/her account is likely to crumble in cross-examination, where there has been an effective cross-examination of important prosecution witnesses and/or where the defendant's case is fully set out in his/her interview and there is little the defendant is able to add. There may also be tactical reasons for not calling a defendant, particularly where s/he has a bad character and the credibility of prosecution witnesses has been substantially challenged in the course of the prosecution case or, in those circumstances, the defendant's bad character comes to be revealed to the jury by the prosecution.[3] There may also be good legal arguments that an inference should not be drawn from the defendant's silence, for example, relating to his/her mental state or intelligence and that would be a factor for the advocate to consider in deciding whether or not to call the defendant.

12.20   The decision, one way or the other, may need to be kept under constant review. Practice varies, but the advocate may decide to have a written endorsement from a defendant if s/he decides not to give evidence, to avoid the possibility of criticism from him/her at a later stage. The wording of such an endorsement is generally as follows: 'I have been advised by my counsel/solicitor that I am free to give evidence or not and s/he has advised me that the judge can direct the jury to draw an inference from my decision not to go into the witness box, and I have decided of my own free will not to give evidence'.

2   *R v Cowan* (1996) 1 Cr App R 1, CA.
3   *R v Butterwasser* [1947] 2 All ER 415; (1948) 32 Cr App R 81, CA.

12.21   The endorsement should then be signed by the defendant and dated, preferably in the presence of the solicitor's representative. Once the defence case commences, the judge will ask the defence advocate whether the defendant has been advised of the consequences of not giving evidence, ie, that an inference may be drawn, before asking whether s/he intends to call the defendant. At a later stage, the judge will generally ask for representations to be made (in the absence of the jury) about whether, if the defendant does not give evidence, it would be an appropriate case for a direction on adverse inference to be given by him/her to the jury.

Defence witnesses

12.22   Depending on the nature of the defence, different categories of defence witnesses may be called in addition to the defendant, for example, alibi witnesses, or witnesses present at the scene who can describe the defendant's non-participation in a particular offence or describe the actions of the victim or the defendant in a different way from that presented by the prosecution witnesses. Character witnesses may also be called, although this would usually only happen where the defendant is of good character or is to be treated as a person of good character under a *Nye* direction.[4]

Advance disclosure – CPIA 1996 s5

12.23   A vital new provision requiring careful consideration is the defendant's obligation to provide advance disclosure of his/her case in all Crown Court cases, under Criminal Procedure and Investigations Act (CPIA) 1996 s5. Before this section came into force, the defence was only obliged to give advance particulars of any alibi and the names and addresses of any alibi witnesses whom the defence intends to call (pursuant to Criminal Justice Act 1967 s11).

12.24   Now, under CPIA 1996 s5(5) (which came into force on 1 April 1997), the defendant must give a defence statement to the court and the prosecutor within strict time limits (see para 9.4). It is too soon to tell whether the prosecution advocate will be able to refer to the defence statement as part of its case, to strengthen it for the purposes of a defence submission of no case to answer, for example, in a case where the identification evidence given was weak but where

---

4   See *R v Nye* (1982) 75 Cr App R 247, CA.

the defendant has admitted presence and even involvement in the offence alleged. However, it is clear from the Act that, with the leave of the judge, the prosecution would be able to comment where, for example, a different defence is run at trial or where an alibi witness has come forward who is not referred to in the defence statement.

12.25   It is always important for the defence advocate to advise the defendant whether or not to call particular witnesses, often after discussion with the solicitor who took the proof of evidence. The defence advocate will need to consider whether the witness is likely to be honest, reliable, credible and able to stand up to cross-examination. The adage – that it is often better to call one good witness only than one good witness and a number of less impressive witnesses – is a good one. Strength in numbers of defence witnesses is only worth while if those witnesses are going to be effective and complementary witnesses in court. Cross-examination of discrepancies between defence witnesses' evidence can be fatal to the defendant's case.

Closing speeches

12.26   At the close of all of the defendants' cases, the prosecution advocate will usually make a closing speech, except if the case has been short and where the defendant(s) did not give evidence. The closing speech should sum up the case by referring to a number of prosecution points which support its case on the criteria but it should be made fairly and consistent with the evidence which has been adduced (which will probably vary from how the case was opened). Under the new provisions brought in by the CPIA 1996, the prosecution advocate (with the leave of the judge) would probably be entitled to comment on any differences between the defence statement and the defence case as heard by the jury (see para 9.7).

12.27   After the prosecution closing speech, closing speeches are made on behalf of all of the defendants. The judge would not usually allow speeches to take place late in the afternoon and will often not allow a prosecution speech to end on one day and a defence speech to commence the following morning.

12.28   It is difficult to give any advice on how to make a defence closing speech, as every advocate will have his/her own style and every case will have its own peculiarities. However, what is commonly regarded as a good way to prepare a closing speech is to write down a number of points, which can be developed in the course of the speech in support of the defendant's case.

12.29   Particularly important points to note are the burden and standard of proof, the law applicable to the charges the defendant is facing and particular evidential points which the advocate believes support the defendant's case. It is probably fair to say that the vast majority of cases which are won by the defence are by attacking the prosecution's case, as opposed to concentrating on the defendant's own evidence (particularly as the judge has decided that the charges are fit to go before a jury). So, for example, if conflicts can be exposed between prosecution witnesses or there are aspects of the prosecution's case, when opened, which can no longer be supported after the evidence has been heard, these are points the defence advocate would probably wish to bring out forcefully before the jury.

12.30   An unpleasant experience which unfortunately happens regularly to defence advocates, can be termed the role of the 'second prosecutor'. The defence advocate might feel the need to redress the balance in advance of the judge's summing-up in his/her closing speech. This happens when a prosecution-minded judge finds him/herself unable to control his/her personal view of the case in the course of the trial and proceeds to ask the defendant nasty questions and seeks to plug any gaps in the prosecution's case which s/he thinks may exist. The judge in those circumstances can make the defence role particularly difficult, with meaningful looks, shrugs and prosecution-favouring directions to the jury.

12.31   However, sometimes the judge's attitude can be used to the defence's advantage, by, for example, employing subtle tactics, such as knowing sighs and looks to the jury. In addition, in the course of the closing speech the defence advocate may make reference to the 'anti-judge correction factor'. This technique (which should be undertaken carefully and may annoy or even infuriate the judge) is to remind the jury that it is for them to consider the evidence and not to rely on speeches or even comments made by the judge. An unobjectionable but powerful way to express that is to make a comment, such as, 'His/Her Honour may also comment on matters of evidence but will, no doubt, do so in a fair manner as between the parties and will remind you that you are free to accept or reject any of his/her comments'.

12.32   Speeches will inevitably vary in length depending on the complexity and length of the trial, but it is generally advisable not to give a speech of excessive length because some of the best points may be lost. Typically, a defence closing speech will be between 20 and 30 minutes in length for a trial of around two or three days. It is essential to be polite, even flattering, towards the jury. An advocate may choose to be apologetic about the length of the speech or, where some false point has been made during the trial, to remind the jury of the advocate's own personal failings which may assist in getting the jury on his/her side. It is always nice if an illustrative and perhaps humorous story far removed from the facts of the case can be introduced, but in most cases that simply is not possible and the defence advocate should not worry if s/he simply restricts him/herself to the facts of the case before the jury. There is potential to get carried away in closing speeches, which can be harmful to the defendant.

Summing up

12.33   Once the defence speeches have ended, all that remains before the jury's deliberations is the judge's summing-up. A very careful note will need to be taken and, failing shorthand, it is useful to use many abbreviated forms of common words which the judge would be likely to use.

12.34   Generally, the judge will go through a formulaic style of summing-up. This is partly because s/he has been provided with a series of standard guideline directions. Usually it would begin with the division of functions between judge and jury, reminding them that they should try the case on the evidence and that the evidence is a matter for them and them alone, the burden of proof and standard of proof, taking the jury through the indictment and directing them on the legal ingredients and reminding them to try each defendant separately and on each count separately, giving a good character direction where appropriate, directing them to treat all witnesses equally, and reminding them that the defendant does not need to give evidence. The judge may also direct the jury that they can draw adverse inferences from the defendant's failure to answer police questions and/or to give evidence and/or from a failure to provide or departure from the defence statement.

12.35   After these important preliminary matters, the judge will then summarise the evidence in the case. Usually, but unimaginatively, the judge will summarise the evidence of each witness chronologically and ought to remind the jury of significant points made in cross-examination of the prosecution witnesses. S/he must then remind the jury of the defendant's case and evidence called on behalf of the defence. As indicated above, many judges would prefer to see a conviction at the conclusion of a trial and may seek to assist in that regard by making unfavourable comments on the evidence. If this is done subtly and infrequently, and providing that the judge has reminded the jury of the salient features of the defence case, and has reminded the jury in the dismissive but effective phrase '... but remember, members of the jury, that is a matter for you ...', that is one of the difficulties that the defence advocate will have to endure.

12.36   Having completed a resumé of the evidence, there are a number of further matters which the judge would need to direct the jury on, for example, the appointment of a foreperson and directing them that at that stage only a unanimous verdict would be acceptable.

12.37   Sometimes, at the conclusion of the summing-up, the judge asks the advocates if there is anything further either of them would wish to say, but usually the bailiff would then immediately swear to keep the members of the jury in his/her charge and they would retire to consider their verdict. Exhibits in the case, including the defendant's interviews, are generally kept on a table in front of the clerk, but the jury will be told that they can see and consider any of the exhibits in the course of their deliberation (except where the particular exhibit is potentially dangerous or harmful). Once the jury have retired, assuming that the judge has not asked whether anything has been omitted or requires to be corrected in the presence of the jury, it is open to the defence advocate to raise any legal or evidential matter with the judge. Generally, it is not worth asking the judge to bring the jury back if s/he has got a minor evidential matter wrong but if there has been a substantial misunderstanding of a significant point, it is the defence advocate's duty to correct the judge and ask him/her to deal with that matter correctly by recalling the jury.

The jury in retirement

12.38   Once the jury has retired, if the defendant has been on bail, it is usual to ask for bail within the precincts of the court. The judge will almost certainly give an indication that s/he will not take a verdict between 1 and 2 o'clock.

12.39   In the course of their deliberations the members of the jury may pass a note through to the court which may require the consideration of the judge and advocates. If so, all parties will be asked to attend the court and the note will be passed to the advocates, having already been seen by the judge, before the court reconvenes. Often, questions will be asked for clarification or elaboration on a matter of evidence and the judge will ask for both advocates' view before directing the jury on the point. Sometimes a jury will wish to have directions of law repeated or clarified.

12.40   Some notes are not passed to the advocates by the judge. The most obvious and important example is where the jury members have indicated that they are not agreed and have given an indication of numbers in favour of conviction and numbers in favour of acquittal. A note of that sort is kept private by the judge.

The verdict

12.41   When the parties are recalled to court, it is always useful to find out from the clerk or usher whether there is a note or whether the jury has reached a verdict, because the defendant can then be warned of the position. A third possibility is where the jury has not reached a unanimous decision and the judge has decided that it is appropriate to give a majority direction. This cannot be before a period of a maximum of two hours ten minutes has elapsed since the jury retired to consider its verdict.[5] In those circumstances, the judge would tell the advocates that s/he proposes to give such a majority direction before the jury is recalled.

12.42   Once that has happened, the clerk of the court would usually ask the foreperson whether the jury has reached a verdict against any of the defendants on any count and if the jury is not agreed on all counts involving all defendants, the judge will give a majority direction, which in the case of 12 jurors would be, for example, 'members of the jury, the time has now come where I can accept a majority verdict, which is a verdict of which at least ten of you are agreed, but please, members of the jury, do try nonetheless to reach a unanimous verdict, but if that is not possible, as I have indicated, I can accept a verdict of which at least ten of you are agreed'. If one juror has been discharged because, for example, s/he is ill or otherwise deemed by the court not to be appropriate to continue to try the case in the course of a trial, the only acceptable majority verdict would be 10:1. If there were only ten jurors left, the only acceptable majority verdict would be 9:1.

---

5   *Practice Direction (CA) (Crime: Majority Verdicts)* (1967) 54 Cr App R 373.

12.43   Once a verdict has been reached, the defendant will be asked to stand up and the clerk will ask the foreperson to deliver the verdict or verdicts. If the defendant is found not guilty on all counts, the defence advocate should immediately ask for the defendant to be discharged, and where appropriate, make an application for a defendant's costs order out of central funds, which would usually be limited to travel expenses in the magistrates' court and the Crown Court and a revocation of the defendant's legal aid order and remittance of any contributions already made.

12.44   The Contempt of Court Act 1981 prevents enquiries into the reasons why juries reach their verdicts and that has helped create an atmosphere of distance between defence advocates and the jury. However, if the jury acquits the defendant of all counts, a mouthed thank you to the jury as they are discharged would not be likely to attract criticism.

12.45   If the defendant is found guilty on one or a number of counts, s/he is asked to sit down, and the case proceeds to the question of sentencing. If it appears likely that the defendant will not be sentenced on the same day, the jury will usually be discharged, although the judge may inform them that they are welcome to return on the sentencing date to hear the final outcome.

Change of plea in the course of the trial

12.46   It sometimes happens that a defendant wishes to change his/her plea to guilty to some or all of the counts s/he faces, or the prosecution is prepared to accept a new and lesser charge. If that situation arises, the usual procedure is for the defendant to be re-arraigned in the absence of the jury and to enter the relevant plea(s).

12.47   However, as the defendant is in the charge of the jury once it has been empanelled, the verdict(s) (which must be guilty on the defendant's admission(s)) must be obtained from a foreperson usually nominated by the judge, and on his/her direction via the court clerk. The trial may then continue against other defendants or concerning the defendant on other charges, although there may be an application to discharge the present jury and begin a new trial. If the guilty plea(s) conclude the trial, the defendant would be in a position to be sentenced, as though there had not been a trial in the first place.

Checklist for Crown Court trial

1) Pre-trial preparation will include establishing the nature of the defendant's case, the areas of challenge to the prosecution case and the availability of defence witnesses and the advisability of calling them.
2) Are there any legal rulings which should be sought from the judge? Can a ruling be avoided by agreement with the prosecution advocate? If not, establish the appropriate stage to make submissions.
3) Consider whether a submission of no case to answer can properly be made on at least one charge at the close of the prosecution case.
4) Advise the defendant about the potential effects of not giving evidence under Criminal Justice and Public Order Act 1994 s35.
5) Prepare the closing speech with a number of points written down in advance.
6) Take a careful note of the judge's summing-up.
7) If the defendant is convicted, advise orally and later in writing, if required, on the prospects of a successful appeal.
8) If the defendant is acquitted, apply for his/her discharge and costs out of central funds.

Available sentences

Pre-sentence reports

13.1   In most cases, the defendant will not be sentenced until a pre-sentence report has been obtained pursuant to Criminal Justice Act 1991 s3 or s7. It is only where the sentencing tribunal considers that the offence is not serious enough to merit either a custodial or community sentence, or that it is so serious that not only is a custodial sentence inevitable but that the sentencing tribunal would gain little or no assistance from such a report in determining the appropriate length of the sentence, that sentencing would proceed without a report. The sentences which may be imposed without a pre-sentence report are discharges, fines and probation, supervision or attendance centre orders. A pre-sentence report must be obtained where a community service order or combination order is imposed or where a supervision order or a probation order is intended to be imposed with specific requirements with which the defendant must comply.

13.2   Under Crime (Sentences) Act 1997 s50, which came into force on 1 March 1998, the prosecution advocate now has the right (although rarely exercised) of seeing the pre-sentence report before sentence, in order to check the factual basis of the offences, and where appropriate, that the defendant's version has been accurately set out and accepted.

13.3   It is essential for the advocate to advise the defendant to co-operate very fully with the probation officer, who will be the author of the report, and to attend interviews and discuss personal matters as fully as possible with him/her. If there has been lack of co-operation by the defendant then s/he will be at a considerable disadvantage when the sentencing options available to the court are considered. The defendant would not be seen in a good light unless there was a very good reason for his/her failure to co-operate.

Deferred sentences

13.4   The case may also be delayed for sentence under Powers of the Criminal Courts Act 1973 s1, which gives the court the option of imposing a deferred sentence. The period of deferral is usually in practice six months and requires the defendant's consent. Once the period of deferral has been completed, the defendant will come back to court with an updated pre-sentence report. If the defendant has committed no other offences and has co-operated with any conditions imposed upon him/her when the deferred sentence was imposed, s/he will have a legitimate expectation of receiving a non-custodial sentence.[1] The defendant should be warned, however, that if s/he commits other offences or breaches the terms of deferral, the almost inevitable disposal on the return date will be custody.

Criteria for custodial sentences

13.5 Criminal Justice Act 1991 ss1 and 2 set out the criteria to be considered by the court before the imposition and determining the length of a custodial sentence. The three bases for imposing such a sentence are where the offence is in itself so serious, that the offence is of a violent or sexual nature and it is necessary for the protection of the public or where the defendant has refused consent to a community penalty. If the defendant is over 21 years old at the date of conviction, s/he would be sent to prison. If s/he is less than 21, s/he will be sent to a Young Offender Institution.

13.6 In the magistrates' court, there are important limitations on the periods of custody which may be imposed. This is relevant to whether the magistrates' court accepts jurisdiction in regard to the case at the outset or subsequently when it considers its sentencing options. Under Magistrates' Courts Act 1980 ss31, 32, 132 and 133, the maximum sentence that can be imposed for one offence by a magistrates' court is a period of six months' imprisonment and for a series of offences, the maximum total sentence is 12 months' imprisonment.

Extended custodial sentences

13.7 In very special circumstances, under Criminal Justice Act 1991 s2(2)(b), it is possible for any court to impose a 'longer than normal' sentence. This is known as an extended sentence of imprisonment. The prerequisite would be where the offence is of a violent or sexual offence and where the court thinks that it is necessary to protect the public from serious harm from the defendant. It would be necessary for the court to state why an extended sentence is to be imposed. If the court is contemplating such a sentence, it would usually indicate

1   *R v George* (1984) 6 Cr App R (S) 211, CA; *R v Gillam* (1980) 2 Cr App Rep (S) 267, CA.

that it is of that view and give the defence advocate the opportunity
to make submissions about why that course should not be adopted.

13.8   In addition, new provisions under Crime and Disorder Act 1998
ss58–60 permit the court to impose an extended sentence
comprising both the custodial term and a further period known as
the 'extension period', whereby the defendant is on licence for that
further period, if s/he has been convicted of an offence of a sexual or
violent nature. The extension period can be for up to ten years in the
case of a sexual offence, or five years in respect of a violent offence.
The sentence cannot be imposed for an offence of violence unless
the custodial term imposed is less than four years' imprisonment.

Repeated offences

13.9   Under new provisions brought in by Crime (Sentences) Act 1997 ss2
and 3 (effective from 1 October 1997), a mandatory life sentence will
be imposed on a defendant aged over 18 years convicted of a second
serious offence (defined by s2(5)) unless there are 'exceptional
circumstances' relating either to the defendant or to either of the
offences which justify a court not imposing that sentence. A
sentence of a minimum of seven years' imprisonment will be
imposed on a defendant aged over 18 years for a third conviction for
Class A drug trafficking unless there are 'specific circumstances'
relating either to the defendant or to any of the offences which would
make that sentence unjust in all the circumstances.[2]

13.10   Further provisions under s4 relating to a maximum sentence of
three years' imprisonment for a third domestic burglary have not yet
been brought into force.

Multiple offences

13.11   Where custodial sentences are imposed for a number of offences, an
important issue is whether those offences will be made concurrent
or consecutive. The general principle is that consecutive terms
would not be imposed for offences which arise out of the same
transaction or incident, whether or not they arose out of precisely the
same facts.[3] However, much is left to the discretion of the sentencing
court, although the court would always have to be mindful to
consider the totality of the sentence imposed. There may be

2   Crime (Sentences) Act 1997 s3(2).
3   *R v Lawrence* [1990] Crim LR 276; (1989) 11 Cr App R (S) 580, CA.

exceptional circumstances even where the offences arise out of the same transaction justifying consecutive sentences, for example, an assault on an arresting police officer following the commission of another offence.

13.12   If the offences do not arise out of the same transaction and are therefore separate in time, consecutive sentences are generally imposed, particularly where subsequent offences were committed when the defendant was on bail for the first offence. Offences committed on bail are treated as an 'aggravating feature' and it is worth checking from discussion with the defendant and the prosecution advocate whether this additional feature requires consideration. Similarly, if the subsequent offences involve violence, in particular, an attempt to resist arrest or possession of a firearm at the time of the commission of the earlier offence, consecutive sentences would usually be imposed.

13.13   Where a number of consecutive sentences are imposed, as indicated, the court would need to consider the aggregate sentence to determine whether it is just and appropriate taking the offences as a whole. It is worth reminding the court of the 'totality principle' which is preserved by Criminal Justice Act 1991 s28(2)(b). The court will also bear in mind the period of time the defendant has spent on remand in custody and if s/he has served a sentence of imprisonment on another matter since the commission of the present offence or offences.

Suspended sentences

13.14   The option of a suspended sentence of imprisonment used to be advanced regularly pursuant to Powers of Criminal Courts Act 1973 ss22–24. This was a very useful form of sentence as it marked the severity of the offence by a custodial sentence but, where the sentence of imprisonment would otherwise have been for not more than two years, enabled the court to suspend that sentence for a period of between one and two years on the express basis that should the defendant get into further trouble, s/he would almost inevitably have that sentence of imprisonment enforced as well as being sentenced for the subsequent offence.

13.15   However, the power of the court to impose suspended sentences was substantially curtailed by Criminal Justice Act 1991 s5. Amendments introduced to ss22(2) mean that a suspended sentence cannot be imposed unless first, the case is one in which a sentence of imprisonment would have been appropriate even without the power to suspend the sentence and second, the exercise of that power can be justified by the 'exceptional circumstances' of the case.

13.16   It is difficult to define what would constitute 'exceptional circumstances', but matters such as good character, youth and an early plea of guilty are not treated as exceptional circumstances because they are common features of criminal cases.[4] At one stage, it was commonly believed that 'exceptional circumstances' was limited to the circumstances of the offence as opposed to the offender, but the Court of Appeal has now held that the expression can apply to the circumstances of the offender.[5] However, in many cases, the courts have declined to find 'exceptional circumstances' where there has been a combination of mitigating factors relating to both the offence and the offender and it is probably realistic to observe that the defendant would be unlikely to receive a suspended sentence unless there are remarkable features to the case justifying a departure from usual principles and which otherwise would have resulted in a custodial sentence. It is, therefore, unusual for the court to be thinking in terms of a suspended sentence and the best way to deal with this possible option may be for the defence advocate to suggest it tentatively to the court to see if there is any possibility of the tribunal accepting that there may be 'exceptional circumstances'. If a doubtful or lethargic response is received, it may be best not to pursue that option.

Length of sentence

13.17   Although the maximum sentence for quite a number of serious criminal offences is life imprisonment, in practice only the most serious types of case of that offence would attract that sentence. The exception is for the offence of murder, for which the sentence of life imprisonment remains mandatory, with the possibility that the trial judge (it would always be a judge) making a recommendation that the defendant should serve a minimum term of imprisonment.

13.18   A recent *Practice Direction (Custodial Sentences: Explanations)* (1998) *Times* 24 January, a copy of which appears at appendix N, has been introduced by Lord Bingham LCJ whereby judges are now required to explain to the defendant where a custodial sentence is

---

4   *R v Okinikan* [1993] 1 WLR 173; [1993] 2 All ER 5; (1993) 96 Cr App R 431; (1993) 14 Cr App R (S) 453; [1993] Crim LR 146, CA.

5   *R v Weston* [1995] Crim LR 900; (1996) 1 Cr App R (S) 297, CA.

imposed, exactly what period will be served and the consequences for the defendant if s/he re-offends during the currency of the licence period after release. This will help clarify any confusion which the defendant may have when sentenced to a term of imprisonment, but it will still be worth explaining the true effect of the sentence afterwards.

Bind-overs and discharges

Bind-overs

13.19 Bind-overs and discharges are at the other end of the sentencing spectrum. There are a number of different powers which a court may use to impose a bind-over. A convicted defendant may be bound over to come up for judgment when called under Powers of Criminal Courts Act 1973 s1(7). There are analogies with binding over to come up for judgment with a deferred sentence because the defendant's sentence is postponed on condition to be of good behaviour and the defendant will be required to enter into a recognizance in an amount which will be forfeited if s/he fails to keep the peace.

13.20 In addition, a defendant or any person may be bound over to keep the peace under the Justices of the Peace Act 1361. The use of this power to bind over to keep the peace does not depend on a conviction and may even be used against a defendant who has been acquitted by a jury. It is a potentially very useful device to enable a case to be resolved without a full trial as the prosecution advocate may be prepared to offer no evidence against a defendant on the condition that s/he agrees to being bound over. This would usually be for a period of 12 months in a recognizance of between £50 and £200, depending on the defendant's means. If that course is to be adopted, it would need to be with the express approval of both the defendant and the court, who would ultimately sanction such a disposal, but it would be for the prosecution advocate to explain why the CPS has decided to take that course. Increasingly, the use of a bind-over to resolve the matter is used more sparingly because the CPS is adhering, quite rigidly, to specific guidelines in determining whether a case should be prosecuted through to trial. Nonetheless, in an appropriate case, it remains a possible way of disposing of a case where the offence charged is not particularly serious and where, for example, the defendant has few or no previous convictions and the consequence of a conviction would be particularly serious. It may, therefore, be very useful in the right case for the defence advocate to canvass the possibility of a bind-over with the prosecution advocate. The defendant must be made aware that a bind-over does not count as a conviction but, nonetheless, there is an implicit recognition on his/her part that his/her behaviour is marked by the imposition of a bind-over and the defendant would need to be warned that should s/he become involved in further trouble, s/he would be liable to forfeit the sum entered into by recognizance. Sometimes, defendants feel very strongly about the charge and would prefer to fight the case, even when a bind-over is on offer and the risk of a conviction remains and it is not generally very wise to press the defendant too hard into accepting the alternative course even where the advocate feel that it would be in his/her best interests.

Discharges – absolute and conditional

Absolute discharges

13.21   Absolute discharges are extremely rare and are only imposed where the defendant has committed the most technical of criminal offences and where it is one of strict liability or where there are particular extenuating circumstances all but excusing the defendant from the commission of the offence.

Conditional discharges

13.22   By contrast, a conditional discharge is much more frequently imposed, (particularly in the magistrates' court) where the offence is not particularly serious and where good mitigation is available, including the defendant's previous good character and an early plea of guilty. A word of caution: in quite a number of pre-sentence reports, the possibility of the imposition of a conditional discharge is recommended. If the case is clearly too serious for such a disposal, it is advisable to ignore that recommendation as it may simply annoy the sentencing tribunal. Nonetheless, in the right case, where the court intends to deal with the matter relatively leniently, the operation of a conditional discharge is very useful, as it leaves open the possibility of the defendant being re-sentenced for the offence, if s/he commits a further offence during its activation period.

Probation orders

13.23   A probation order may be imposed against any defendant aged 16
        years or over. If conditions are intended to be imposed, a pre-
        sentence report would usually first need to be obtained, unless the
        court considers it unnecessary to obtain one (see para 13.1). The
        period of an order can be for between six months and three years,
        usually for one to two years, in practice. The type of conditions that
        may be attached to such an order would include residence at a
        particular address; performance of specified activities up to 60 days;
        attendance at probation centres for up to 60 days; consent to
        treatment for a mental condition or for a drug or alcohol dependency.

Community service orders

13.24   A community service order is an order that the offender perform,
        without pay, work which is deemed to be of virtue to the community.
        A community service order may be imposed against any person aged
        16 years or older charged with an imprisonable offence for a period
        between 40 hours and 240 hours. Before imposing a community
        service order, a pre-sentence report will usually need to be obtained
        to assess the defendant's suitability (although it is no longer a pre-
        requisite to the imposition of a community service order for there to
        be a report).[6]

Combination orders

13.25   Under Criminal Justice Act 1991 s11, it is now possible to make a
        combination order combining a community service order and a
        probation order for any defendant aged 16 years or over convicted of
        an imprisonable offence. The minimum length would be 12 months'
        probation and 40 hours' community service up to a maximum length
        of three years' probation and 100 hours' community service. A pre-
        sentence report will usually be obtained before a combination order
        can be imposed, unless the court considers it unnecessary. This form
        of sentence is particularly useful where the court would not otherwise
        consider a community order appropriate, as it increases the scrutiny
        by probation officers of the defendant and marks the disapproval of

6   Criminal Justice Act 1991 s7(3A).

the court of the offences committed by the defendant, without placing the defendant into immediate custody. In practice, the pre-sentence report would usually be recommending whether a probation order, community service order or combination order ought to be imposed and it will be for the advocate to seek to persuade the court to adopt one of the recommendations contained within that report.

Fines

13.26   Both the magistrates' court and the Crown Court may impose financial penalties. In the magistrates' court, there is a maximum limit of £5,000, unless the relevant statute prescribes a different figure. There is no financial limit in the Crown Court, unless the relevant statute prescribes a maximum figure, although the court is required to consider the defendant's financial circumstances to determine the amount of the fine. Where a fine is ordered to be paid by instalments, the court is required to consider the period by which the defendant must repay the full sum. This may be as long as three years. If a financial penalty is imposed, the court would usually allow instructions to be taken by the advocate from the defendant about how long s/he would need to repay the sum imposed and at what rate. However, in the course of mitigation, the advocate would usually be asked to give a full breakdown of the defendant's means and liabilities, if the court appears to be considering a financial penalty, and it is essential to have full details of the defendant's financial position. Under Criminal Justice Act 1991 s18, before fixing the amount of the fine, the court is obliged to consider the defendant's financial circumstances as well as the seriousness of the offence and other circumstances of the case.

Compensation orders

13.27   Under Powers of Criminal Courts Act 1973 s35, a compensation order may be imposed against the defendant compensating the victim for personal injury, loss or damage. It is a useful expression of the defendant's contrition for the advocate to advance that the defendant is willing to pay appropriate compensation (subject to means) following an offence of assault or criminal damage. Where the court considers that it would be appropriate both to impose a fine and to make a compensation order but the defendant has insufficient means to pay both, the court would give preference to the award of compensation.[7] A compensation order may be imposed in addition to another sentence or it may be the whole sentence. Guidance on the amount of compensation to be awarded in personal injury cases is contained in a Judicial Studies Board booklet,[8] which is updated regularly, as well as the Magistrates' Courts Association's *Sentencing Guidelines* (1994) which magistrates will have been provided with by the Lord Chancellor's Department.

Other orders

13.28 Other orders may be imposed by the court in appropriate cases, including restitution orders, deprivation and confiscation orders, and confiscation orders under the Drug Trafficking Act 1994. There is a complex procedure involved in drug trafficking offences which is outside the scope of this book but which involves identifying whether the defendant has 'benefited from drug trafficking' and thereafter determining 'the amount to be recovered'. Sometimes, a hearing on these issues can take a number of hours where issues concerning benefit and the amount to be realised are challenged by the defendant and may involve live evidence being adduced, there having been a statement served by a customs officer seeking recovery of a specific amount under a confiscation order. This area is covered in *Archbold* at para 5-419 and you would be well advised to look at a specialised text book on this area, before appearing in a contested Drug Trafficking Offences Act hearing.

13.29 Other less common orders include exclusion orders from sporting events under the Public Order Act 1986, restriction orders under the Football Spectators Act 1989, exclusion orders from licensed premises, disqualification of company directors under the Company Directors Disqualification Act 1986 and deportation orders under the Immigration Act 1971.

13.30 New orders have been introduced by the Crime and Disorder Act 1998, including a drug treatment and testing order[9] whereby a defendant aged over 16 years may be subject to such an order for a

---

7 Powers of Criminal Courts Act 1973 s35(4A).

8 Judicial Studies Board, *Guidelines for the Assessment of General Damages in Personal Injuries Cases* (4th edn, 1998, Blackstone Press).

9 Crime and Disorder Act 1998 ss61–64.

period of between six months and three years and in respect of
young offenders, further orders set out include a parenting order,[10] a
reparation order,[11] an action plan order,[12] and a detention and
training order.[13] (See further generally chapter 15.)

Mental Health Act 1983

13.31   The only other significant type of sentence in an adult court is an
order under the Mental Health Act 1983, in particular, the powers
which the court has to order the admission of a defendant to hospital
under Mental Health Act 1983 s37 and, additionally, to impose a
restriction order restricting the defendant's discharge from hospital
under Mental Health Act 1983 s41. Again, the legislation is quite
complex and requires careful consideration. The Mental Health Act
1983 applies where the defendant is suffering from 'mental disorder'
defined by s1. There are specific requirements concerning the
obtaining of medical evidence before the imposition of a hospital
order and interim orders can also be imposed. If there is a possibility
of a sentence under the Mental Health Act the advocate should study
carefully the provisions contained in the Act to be sure that s/he has
obtained the relevant evidence necessary. Often, it is clear that a
Mental Health Act order would be appropriate, but the prosecution
advocate (or judge) may be advancing the necessity of a restriction
order whereas the defendant would often not wish it to be imposed.
The test for the court is whether, having regard to the nature of the
offence, the antecedents of the defendant and the risk of his/her
committing further offences if set at large, it is necessary for the
protection of the public from serious harm to restrict the defendant's
discharge from hospital, either without limit or time or for a period
as specified by the judge. There is provision for the judge to listen to
evidence in open court from an appropriate medical practitioner
before imposing the order. A summary of the provisions of the
Mental Health Act 1983 is set out in *Archbold* at paras 5-533 to 5-560.

10 Ibid ss8 and 9.
11 Ibid ss67 and 68.
12 Ibid ss69 and 70.
13 Ibid ss69–73.

Checklist for sentencing

1) Take full instructions on the defendant's antecedents to check that no previous conviction is challenged.
2) Prepare a summary of mitigation points as a checklist.
3) Be prepared to deal with any aggravating features of the offence.
4) Advise the defendant to co-operate in the preparation of reports.
5) Advise the defendant orally and, if necessary, in writing, on the merits of an appeal against sentence.
6) Explain to the defendant what the sentence means in practice and what could occur if further offences are committed during the currency of any period specified by the court.

CHAPTER 14

Sentencing – adults

14.1   Sentencing procedure in the magistrates' court and the Crown Court is similar for defendants over 17 years old (although of course the sentencing powers in a magistrates' court are more limited both in terms of financial and custodial penalties). This chapter will, therefore, deal with the sentencing of adults, while chapter 15 will cover the sentencing of young people.

The adult court

Guilty pleas

14.2   Where a defendant has pleaded guilty or been found guilty, the next issue to be resolved is his/her sentence.

14.3   Following a guilty plea or pleas tendered by the defendant that are acceptable to the prosecution advocate, s/he will then open the facts. This is usually unnecessary following a trial as the tribunal will have heard all about the circumstances of the offence or offences already. The defendant's antecedents (personal details and previous convictions) will be summarised. Usually only recent and relevant convictions will be referred to. Check with the defendant that the convictions are accepted and obtain some details, if possible, about those matters. If a conviction is disputed, it may be necessary for the sentencing hearing to be adjourned to check it. Otherwise, the tribunal can indicate that it will make no difference to sentence, in which case the disputed conviction can be ignored and the hearing can proceed.

Newton hearings

14.4   The basis of the guilty plea or pleas may be significant, because the CPS may not necessarily accept the basis tendered by the defendant, ie, there may be a substantial difference of fact.

14.5   It is therefore important for the defence advocate to discuss the basis of the plea or pleas of guilty first with the defendant and then with the prosecution advocate in order to assess whether there is a large discrepancy between the versions. It is possible to ask the prosecution advocate not to open a particularly contentious issue, if it does not alter an assessment of the overall seriousness of the admitted offence or offences. However, there will be occasions where the defendant's version of the circumstances of the offence or offences, while still amounting to a guilty plea or pleas, differs significantly from the version put forward by the prosecution advocate. In those circumstances, it may become necessary to have a Newton hearing. In circumstances where the defendant pleads guilty, but puts forward a version of facts differing significantly from the version put forward by the prosecution advocate, the sentencing tribunal must resolve the issue before passing sentence and should not pass sentence without determining which version of the facts is accepted.[1] Where the prosecution advocate is aware that there is a marked difference between the parties, s/he will notify the judge and leave it for him/her to determine whether a Newton hearing would be appropriate. Even where the prosecution advocate accepts a version of the facts put forward by the defence advocate, the sentencing tribunal is not bound by that version and may, nonetheless, direct that a Newton hearing takes place, although this is rare in practice.

14.6   The procedure to be followed, where conflicting versions of the circumstances of the offence are put forward, was set out by Lord Lane LCJ in *R v Newton*[2] where he said that in some cases it was possible to obtain an answer from a jury, where the different versions could be reflected in different charges in the indictment. The second method was for the judge him/herself to hear the evidence of one side and another, and come to his own conclusion, acting so to speak as his own jury. The third possibility was for the judge to hear no evidence, but to listen to the submissions of counsel: but if this course is adopted, 'if there is a substantial conflict between the two sides ... the version of the defendant must so far as possible be accepted'.

14.7   If the sentencing tribunal directs that a Newton hearing should take place, it is the duty of the prosecution advocate to assist the court by calling evidence and testing any evidence called on behalf of the defence. What actually happens at a Newton hearing is that evidence is called as in a trial (with examination-in-chief, cross-examination and re-examination). The standard of proof for the sentencing tribunal is the usual criminal standard, but the important consequence which the advocate must advise the defendant about, is that where his/her version is rejected, the sentencing tribunal will withhold some part of the discount which the defendant would usually receive in recognition of his/her plea of guilty.[3]

1   *R v Brown (Walter Thomas)* (1981) 3 Cr App R (S) 250, CA.
2   (1983) 77 Cr App R 13, CA.
3   *R v Stevens* (1986) 8 Cr App R (S) 297; [1987] Crim LR 139, CA.

14.8   From a defence point of view, Newton hearings are to be avoided wherever possible because of the risk of loss of credit for a guilty plea. In addition, the process of giving live evidence means that the defendant's credibility is put in issue. If the defendant is unsuccessful, it becomes difficult for the advocate to put forward the remorse of the defendant with the same degree of sincerity.

Exceptions to need for a Newton hearing

14.9   There are some situations where a Newton hearing is unnecessary. The most important is where the difference in the two versions is regarded as immaterial to the sentence, in which case the sentencing tribunal should proceed on the basis of the defendant's version.[4] Where the defence advocate has not succeeded in persuading the prosecution advocate to accept or at least not oppose his/her version of the circumstances of the offence, or to refrain from referring to a contentious issue, s/he should seek to persuade the sentencing tribunal that a Newton hearing is not necessary.

14.10   A further exception for the requirement of a Newton hearing is where the defence version is 'manifestly false' or 'wholly implausible'.[5] It is important for the advocate to advise the defendant on the possibility of the sentencing tribunal rejecting the defence version in circumstances where it is clearly incapable of belief. In certain circumstances it may be necessary to take a strong line with a defendant who is instructing the advocate to argue that version of the offences when mitigating.

14.11   A third exception is where the prosecution advocate is not in a position to contradict matters put forward by the defence as mitigation concerning the background to the commission of the offence or other circumstances, although the sentencing tribunal is not bound to accept the truth of the matters put forward by the defendant even if they are not challenged by the prosecution.[6] Before the hearing, the prosecution advocate may be able to confirm that s/he will not seek to oppose the basis on which those mitigating factors are placed before the court and it would be unusual for the judge to go behind the version put forward by the defence advocate in those circumstances.

---

4   *R v Hall (Terence)* (1984) 6 Cr App R (S) 321; [1985] Crim LR 54, CA.
5   *R v Hawkins* (1985) 7 Cr App R (S) 351; [1986] Crim LR 194, CA.
6   *R v Broderick (Michelle)* (1994) 15 Cr App R (S) 476; [1994] Crim LR 139, CA.

Sentencing

14.12 The general principle is that the defendant will be sentenced for the offence(s) to which s/he has pleaded guilty. A slight variation is where further offences are taken into consideration. The net effect is that the sentence passed by the court can be rightly longer than it would be if it were dealing only with offences to which the defendant has pleaded guilty. Although there is no conviction in respect of the offences taken into consideration, they are, in practice, considered by the judge in ascertaining the appropriate overall sentence.

Offences taken into consideration

14.13 There is a clear benefit for both the CPS and the defendant to have matters taken into consideration (which generally become apparent by the defendant admitting these further offences in interview) in that further offences are cleared up, while the defendant will not be liable to prosecution and conviction for those offences subsequently.

14.14 The procedure is for a schedule to be prepared and served on the defendant or his/her legal representative. Once the defendant has been given an opportunity to consider the offences listed and detailed under the schedule, s/he should sign for those offences, thereby admitting them and stating that s/he wishes to have each and every one of them taken into consideration. If there are any doubts about whether the defendant admits a particular offence, it should not be taken into consideration. Once the schedule has been signed, it is handed up to the clerk of the court who will confirm with the defendant that s/he wishes the following additional number of offences to be taken into consideration by the sentencing tribunal.

Antecedents

14.15 Once the case has been opened by the prosecution advocate, s/he will then refer to the defendant's antecedents, which comprise details provided by the defendant to the police at the time of his/her arrest concerning their personal details as well as any previous convictions and cautions. The prosecution advocate and thereafter the sentencing tribunal will consider which, if any, of the defendant's previous convictions are relevant and will usually not refer to either very old or 'spent' convictions under the Rehabilitation of Offenders Act 1974, or offences of a wholly unrelated character.

There is likely to be an application for costs made by the prosecution advocate, which will vary in size depending on the amount of investigation required into the offence and at what stage the defendant pleaded guilty. If, for example, the defendant pleaded guilty when the case was listed for trial, at least some of the prosecution witnesses would have been asked to attend court, which would incur extra expenditure.

14.16   It can be very helpful to persuade the prosecution advocate to make points on behalf of the defendant in the course of summarising the case. (However, this should be within reason, as otherwise it may have a negative effect on the sentencing tribunal, which might take the view that the CPS are being unduly generous to the defendant.) In particular, matters which the CPS may be prepared to admit in an appropriate case are:

1) the defendant's guilty plea at an early stage,
2) his/her co-operation with the police including admissions in interview,
3) his/her co-operative nature generally with the police,
4) assistance given to the police in respect of other persons, or
5) the saving of considerable police time by providing important information about the extent of the offences, the limited nature of the injuries inflicted on the victim or any provocation by the victim before the commission of the offence.

Mitigation points

14.17   As with all other areas of advocacy, advocates will have their own style about how best to advance mitigating factors on behalf of the defendant. However, there are a number of standard matters which the court will regard as appropriate mitigation in all cases.

Guilty plea

14.18   By far the most important mitigating factor is the defendant's guilty plea. That has always been regarded as strong mitigation and has now been given statutory recognition by Criminal Justice and Public Order Act 1994 s48.

14.19   The sentencing tribunal will give a maximum discount of a third where the defendant indicated a guilty plea at the earliest opportunity and it follows that the later the indication is given, usually the smaller discount will be given. Less than a full discount will be given where the defendant entered a guilty plea on the first day of trial or even during the course of the trial, where s/he disputed a material issue requiring a Newton hearing and his/her version was not accepted, and where the defendant had no realistic defence and therefore in effect, was forced to plead guilty.

14.20   When advancing a guilty plea, it is worth emphasising that the guilty plea has saved time and expense and has avoided the necessity of prosecution witnesses coming to court. It is also important to refer to the defendant's remorse, as reflected by his/her plea.

Admissions and co-operation

14.21   A related, although separate, mitigating factor is admissions made by the defendant to the police in interview or when first apprehended and/or where considerable time has been saved by the defendant providing assistance to the prosecuting authorities about other offences of which s/he was not originally suspected, or which results in the proceeds of the offences being recovered.

14.22   A further way in which the defendant may have assisted the police is if s/he has provided a statement to the police implicating potential co-defendants which has resulted in those other persons pleading guilty, or if they have continued to contest the matter, the defendant has given evidence on behalf of the prosecution in their trial. This is referred to as turning Queen's evidence. If a defendant provided a statement to the police and then gave evidence in accordance with that statement, that would be a strong mitigation point to advance, particularly if the evidence against the co-defendants was weak without the assistance of the defendant.

14.23   A defendant may have assisted the police with regard to providing names of other persons, particularly the names of persons more deeply and seriously involved in the commission of the offences. Evidence of this nature is sensitive and it may be necessary to refer to this aspect of mitigation by the defence advocate seeing the sentencing tribunal with the prosecution advocate in chambers. Sometimes, it is possible for a letter to be obtained from a senior police officer confirming that the defendant has assisted in providing information relating to other persons not presently before the court and when mitigation takes place afterwards in open court, it is only necessary to refer in passing to the matter referred to expressly in chambers by stating that 'the defendant has substantially assisted the police in their enquiries'.

Age

14.24   Another aspect of mitigation of importance is the defendant's youth (generally interpreted as meaning not older than in their early twenties). It may be possible to submit that s/he is more easily influenced by his/her peers, may be immature, or that s/he was in a particularly stressed phase in his/her life, since when s/he has matured. It is very useful to stress that the effect of even a short custodial sentence being imposed on a young person will generally have a deeper impression than for a mature adult.

14.25   The defendant's lack of relevant previous convictions is of particular importance. This point may be argued forcefully with the defendant of more mature years on the basis that the defendant is now a mature adult and has lived an honest and industrious life before the commission of the present offences.

Personal factors

14.26   Mitigation which is personal to the defendant should also be advanced, for example, loss of employment or of a job opportunity caused by the conviction, the evidence of a long-standing relationship with a partner and/or contact with children, ill-health since the offence(s) came to light, financial difficulties which the defendant was under at the time of the offence(s), and other stressful factors influencing the defendant to commit the offences.

14.27   It may also be possible to advance reasons why the defendant may be less likely to continue offending, for example, the continuing support of his/her family or partner, helpful recommendations contained within the pre-sentence report, especially whether the defendant remains at serious risk to the public of re-offending, the fact that the defendant has cut off association with persons influencing him/her to commit crime or the fact that s/he had ceased taking drink and/or drugs which may have influenced or even been the motive behind the commission of the offences.

14.28   Other examples of personal mitigation are the effect a custodial sentence would have on the defendant, in particular, if s/he is young, very old or not in good health (physically or psychologically) and whether there are clear indications that the defendant is intending to reform him/herself. The defendant's work record can also be an important point in mitigation.

Nature of the offence(s)

14.29 Some features of the offence(s) committed by the defendant can be either mitigating factors or aggravating factors. If there are mitigating factors, for example, the offences(s) are at the lower end of the scale of offences or the proceeds of the crime have been recovered, the advocate should refer to them. If there are any potentially aggravating features, it is the duty of the prosecution advocate to state them to the advocate before the sentencing hearing, first, to alert the advocate and the defendant to the fact that the judge will be informed of them and second, to check whether those aggravating features are disputed by the defendant, because it may be necessary for a Newton hearing to take place on another date.

14.30 Examples of features which may be either mitigating or aggravating are where the scale is relevant to the seriousness of the offence, whether violence was used, whether weapons were used, whether the property was recovered and its value, the type of victim, ie, whether vulnerable or not, whether the offence was against a public servant or an abuse of trust, the extent of personal financial gain, whether the offence was pre-meditated, whether there was a racial motivation,[7] the time of day or night when the offence was committed and the role played by the defendant, ie, whether s/he was the ringleader or played a lesser role.

14.31 Other aggravating features would include the prevalence of the offence in a particular area. This might justify a sentence of deterrence if the defendant has relevant previous convictions and/or has demonstrated a failure to respond to previous sentences.[8]

Presentation in court

14.32 It is sometimes very difficult to make pleas in mitigation sound fresh and it is hard to avoid resorting to commonplace expressions such as 'the clang of the prison gates' or 'the defendant has had the "Sword of Damocles" hanging over him for X months'. Usually sentencing tribunals will accept that there are a limited number of ways to make the same point. Advocates may find it helpful to list the best features of mitigation and inform the tribunal at the outset that they have, for

7 Under Crime and Disorder Act 1998 ss28–32, new offences of assault, criminal damage, public order and harassment which is 'racially aggravated' have been introduced.
8 Under Criminal Justice Act 1991 s29.

example, the following seven points to make. This has the real benefit of brevity and clarity, which will often be appreciated by the tribunal.

14.33   When completing the plea in mitigation it is generally worth summarising briefly the best points in mitigation. If there is a pre-sentence report and the recommendation is a non-custodial option, it is worth urging the sentencing tribunal to take that course. However, advocates should not be unrealistic with their submission and, if the offence is a serious one, should accept that a custodial sentence would usually be imposed and seek to persuade the court not to take that course. If it is clear that only a custodial sentence can properly be imposed for the offence or the sentencing tribunal has already indicated that s/he is only considering a custodial option, all that is left in conclusion is to seek to urge the court to make the sentence as short as possible. Having completed all the submissions, before concluding, advocates should ask the sentencing tribunal if there is any way that they can be of further assistance to the court.

14.34   When the magistrates or judge impose the sentence, in any event advocates will need to take a full note in case they want to appeal and to advise the defendant about the prospects of an appeal.

14.35   Once the sentence has been passed, including any additional orders relating to costs, forfeiture or destruction, if the defendant is given a custodial sentence, s/he will be taken down immediately and should be seen in the cells afterwards. If a non-custodial option is imposed, the defendant will be discharged, although advocates would wish to advise the defendant about the requirements that the sentence imposes on him/her outside the court. It may also be necessary to speak to the court probation officer if a community sentence has been imposed. Once all the matters relating to sentencing have been completed, advocates should bow slightly and leave court once there are other advocates in the courtroom. If advocates are satisfied with the sentence, it is customary to indicate their gratitude to the tribunal before leaving.

Appeals

14.36   Once sentencing has been completed, it will be necessary to consider whether to appeal, the sentence imposed. The defendant should be advised orally and, if requested, and if the sentence is appealable, the advocate should draft an advice on appeal against sentence and grounds of appeal. In rare circumstances, it may be possible to return to the court which imposed the original sentence under the 'slip rule',[9] which allows the sentencing tribunal to correct an unlawful sentence previously imposed. Usually, one or both advocates would suggest to the judge's clerk to re-list the case, but occasionally the court itself will rely on the 'slip rule'. This would happen where it decides that the appeal would inevitably or at least be highly likely to succeed and in order to save both costs and the sentencing tribunal's face, the slip-rule device can be usefully employed, and the defendant will be re-sentenced by the same tribunal.

9   Pursuant to Supreme Court Act 1981 s47.

Sentencing – young people

Introduction

15.1   The procedure in the youth court is much more informal than for adults in the magistrates' court. The defendant would usually be referred to by his/her first name and the court of three magistrates would include at least one person of each gender. There will always be reporting restrictions in the youth court[1] (although these can be lifted following conviction) and usually there would need to be a parent or guardian present with the defendant in court. The defendant would not surrender to a dock but would simply be sitting behind the defence advocate. The proceedings would usually be held with only parties involved in the case being present.

15.2   The full trial procedure in the youth court is very comprehensively set out in *Defending Young People in the Criminal Justice System* by Mark Ashford and Alex Chard (LAG, 1997) and we do not propose to repeat it here. Instead, the remainder of this chapter is limited to the sentences that can be imposed for young offenders, and which would not be open to adult defendants or where the possible sentences for young offenders are limited.

Custodial sentences in the youth court

15.3   As far as custody is concerned, in the youth court, it is not possible to sentence any child or young person under 15 years old to custody. In a case where the offence merits a greater penalty than is permitted by the scheme of maximum penalties for detention in a young offender institution (YOI),[2] the proper course is for the magistrates to commit the defendant for sentence under Magistrates' Courts Act 1980 s37 to allow for the possibility of a Children and Young Persons Act (CYPA) 1933 s53(2) order being made (see below at para 15.9).

15.4   Between the ages of 15 and 17 years, a child defendant may be detained in a YOI for a maximum period of six months for one offence or 12 months for two or more indictable offences.

Custodial sentences in the Crown Court

15.5   There are a number of forms of custodial sentence which may be imposed in the Crown Court for defendants under the age of 21

1   Under Children and Young Persons Act (CYPA) 1933 s49.
2   Provided by Criminal Justice Act (CJA) 1982 ss1A and 1B.

years. Unlike other sentences, in respect of all those forms of sentence, the relevant date is the date of conviction.[3] The judge must explain the practical effect of the sentence of detention as s/he would for an adult defendant.

15.6   The court may sentence a young offender aged between 15 and 21 years to a term of detention in a YOI.[4] The maximum term of detention in respect of an offender under the age of 18 years is two years. The maximum term in respect of an offender aged between 18 and 21 years is the same as the maximum term of imprisonment that it may impose for that offence.

15.7   The court must sentence a young offender of any age under 21 years to custody for life on conviction for murder (or any other offence with a mandatory life sentence).[5] For a young offender aged under 18 years, the mandatory sentence for murder is detention during Her Majesty's pleasure.[6] The judge may also indicate (as with an adult defendant) the minimum period the defendant should serve, which is referred to as 'the tariff'. This is intended to reflect the seriousness with which the court treats the offence.

15.8   The court may also detain a young offender aged between 18 and 20 years inclusive for default or contempt of court,[7] but by far the most important provision concerning detention in a YOI is CYPA 1933 s53(2).

15.9   The provisions of CYPA 1933 s53(2) and (3) (as amended by the Crime (Sentences) Act 1997) allow for the possibility of sentencing young offenders between the ages of 10 and 17 years inclusive in the Crown Court, to sentences in excess of two years' imprisonment for certain serious offences. For example, where an adult defendant could receive a maximum sentence of not less than 14 years' imprisonment for an offence of indecent assault on a woman or man or, in respect of a young person aged between 11 and 12 years inclusive only, causing death by dangerous driving, or reckless driving while under the influence of drink or drugs. In theory, that could cover offences such as handling stolen goods, residential burglaries and robbery.

---

3   *R v Starkey* (1994) 15 Cr App R (S) 576; [1994] Crim LR 380, CA; *R v Robinson* [1993] 1 WLR 168; [1993] 2 All ER 1; (1993) 96 Cr App R 418; (1993) 14 Cr App R (S) 448; [1993] Crim LR 143, CA.

4   Under CJA 1982 ss1A and 1B.

5   Ibid s8.

6   CYPA 1933 s53(1).

7   Under CJA 1982 s9 (as amended by CJA 1991 s63(5)).

15.10   In the recent case of *R v AM*,[8] the Court of Appeal reviewed the guidelines previously established in the cases of *R v Fairhurst*[9] and *R v Wainfur*.[10] The court confirmed that, under the provisions of s53(2), the crime concerned should be one of 'exceptional gravity', and the usual two-year limit for detention in a YOI should not be exceeded unless the offence was clearly one calling for a longer sentence. However, contrary to the earlier authorities, if, after much careful thought, the court concluded that a longer sentence was called for, then it should impose whatever it considered to be the appropriate period of detention under CYPA 1933 s53(2) and (3).

15.11   For young offenders under 15 years, detention under s53(2) and (3) is the only form of detention available (save for detention at Her Majesty's pleasure). Where sentences of detention are called for, for young offenders of this age, the court determines the appropriate term to be imposed.

15.12   If the young offender is to be sentenced for a number of offences, for which only some could qualify for detention under s53(2) and (3), the court is entitled,[11] in considering whether to pass a custodial sentence and, if so, of what length, to take account of the seriousness not only of the offence in question but also of the combination of that offence and of one or more of the other offences associated with it as defined by Criminal Justice Act 1991 s31(2), which would cover offences which were not necessarily part of the main offence.

15.13   By Crime and Disorder Act 1998 ss73–76 (due to be brought into force in Summer 1999), the court may impose a detention and training order for a period of up to two years, whereby the period of supervision begins when the young offender is released and is completed at the end of the term (or any earlier period ordered by the Home Secretary). Before such an order is imposed for a young offender aged under 15 years, the court must be satisfied that s/he is a persistent offender, and for a young offender under 12 years, it must be satisfied that only a custodial sentence would be adequate to protect the public from further offending by him/her.

---

8   (1997) *Times* 11 December, CA (Crim Div).
9   [1986] 1 WLR 1374; [1987] 1 All ER 46; (1987) 84 Cr App R 19; (1986) 8 Cr App R (S) 346; [1987] Crim LR 60, CA.
10 (1997) 1 Cr App R (S) 43; [1996] Crim LR 674, CA.
11 Under CJA 1991 ss1 and 2.

Community sentences

Attendance centre orders

15.14 Community disposal penalties available in the youth court include attendance centre orders under Criminal Justice Act 1982 ss16 and 17 which may be imposed for young offenders aged between 10 and 20 years old with a length of between 12 hours and 24 hours for children aged between 10 and 14 years, and 36 hours for young persons aged between 16 and 17 years of age. A pre-sentence report is not required before making such an order. An attendance centre order is the most significant of the youth court penalty options and would often be the appropriate sentence for a young offender, except in the most trivial or serious of cases.

Supervision orders

15.15 A supervision order may be imposed under CYPA 1969 s7(7)[12] for young persons aged between 10 and 17 years inclusive, of no minimum length but up to a period of three years. Conditions may be imposed on a supervision order[13] including intermediate treatment for up to 90 days, specified activities to be performed for up to 90 days or education or residence conditions for up to six months.

Other orders

15.16 Probation orders, community service orders and combination orders are available for young offenders in the youth court where the defendant is aged over 16 years. These types of sentence are covered more fully in chapter 13.

15.17 For a young offender aged under 18 years, (except where the offence or any other offence associated with it is triable only on indictment), a pre-sentence report will be obtained before the imposition of one of these types of sentence, unless previous pre-sentence reports had been obtained and were available for the court to consider.[14]

---

12 As amended by Crime and Disorder Act 1998 s71.
13 Under CYPA 1969 ss12, 12A, 12AA, 12B, 12C and 12D.
14 CJA 1991 s7(3B).

15.18   Under new provisions set out in Crime and Disorder Act (CDA) 1998 ss8 and 9, the court may impose a parenting order requiring a parent or guardian to comply with specific requirements in the order for up to 12 months, and to attend for a specified period of counselling or guidance sessions from the appropriate 'responsible' officer, defined as a probation officer, social worker or member of a youth offending team.

15.19   Under CDA 1998 ss67 and 68, the court may impose a reparation order requiring the young offender to work for up to 24 hours for the community at large or for a specified person (including the victim) if consent is given by that person, except where the sentence proposed is custody or a community service order, a combination order or a supervision order with specified requirements.

15.20   An action plan order may be imposed under CDA 1998 ss69 and 70, whereby the court having obtained a written report from the responsible officer, may order the young offender to comply with an action plan within three months and place him/her under the supervision and control of that relevant responsible officer.

15.21   Under CYPA 1933 s55, it is open to the youth court to order a fine or compensation to be paid by a parent or guardian, if the court considers that the imposition of a financial penalty, as part or whole of the sentence, is appropriate, unless that person cannot be found or it would be unreasonable to make such an order, having regard to the circumstances of the case.

Checklist for sentencing young people

1) Meet the family and/or social worker in attendance before the hearing.
2) Explain to the defendant and his/her parent or guardian, if appropriate, what will happen in court and the sentencing options available and likely to be imposed and their implications.
3) Advise the defendant about the sentence actually imposed. What does it mean in practice? Is it worth appealing?

CHAPTER 16

Breach proceedings following the imposition of community sentences

Probation, community service or combination orders

16.1   If an adult or young offender breaches a community service order previously imposed, various options are available to the court depending on the type of community sentence imposed. In the case of probation orders, community service orders or combination orders, where the defendant has failed, without reasonable excuse, to comply with the requirements of the order, the sentencing court may allow the order to continue and as far as the breach is concerned:

1) take no action;
2) impose a fine not exceeding £1,000;
3) impose a community service order of between 40 and 60 hours (if the existing order is a community service order, the total of both orders must not exceed 240 hours); and
4) in the case of a probation order, impose an attendance centre order, in addition.[1]

The court may revoke the order and re-sentence the defendant or, if the defendant was a young offender and the order was made in the Crown Court, the youth court may commit the defendant to the Crown Court to be dealt with there.

16.2   If the court is contemplating re-sentencing the defendant, advocates should ask the court to take into account the extent to which the defendant has complied with the order[2] and the time spent on remand before the imposition of the community sentence[3] which would be deducted from a custodial sentence, if imposed. The court should also take into account any guilty plea in relation to the original offence.[4]

Attendance centre or supervision orders

16.3   In the youth court, where there are breach proceedings in respect of an attendance centre order or supervision order, the powers available to the court are more limited.

---

1   Criminal Justice Act (CJA) 1991 Sch 2 para 3(1).
2   Further to CJA 1991 Sch 2 paras 3(2)(a) and 4(2)(a) for the youth/magistrates' court and the Crown Court, respectively.
3   *R v McDonald* (1988) 10 Cr App R (S) 458, CA.
4   As required by Criminal Justice and Public Order Act 1994 s48.

Attendance centre orders

16.4 For breach of an attendance centre order, where the defendant has either failed without reasonable excuse to attend or, while attending, has committed a breach of the Attendance Centre Rules 1995,[5] the court may take no action, impose a limited fine (up to £1,000 or, if the offender is under the age of 14, up to £250) or revoke the order and re-sentence the defendant.[6]

Supervision orders (and detention and training orders)

16.5 For breach of a supervision order,[7] the defendant must have failed to comply with the requirements of the order and it must still be in force at the relevant date. In those circumstances, the court may allow the order to continue and take no action, impose a fine (up to £1,000 or, if the offender is under the age of 14, up to £250), impose an attendance centre order for the breach, or discharge the order and impose a fine or an attendance centre order.

16.6 Although Children and Young Persons Act 1969 s15 confers the general power to discharge the order and re-sentence the defendant, s15(3) does not extend the power to the passing of a sentence of detention in a young offender institution. However, in certain specified circumstances, s15(4) does allow for the substitution of such a sentence of detention for a failure to comply with a requirement included in pursuance of s12A(3)(a) of the Act. If the sentencing court imposes a supervision order as a direct alternative to detention and makes directions that the defendant is to participate in specified activities, the court must state in open court what it is doing, so that if there is a breach, the court has power to impose a sentence of detention.[8]

16.7 Once the provisions concerning detention and training orders have been implemented, under Crime and Disorder Act 1998 ss77 and 78, there are provisions covering breach of the supervision requirements. The court may fine the young offender, or sentence him/her to detention for between three months and the remainder of the term of the original order and, if a further offence is committed during the currency of the supervision period, the court

5   SI No 3281.

6   CJA 1982 s19(3).

7   As amended by Crime and Disorder Act 1998 s72.

8   Children and Young Persons Act 1969 s12D.

may order detention for any period up to the remainder of the term to be served as well as having the power to sentence the offender for the new offence.

Breach proceedings

16.8   In practice, the defendant would be ill-advised to contest the breach proceedings, unless s/he has a reasonable excuse for non-compliance. Instructions would need to be obtained on this issue before the hearing. Otherwise, it is important to stress good mitigating factors available to the defendant since the imposition of the community sentence and to seek, where possible, to avoid a more severe penalty being imposed. For an adult defendant in the Crown Court, a substantial breach of a community sentence is very likely to result in the imposition of an immediate custodial sentence. The rationale is that the defendant would have been warned at the time of the original sentence that the community disposal was a direct alternative to custody and that on breach, s/he would therefore be at substantial risk of a custodial sentence. Otherwise, the wrong signals would be sent out with regard to the deterrent effect of a non-custodial option being imposed initially.

16.9   If the defendant commits further offences of a similar nature during the operational period of a conditional discharge or suspended sentence, or has not yet completed a community penalty, s/he should be advised of the risk of receiving a custodial sentence both for the original offence(s) (if serious enough to justify custody) or the imposition of part or all of the remainder of the term in the case of a detention and training order (in effect after Summer 1999) and consecutive sentences for the offences committed subsequently. Mitigation will, therefore, need to be tailored in respect of the original offence(s), the subsequent offence(s) and the appropriate disposal in respect of both series of offences.

Appeals

Appeals to the Crown Court

17.1   A defendant convicted by a magistrates' court may appeal to the Crown Court against conviction and/or sentence.[1] Leave is not required and, therefore, the appeal is the defendant's right. However, if the defence lodges an appeal to the High Court on a question of law or jurisdiction under Magistrates' Courts Act (MCA) 1980 s111(1), then a right of appeal against the decision of the magistrates' court to the Crown Court ceases.

17.2   Assuming that the defendant wishes to appeal against conviction and/or sentence, notice of appeal must be lodged. On the notice, the grounds of appeal need to be stated, but this can be dealt with very quickly. If the defendant is appealing against conviction, this section can usually be completed by words such as: 'the decision of the magistrates' court was against the weight of all the evidence' and as far as an appeal against sentence is concerned, 'the sentence was manifestly excessive and/or wrong in principle'. Often, the defendant is upset about his/her conviction or sentence immediately after the case is heard and a notice of appeal can usually be lodged at the court that day, although notice of appeal can be given up to 21 days after the day on which the decision appealed against is given.[2] Reasons need to be supplied.[3] If a defendant wishes subsequently to lodge an appeal, that can be done (usually without risk to costs) up to the third day before the appeal date.[4]

17.3   The wide powers of the Crown Court on appeal are set out under Supreme Court Act 1981 s48. They include costs orders for both the magistrates' court and the Crown Court hearing, ie, if the appeal is successful, the defendant may recover the costs in both courts, whereas if it is unsuccessful, s/he may be liable to pay the costs incurred in the higher court as well as the costs below if they have not already been paid, because the costs order in the magistrates' court may have been suspended pending the outcome of the appeal.

17.4   The appeal is by way of re-hearing.[5] Therefore, procedurally, although the appeal is brought by the defendant (appellant), the prosecution (now the respondent) advocate proceeds by opening the case and calling the evidence in support of the conviction (or for an appeal against sentence, simply opens the facts).

---

1   By MCA 1980 s108(1).
2   Crown Court Rules r7(3).
3   Ibid r7(5).
4   Ibid r11.
5   Supreme Court Act 1981 s79(3).

17.5   The prosecution advocate is not necessarily limited to calling the evidence called in the magistrates' court, nor does s/he have to call all the evidence previously called. In that way, the prosecution has a potential advantage at the re-hearing because perceived weak evidence can be discarded and other aspects of the prosecution case can be strengthened.

17.6   As with a magistrates' court trial, it is open to the defence advocate to make a submission of no case to answer at the conclusion of the prosecution's case. If there is a case to answer, the appellant's case is then heard. As with the prosecution, the appellant's case is not limited to evidence called in the lower court, nor does the defence advocate have to call all the evidence previously adduced if not considered to be tactically advisable, or it is simply not possible for a particular witness to attend.

17.7   When all the evidence has been heard, the defence advocate can make a closing speech similar to the procedure in the magistrates' court.

17.8   The composition of the tribunal is a Crown Court judge and two lay magistrates (who cannot be the same magistrates who first heard the case). The power and influence of the judge over the lay magistrates should not be underestimated. Although it is open to the Crown Court to reach a decision by a majority, that is rarely expressed in open court and it would be unusual to expect two strong-minded lay magistrates only to be the majority. The Crown Court will not be told the details of the sentence until determination of the appeal against conviction, in case this may influence their decision on the merits of the appeal.

17.9   Often, appeals against conviction and/or sentence are heard on Fridays. They must be heard on a day where it will be convenient to obtain magistrates to sit with the judge in the Crown Court.

17.10   It is often quite difficult to advise a defendant about whether it is worth while to appeal to the Crown Court following conviction and/or sentence. An unsuccessful appellant needs to be warned that s/he is likely to have to pay not only the costs incurred in the magistrates' court but also the additional costs in the Crown Court, which are substantially larger. In addition, the appellant needs to be advised that if there is an appeal against conviction, sentence is at large, leaving open the possibility (although quite rarely exercised in practice) that the Crown Court may impose a heavier sentence than that imposed in the magistrates' court. That factor is particularly important where the magistrates have fudged the issue by not dismissing the case as they ought to have done, but instead finding the case proved but giving the defendant a far lighter sentence than would be appropriate for the particular offence. The most obvious example of this is on a charge of assault against a police officer, where the evidence was weak and the magistrates have convicted the defendant but imposed a proportionately light sentence.

17.11   Despite the risks, there will be cases where the advocate and/or the defendant have a sense of grievance at magistrates' decision on conviction and/or sentence and, consequently, where it would be right to advise in favour of an appeal.

17.12   On occasions, the prosecution advocate will not contest an appeal against conviction. An example may be where a defendant was convicted in his/her absence on a road traffic matter where the relevant documentation confirming his/her innocence is only produced at or before the Crown Court hearing. In those circumstances, the prosecution advocate, having considered the material, as respondent, would offer no evidence and the appeal would be allowed by the court without hearing sentence.

17.13   If an appeal against conviction is allowed, an application for costs out of central funds for both the Crown Court and the court below can be made. Similarly, if an appeal against sentence is allowed, an application for costs out of central funds can be made for the Crown Court hearing. If there is an appeal against conviction and sentence and only the appeal against sentence is allowed, it is probable that the Crown Court will impose a costs sanction of a proportion of the prosecution's costs to be paid by the appellant in the Crown Court.

17.14   Although the appellant has a right of appeal and the appeal is by way of a full re-hearing, the appellant does not stand in precisely the same shoes as s/he could before the earlier trial. It will, generally, be an uphill struggle if the appeal is contested by the CPS, as the court will be aware of a previous adverse finding against the appellant. However, legal arguments, concerning, for example, the admissibility of evidence or where there is an allegation of impropriety on the part of police officers, are more likely to be fairly and properly considered by a judge than lay magistrates. Consequently, the prospects of a successful appeal before a tribunal which includes a judge may be greater in certain types of case.

17.15   The appeal hearing generally only takes about half the time that the trial took before the magistrates' court. There are two reasons for this. First, as the evidence has already been heard once (unless there is considerable new evidence), there will generally be notes available from the magistrates' court hearing, resulting in the whole process being quicker. Second, the judge (with his/her colleagues) will tend to pick up the points much quicker than the lay magistrates. As with a trial in either the magistrates' court or the Crown Court, it is always sensible to speak to the prosecution advocate before the hearing to see if there are areas of evidence which can be agreed and to clarify the issues between the parties.

Appeals to the High Court

17.16   An appeal can be lodged from the magistrates' court directly to the High Court.[6] This process is known as 'appeal by case stated'. It bypasses the Crown Court and it is not possible to appeal thereafter to the Crown Court, although it is possible to appeal to the Crown Court first and thereafter to appeal to the High Court by way of case stated.

17.17   Appeal by way of case stated is limited to an appeal on a matter of law only. If the issue is one of mixed fact and law, the proper appeal process is to the Crown Court. If, however, the question for the appeal court is one of pure law, there is a particular procedure which must be followed to take the case to the High Court, either from the magistrates' court or from the Crown Court.[7]

17.18   Assuming that the matter is a question of pure law, the advocate will still need to decide whether to appeal by case stated or to take judicial review proceedings under Supreme Court Act 1981 ss29 and 31. There is some similarity between the appeal procedures by case stated and judicial review. In general, judicial review will only be possible on a matter relating to trial on indictment where the defendant is claiming that the decision reached by the lower court is either: a) in excess of jurisdiction, b) in breach of the rules of natural justice, c) an error of law on the face of the record, or d) so unreasonable that no reasonable tribunal properly directing itself could have reached that decision.[8]

17.19   An application for leave to move for judicial review would be made under Supreme Court Act 1981 s31. The applicant would be seeking relief by the orders of mandamus, prohibition or certiorari as well as possibly declarations and/or injunctions to quash the decision of the lower court and/or to compel it to act in a way directed by the High Court. The procedure for applying for judicial review is set out under Rules of the Supreme Court 1981 Order 53.

---

6   Under Magistrates' Courts Act 1980 s111.

7   Under Supreme Court Act 1981 s28.

8   *Associated Picture Houses Limited v Wednesbury Corporation* (1948) 1 KB 223, CA.

The grounds of challenge need to be set out together with an affidavit, known as Form 86A.

17.20   It is a two-stage procedure – the first stage being an application for leave. Unless leave is granted out of time, an application for leave must be made within three months of the decision which is sought to be challenged.

17.21   By Supreme Court Act 1981 s29(3), only 'matters relating to trial on indictment' are amenable to judicial review (or on appeal by way of case stated).[9] Examples of matters which have been held to be relating, and not relating, to trial on indictment are set out in *Archbold* at paras 7-9 to 7-12.

17.22   The principles governing the granting of discretionary relief which the High Court (sitting as the Divisional Court) will consider are whether the lower court has executed its jurisdiction, has acted in breach of the rules of natural justice or has made an error of law on the face of the record, or the decision was *Wednesbury* unreasonable.

17.23   An appeal by judicial review requires the granting of civil legal aid, which should cover the creating of the relevant documentation and the advocate's appearance at the leave hearing and, if leave is granted, at the full hearing. Usually, at the leave stage there will be no prosecution advocate at court, although, at a full hearing there would be. Of course, the essential challenge was to a decision of the lower tribunal and would not be aimed directly at the prosecution. The lower tribunal itself would not have its own legal representative at court.

17.24   If an application for judicial review is successful, the decision of the lower court would usually be quashed, but there is no power to remit the matter back to the lower court. To quash a conviction therefore would require ensuring that the appeal was reinstated before the lower court in front of a different bench. It does not automatically follow that just because the applicant has succeeded in the High Court that the conviction will be quashed, as there may, for example, have been a breach of natural justice, in which case the prosecution may proceed with the re-hearing which would be treated as a new hearing before the differently-constituted lower court.[10]

Case stated

17.25   If the question was one of pure law and the advocate believes that the lower court has misapplied it, but not in a way which could be

---

9   *Re Smalley* (1985) AC 622, HL.
10   *R v Leeds Crown Court ex p Barlow* (1989) RTR 246, DC.

described as being *Wednesbury* unreasonable, the proper form of appeal would usually be by case stated.

17.26   To appeal by case stated, the lower court will be asked to state the case, which in the magistrates' court is usually done by the clerk to the justices. That will set out the background of the case with certain facts stated within it, the findings of the magistrates based on those facts, and the question(s) of law which the defence advocate seeks to raise in the High Court. Often, the court will ask the advocate to draft the question or questions in advance on its own draft and incorporate that within the statement of the case.

17.27   For the purposes of the hearing, in addition to the statement of the case, a skeleton argument, together with any authorities being relied on and a chronology of events both before and after the hearing in the lower court will be necessary. It is important to realise that the High Court will not make any findings of fact outside what is contained in the statement of case and therefore the content of the statement is vital and, unfortunately, may omit matters that the advocate regards as relevant. Once the advocate has seen a copy of the draft statement, if it contains errors or omissions, s/he should contact the court immediately to seek to rectify the position because although further evidential matters may be raised at the hearing in the High Court, in practice, the judgment is most unlikely to depart from the facts contained within the statement.

17.28   There is unlikely to be representation on behalf of the magistrates themselves, but the CPS is usually represented and will almost certainly seek to uphold the decision of the magistrates as being correct in law. Unlike the procedure in an appeal in the Crown Court, the defence advocate will proceed first and the prosecution advocate will respond, before the defence will have the final comment.

17.29   If the defence argument succeeds in the High Court, the court will answer the questions in a way that usually requires the case to be remitted back to the lower court, but depending on the questions being asked, an acquittal may follow thereafter. Otherwise, the lower court will be asked to reconsider certain matters. This will not necessarily result in a departure from the conclusions once the questions have been properly considered by the court.

17.30   If the appellant is successful in the High Court, costs may be asked for out of central funds, although they are most unlikely to be awarded against the lower court directly. If the appellant is unsuccessful, a costs order is likely to be imposed, although, of course, the appellant may be legally-aided. Legal aid for an appeal by case stated or judicial review would be civil legal aid, unlike any other type of criminal appeal process.

17.31   If you wish to appeal from the decision of the High Court, the appeal would lie directly to the House of Lords but leave from either the Divisional Court or the House of Lords would be necessary. Leave would not be granted unless the Divisional Court certifies that a point of law of general public importance is involved in its decision, and it appears to that court or to the House of Lords that the point is one which ought to be considered by the House of Lords.[11] A right of appeal to the Court of Appeal from any judgment of the High Court, or any criminal cause or matter is specifically excluded.[12]

Appeal to the Court of Appeal

Law

17.32   An appeal against conviction lies not only where the Court of Appeal has granted leave, but where the judge of the court of trial grants a certificate that the case is fit for appeal.[13] If a point is to be argued before the Court of Appeal, it is open for the advocate to argue for a certificate before the trial judge, although, in practice, this is very rarely granted, as it is effectively a concession by the judge that his/her decision may be inherently defective. The threshold test for granting a certificate is, in any event, a high one, not simply that there are arguable grounds of appeal but where the chance of a successful appeal is substantial.[14]

17.33   The sole test now applicable for allowing an appeal against conviction under Criminal Appeal Act 1995 s2(1) is when the conviction is deemed unsafe.

1734   The proviso which had previously existed, whereby the Court of Appeal could dismiss the appeal even if the legal point(s) in the appeal had merit, if it was satisfied that no miscarriage of justice had occurred, is no longer part of the law.[15]

17.35   The possible grounds of appeal are numerous. These may include:

   1) a misdirection or non-direction by the trial judge,
   2) a failure by the trial judge to refer to the defence,

---

11 Administration of Justice Act 1960 s1.
12 Under Supreme Court Act 1981 s18(1).
13 Under Criminal Appeal Act 1958 s1.
14 *Practice Direction (Crime: Bail Pending Appeal)* [1983] 1 WLR 1292; (1984) 78 Cr App R 40 para 4.

3) improper comment made during the course of the trial by the trial judge,
4) wrongful admission or exclusion of evidence,
5) defects in the indictment,
6) not upholding a submission of no case to answer,
7) conduct of the appellant's previous legal representative,
8) prejudicial publicity,
9) non-disclosure of material evidence, and
10) material irregularities in relation to the jury or the verdict.

17.36 If the Court of Appeal allows an appeal against conviction, the conviction will be quashed. However, a re-trial may be ordered.[16] The Court of Appeal, in deciding whether to order a re-trial, will take into account the length of time since the commission of the alleged offence and whether the appellant would suffer prejudice by having a re-trial. If there has been fresh evidence received before the Court of Appeal which clearly establishes the appellant's innocence, no re-trial will be ordered.

17.37 It is rare for fresh evidence to be heard before the Court of Appeal on the basis that it is not intended to be a second jury, but, in an appropriate case, where the justice of the case merits the admission of further evidence, the Court of Appeal has the power to grant leave to admit that evidence.[17]

17.38 If, after granting leave for appeal either against conviction or sentence, the Court of Appeal thinks that the conviction or the sentence is likely to be quashed, and the appellant is in custody, the Court of Appeal has the power to grant bail pending appeal.[18]

17.39 For an appeal against sentence, the possible bases of an appeal are also varied, but may include:

1) where the sentence was not justified by law;
2) where the sentence was based on a wrong factual basis;
3) where the sentencing judge improperly took into account certain matters or failed to take into account matters s/he ought to have done; or
4) where the sentence was manifestly excessive or wrong in principle.

---

15 *R v Graham* [1997] 1 Cr App R 302; [1997] Crim LR 340; (1996) *Times* 28 October, CA.
16 Pursuant to Criminal Appeal Act 1968 s7.
17 Under Criminal Appeal Act 1968 s23.
18 Criminal Appeal Act 1968 s19; Supreme Court Act 1981 s81 and *Practice Direction (Crime: Bail Pending Appeal)* [1983] 1 WLR 1292.

17.40   If the appellant wishes to abandon an appeal or an application for leave to appeal before the hearing, it is necessary for the advocate or the appellant to sign a notice of abandonment.[19]

17.41   At the full hearing, the appellant will usually be produced and it is sensible and reassuring for the appellant and often very useful for the advocate to see him/her in the cells before the hearing even if there has already been a conference. However, a person in custody would not usually be present on an application for leave to appeal or even on an appeal based on a ground involving a question of law alone, unless the Court of Appeal gives him/her leave to be present.[20]

17.42   In the rare situation of considering whether to take an appeal to the House of Lords from the Court of Appeal, the advocate would need the leave of the Court of Appeal or the House of Lords. Leave would not be granted unless it is certified by the Court of Appeal that a point of law of general public importance is involved in the decision and it appears to the Court of Appeal or the House of Lords that the point is one which ought to be considered by the House of Lords.[21] An application for leave to appeal to the House of Lords would need to be made within 14 days of the decision of the Court of Appeal to that court and application to the House of Lords for leave would need to be made within 14 days after the application for leave is refused by the Court of Appeal.[22] For further information concerning an appeal to the House of Lords, see *Archbold*, 1998 edn, at 7-250 to 27-266.

Practice

17.43   At the conclusion of a trial and/or sentence in the Crown Court, the advocate will usually be expected to give an oral advice on possible grounds of appeal to the defendant and to his/her solicitor. The defendant is entitled to have an advice on appeal in writing and the advocate may be requested to draft it. If the advice is negative, that would usually end his/her involvement in the case.

17.44   However, if s/he feels that there are arguable grounds of appeal against conviction and/or sentence, it will be necessary to draft both an advice on appeal and the accompanying grounds of appeal. Practice varies about what should be included in each document, but it is important that there is a full summary of the prosecution case,

---

19   Under Criminal Appeals Rules 1968 r10.

20   Criminal Appeal Act 1968 s22.

21   Ibid s33(2).

22   Ibid s34(1).

the defence case if it is an appeal against conviction, mitigating points for an appeal against sentence and the reasons why the advocate advises that there are arguable grounds of appeal, and any authorities s/he is relying on to support his/her propositions (and any other authorities which are clearly relevant and would have been referred to in the advice). There should also be a summary containing details of where the case was heard, before whom and when, what counts the defendant was convicted of, and his/her sentence. The grounds of appeal is generally a more formal document than the advice. The grounds of appeal against conviction would generally be in the form of: 'The learned judge erred in law in that ...'. The grounds of appeal against sentence would usually be in the form of 'the sentence was manifestly excessive and/or wrong in principle'.

17.45   The advice on appeal and grounds of appeal are placed before a single judge in the Court of Appeal (Criminal Division) who decides whether or not to grant leave to appeal on the papers. If leave is granted, legal aid will usually be granted for the appellant to be represented at a future hearing before the full court, which comprises three other High Court judges sitting in the Court of Appeal. The advocate would be entitled to see any written comments made by the single judge in granting leave, which may give a helpful indication about his/her thinking in granting leave (although, of course, could not be binding on the Court of Appeal judges).

17.46   The registrar of criminal appeals takes over the case once it is in the Court of Appeal and should be liaised with about the papers. Once the advocate has advised that there are grounds for an appeal and once the papers have been lodged, the original instructing solicitor no longer plays a formal role. When legal aid has been granted, the advocate will be sent papers, including a summary of the case, drafted by a case lawyer in the Court of Appeal office, distilled from the prosecution papers and the summing up and/or sentencing remarks of the trial judge. Transcripts will also be obtained of the summing up (on an appeal against conviction) and the sentencing remarks (on an appeal against sentence) and if there are any other transcripts of importance, including particular extracts of evidence or exchanges between the advocate and the judge or the prosecution opening, they would need to be specifically requested in the advice on appeal, or followed up by telephone with the case lawyer. The advocate should check that s/he is happy with the case summary because the Court of Appeal will rely heavily on its contents when delivering judgment. Therefore, if there are mistakes or matters omitted of significance, seek to have the statements corrected before the summary is presented to the Court of Appeal in its final form.

17.47   On occasions, advocates may be assigned cases by the registrar of criminal appeals where the advocate have not acted for the appellant in the court below. This would usually happen where there is a good reason why the appellant should not have the same representation as in the Crown Court, for example, where s/he has made criticisms about his/her previous legal advisers or where there has been a considerable time delay before the process or the appeal processed and the registrar was not satisfied that the papers would be dealt with within a reasonable time frame by the appellant's previous lawyers. Legal aid will often permit a conference with the appellant. This should generally be helpful, particularly if the advocate did not represent him/her previously. If the Criminal Appeal Office does not provide all the papers required, the advocate should inform the case lawyer that s/he wants papers to be returned from the appellant's former solicitors.

17.48   As mentioned above, it is somewhat strange that once a case reaches the Court of Appeal, there is an automatic change of representation at solicitor level. Although many solicitors may retain a personal interest in the case, the formal position is that they no longer have a role to play. Legal aid does not extend to their continued involvement (except in exceptional cases). As a result, in general, the advocate will be the most informed lawyer as the case lawyer will only have limited knowledge of the case, based on the papers before him/her and received at an obviously relatively late stage.

17.49   If leave is refused before the single judge, it may be renewed before the full court, ie, three appeal judges on an oral hearing. There will be no legal aid for this hearing and the advocate would therefore be acting pro bono, but if leave is subsequently granted by the full court, the advocate can apply retrospectively for legal aid to cover the leave application as well as the full hearing.

17.50   The procedure at the full hearing is that the defence advocate will commence the appeal, having had the opportunity to perfect grounds of appeal and the prosecution advocate, who will be represented as respondent on an appeal against conviction only, will be given the opportunity to reply. In advance of the hearing, the CPS will usually serve its submission in response to the grounds of appeal.

17.51   It is important for the defence advocate to consider the grounds that s/he wishes to proceed with before the full court. There may be good tactical reasons to abandon certain grounds if they have little or no prospect of success, on the basis that the other grounds have more substance. That has the effect of indicating to the court that the advocate is pruning the appeal points to concentrate on the best arguments.

17.52 On an appeal against sentence only, the CPS will not usually be represented, unless the appeal against sentence has been launched by the CPS on an Attorney-General's reference where the CPS is submitting that the sentencing of the judge in the court below was too lenient (see para 17.54).

17.53 Generally, judgment is delivered immediately after submissions and is usually substantially prepared in advance by the judge delivering judgment. However, further points which have been raised orally would wholly be included in the judgment. In a complicated or particularly serious case, the appeal may be allowed or dismissed immediately and judgment reserved, or judgment may simply be reserved for a future date.

Attorney-General's reference to the Court of Appeal

17.54 Under Criminal Justice Act 1988 s35, the Attorney-General has the power to refer cases to the Court of Appeal when it appears to him/her that the sentencing of a defendant in the Crown Court for an offence triable on indictment only, or a small number of specified offences triable either way, has been unduly lenient. Where a case is referred to the Court of Appeal, it has the power to review and alter the sentence and substitute a different one. The approach of the Court of Appeal is that it will not intervene unless there was some error in principle in the judge's sentence, or that public confidence would be damaged if the sentence was not altered.[23]

17.55 The approach of the Court of Appeal is to examine the sentence, and decide whether it was outside the range of permissible ones, as opposed to simply whether it would have given a heavier sentence if it had been the trial judge.

17.56 That is of some comfort to the defendant, but, nonetheless, many Attorney-General's references have succeeded and the defence advocate will have the unenviable job of warning a defendant, for example, that although he has not received a custodial sentence before the trial judge, s/he is at risk once more of custody being imposed.

23 *Attorney-General's References (Nos 4 and 5 of 1989)* (1990) 90 Cr App R 366, 358, CA.

The defendant's perception of 'double jeopardy' has the effect of reducing what would otherwise be the sentence deemed appropriate by the Court of Appeal.

17.57   Procedurally, the prosecution advocate commences the reference submitting why the sentence was unduly lenient, and then the defence advocate would essentially be seeking to uphold the trial judge's decision (with authorities if they are helpful), mitigate again on behalf of the defendant and include new matters arising since his/her original sentence. If a custodial sentence is imposed by the Court of Appeal, it will usually require the defendant (who would usually be present) to present him/herself before a local police station within the following few days.

Checklist for appeals

1) Advise the defendant orally on an appeal to the Crown Court. Check whether the appeal is against both conviction and sentence. Ensure that the risks of an appeal are fully explained.
2) Ensure that the time limits for an appeal are met.
3) On the day of a Crown Court appeal, establish the prosecution's position concerning the appeal.
4) If the appeal is successful, make an application for costs out of central funds in respect of both the appeal and the original hearing in the court below.
5) For an appeal to the High Court, ensure that all written documentation has been carefully checked and then lodged with the court in good time.
6) Consider whether to apply for judicial review or appeal by way of case stated.
7) For an appeal to the Crown Court, draft grounds of appeal and an advice on appeal within the time limits and ensure that the grounds of appeal (if necessary) are perfected before the hearing.
8) Establish contact with the registrar of criminal appeals. Check that all the relevant documentation is available for the defence and the court.

CHAPTER 18

Legal aid – conclusion of the Crown Court case

18.1   The taxation note

The taxation note

18.1   Once a Crown Court hearing has been completed, before returning the papers to the solicitors, the advocate should complete his/her claim for fees. Most cases will come within the category of graduated fee cases which have fixed rules of payment for different offences, with uplifts for the number of prosecution papers and witnesses over a certain number and for subsequent attendance at court after the first day.

18.2   However, cases lasting longer than ten days or those of a sufficient seriousness will, or may, come within the category of being non-standard.

18.3   Although it is a fairly laborious process, a non-standard case of reasonable complexity or seriousness would usually justify the time spent in drafting a taxation note and thereby assisting the determining officer to assess the appropriate remuneration pursuant to Legal Aid in Criminal Care Proceedings (General) Regulations 1989 reg 9(5)(b).

18.4   Knowing how best to draft a taxation note is a gradually acquired skill. Important factors to include are:

1) the importance and gravity of the case,
2) the size and complexity of the matter, including the number of documents examined or pursued with due regard to difficulty or length,
3) the degree of skill or specialised knowledge required,
4) the degree of responsibility and other burdens placed on the advocate,
5) the time reasonably expended on the case,
6) all other relevant circumstances, including any assessment of the weight of the case and any observations made by the trial judge, and
7) travelling and hotel expenses if the advocate is entitled to claim them (which depends on the nearness of local advocates).

18.5   Other important matters include:

1) the nature of the defence (including whether it was cut-throat),
2) how difficult it was to obtain instructions and represent the defendant,
3) the consequences of a conviction as far as the defendant was concerned,
4) legal arguments advanced in the course of the trial and whether

       time was saved by admissions of fact,

5) agreeing evidence or otherwise,

6) whether the advocate represented more than one defendant, and

7) the number of indictments the defendant faced.

18.6   The form of a taxation note, generally, would commence with a paragraph explaining where the defendant appeared, before whom and the charges s/he faced. The expected length of trial should be referred to and its actual length.

18.7   A summary of the prosecution case and the defence case should follow. The narrative should then refer to the number of documents, including unused material perused before the trial and legal arguments either advanced or prepared but not advanced for tactical or other reasons.

18.8   There should also be reference to the complexity and seriousness of the case and the potential consequences on conviction as far as the defendant is concerned.

18.9   The resulting taxation note often resembles the reverse of a plea in mitigation, where all aggravating features are accentuated. Before drafting the taxation note, it is often advisable to look at precedents of more senior colleagues, but guidance is now provided in *Archbold* appendix G (1997 edn).

18.10   Not only is it advisable to draft a taxation note in an appropriate case, but it should be done shortly after the case has been completed so that it is still fresh in the memory. Bear in mind that there are strict three-month time limits for claiming fees and if the advocate is out of time, some or all of the claim may be disallowed.

18.11   Notes on taxation need not be limited to effective trials. In an appropriate case, a taxation note can be drafted for a cracked trial which has been fully prepared in the expectation of a trial, or even on complex guilty pleas. Where Queen's Counsel or leading counsel has also been instructed, it is often expected (and certainly appreciated) that the junior advocate will provide the first draft of a taxation note for the leader's consideration.

CHAPTER 19

Solicitor-counsel relationship

A solicitor's perspective

19.1   While an increasing number of solicitors are taking up the option to apply for rights of audience in the Crown Court, for the majority of solicitors, the Crown Courts will remain the principal domain of barristers. That, together with the fact that newly-qualified solicitors are unlikely to pursue that avenue and that recently admitted barristers 'cut their teeth' in the magistrates' court, means that the relationship between solicitors and counsel remains mutually dependent. It remains essential for efficient case preparation and presentation that solicitors and barristers are aware of potential areas of concern that may be obvious, for example, to solicitors, but easily overlooked by barristers. The purpose of this section is, therefore, specifically to highlight to barristers, those areas which, from a solicitor's perspective, ensure that any case runs smoothly.

19.2   Traditionally, barristers in their training have paid little regard to the intricacies of completing legal aid application forms – something traditionally thought of as an aspect of a case solely within the solicitor's ambit. However, newly-qualified barristers/pupils will, as time goes by, appreciate that much of their time is spent in the magistrates' court, often dealing with overnight prisoners appearing at court on the first occasion. As indicated in chapter 2 on legal aid, the responsibility for completion of a legal aid application form is often left to the advocate appearing at the first hearing – often counsel. As such, barristers should ensure that they are fully conversant with the content of legal aid application forms. More importantly, they should be aware of the need to ensure that these are fully completed so that the risk of requisitions being raised by the court legal aid clerk is reduced or, alternatively, and in its worst scenario, having that legal aid application rejected. That may result in both solicitors and barristers being unpaid from the legal aid fund for work properly done. The financial pressures put on solicitors are such that barristers should not take it for granted that they will necessarily receive a fee if legal aid is not granted owing to an error on their part in satisfactorily completing the client's legal aid application form. In addition, errors of that nature will do little to improve a barrister's standing in the eyes of the instructing solicitor, at a time when, for newly-qualified barristers/pupils, good first impressions are of the greatest importance.

19.3   When barristers do attend the magistrates' court, on occasions where they may not be in possession of a detailed brief (as opposed to appearing at the Crown Court when a full brief should be provided), they should ensure that contact is made with the solicitor who has the conduct of the case. They should obtain as much relevant information about that client's case as possible to ensure that any eventuality that may arise from that court hearing can be properly dealt with. In the event that counsel does receive a brief with enclosures, as obvious as it may sound, those papers should be read. There are occasions when it becomes readily apparent that either documentation or information that should be given is missing and the solicitor with conduct of the case should be contacted with a view to 'plugging' any gaps that might have arisen.

19.4   Once barristers have attended the magistrates' court on behalf of a firm of solicitors, it is essential that the result of that hearing is notified to the solicitor as soon as possible after the hearing. This is important for a number of reasons, so that:

1) the solicitor can write to his/her client notifying him/her of the result;
2) the solicitor can carry out any preparatory work as required between that time and the next hearing;
3) the date of the next meeting can be diarised;
4) if the period of remand is to be unusually short (for example, from a Saturday court to a Monday court), the solicitor is aware that arrangements will have to be made to cover that hearing. In such a scenario where a case is adjourned from a Saturday to a Monday, the solicitor should be notified over the weekend. On a practical level, late notification on Monday morning can prove to be extremely disruptive.

19.5   When a barrister attends a committal hearing where the CPS purports to make primary disclosure in accordance with Criminal Procedures and Investigations Act 1996, s/he should make every effort to ensure that all relevant papers are returned to his/her instructing solicitors as soon as possible after that hearing. Where disclosure in accordance with the above provision is made, the 14-day time limit for service of any defence statement starts to run. Any delay in returning the committal bundle reduces the time solicitors have to take instructions on those papers and, thereafter, either for them or for barristers to prepare and serve a defence statement. This may be of particular relevance where the CPS has not served any prosecution statements on solicitors before the committal hearing, ie, solicitors have not had the opportunity to take their client's full instructions on those statements. This is a common occurrence where a client is charged with an indictable only matter. Barristers should be aware that it may take some time for a full proof of evidence to be taken. Clients on bail may not keep appointments to give their solicitors full instructions and solicitors often experience difficulties in arranging early prison visits to see their clients, due to the lack of facilities that exist in many prisons. While it is open to solicitors to apply for an extension of time for the service of defence statements, barristers and their clerks should not treat that possibility as a justification for delay in returning papers to solicitors.

19.6   Once barristers have attended hearings, in cases where they will not be required to attend the next hearing (which should not be taken for granted) any papers supplied to barristers, for example, by the CPS and/or the Probation Service or some other third party, should be immediately sent to solicitors so that case preparation can proceed as quickly as possible. In those circumstances, where the necessary preparatory work is complicated, most solicitors will find it extremely helpful to have a detailed note from counsel setting out that required work. Similarly, barristers should ensure that their clerks return fee notes promptly. Solicitors will no doubt be aware of the three-month time limit for submission of their bills and in magistrates' court proceedings, where those bills cannot be submitted until counsel's fee notes are received, the late submission of those fee notes will do little to endear barristers to solicitors. Returning papers and promptly communicating essential information regarding the outcome of a hearing not only creates a professional image that barristers should strive for, but avoids unwanted delay in solicitors' progressing with case preparation.

19.7   So far as Crown Court briefs are concerned, there may be an understandable tendency on behalf of barristers not to read the brief and study its enclosures too early. The current system of warned lists regularly results in the briefed counsel being unable to conduct the trial. That, however, should not be misconstrued in a way that may lead barristers to believe that papers should not be promptly read and the appropriate advice given at the earliest possible stage. The coming into force of the Criminal Procedure and Investigations Act 1996 in April 1997 imposes rigid time limits for the service of defence statements. The failure to comply with its provisions may be potentially devastating for the client. If that is the case, while the client may vent his/her anger towards his/her solicitors, if the late submission of the defence statement is caused by counsel neglecting to deal with instructions and settling that document promptly, barristers will not be surprised to learn that they will be unlikely to be briefed in future. Similarly, while regretfully, wasted costs orders are becoming an increasingly familiar sight in the Crown Courts. Care should be taken to ensure that from the defence point of view solicitors and counsel liaise fully to ensure that all necessary preparatory steps are undertaken. The effect of that is that barristers should, having considered the brief at the earliest possible stage, settle any necessary advices and send them to their instructing solicitors at the earliest possible opportunity. Failure to send appropriate advices at an early stage (particularly advices that relate to instructing experts), should be dealt with at the earliest possible opportunity so that by the time the plea and directions hearing takes place, usually four weeks after the committal hearing, even if any necessary report has not been obtained, the necessary progress has been made by either applying to the Legal Aid Board for prior authority or by having instructed an expert and awaiting the report. It is particularly annoying for solicitors to send a brief to a barrister at an early stage, only for those papers to be ignored until a matter of a few days before a trial, whereupon the solicitor is given a lengthy list of matters that require urgent attention at that late stage.

19.8   As with all aspects of case preparation, effective communication of relevant information by solicitors to their chosen barrister and the speedy and effective notification by barristers to solicitors about any follow up preparatory work required is an essential element of case preparation and results in a better service for the client and a more stress-free environment for both sides of the profession.

A barrister's perspective

19.9   From the position of the advocate who attends court, the relationship with the instructing solicitor is potentially quite awkward because it is the solicitor giving the advocate the work in the first place. It is, therefore, essential for the advocate to bear in mind that the relationship is a delicate one, which often requires nurturing and a degree of tact.

19.10   The preparation of the brief has been covered earlier in the book, in chapter 8. In general, a barrister may feel a bit annoyed if asked to do some or all of the work which s/he would usually expect a solicitor to have done. In particular, s/he can expect full instructions from the defendant (subject of course to his/her co-operation in attending appointments at the solicitor's office) including, as appropriate, the instructing solicitor's views on the merits and some indication of where the barrister's advice would be welcomed. That may include requesting an advice on evidence, an advice on appeal on conviction and/or sentence and whether s/he feels that a conference would be helpful. The barrister would usually expect to receive a proof of evidence, defence witness statements, all statements and exhibits served by the CPS including transcripts of the interviews and interview tapes, a schedule of unused material and copies of any unused material provided by the CPS. If most or all of these are not received, it is a good idea to give the solicitor a ring and ask (politely) for it. There may be a good reason why it has not been provided, of which the barrister was previously unaware.

19.11   An obvious area of importance is accessibility. If the instructing solicitor is unavailable to return the barrister's calls, (or vice versa) that will mean there is a lack of communication between them. This could obviously affect the defendant's prospects of a successful hearing. If it is proving difficult to establish contact, it can often be a good idea for the barrister to give the solicitor his/her home or mobile telephone number and/or a time when s/he may be contacted. Conferences are useful not just for the barrister's relationship with the defendant but also to establish closer ties between him/her and the instructing solicitor. It is possible to be instructed many times by the same solicitor and yet never have met in person. Sometimes, instructing solicitors will be invited for drinks, which provide an obvious opportunity to get to know the instructing solicitor, although some people feel the artificiality of such a meeting quite strongly.

19.12   One problem for counsel is where the instructing solicitor identifies very closely with the defendant, and his/her case. In such (rare) situations instructions can be drafted almost as if they come from the defendant. That can place unnecessary pressure on the barrister if expressions such as 'the defendant is innocent', or 'you are instructed to ensure an acquittal' are contained within the instructions. A degree of distance between the defendant and the instructing solicitor is to be expected. A closer and more open relationship concerning the defendant's prospects of success can usually be created by telephone contact between barrister and solicitors. The barrister will be able to discuss with the solicitor the possible pleas of the defendant to lesser charges and/or appropriate pleas to the indictment.

19.13   It is always a good idea to maintain some degree of follow-through with the solicitor as a case progresses. However, most instructing solicitors will realise that the barrister is likely to have quite a large case-load and so they will take care not to trouble him/her on every small point that arises. Similarly, telephoning the solicitors should be done with discretion for similar reasons. A delicate balance needs to be established between ensuring that the barrister is updated properly and fully on the progress of the case without every minor detail being cross-checked.

19.14   Where there is a late change of advocate, this can be a source of great irritation to the instructing solicitor (as well as to the defendant). Good liaison will lessen the chances of that happening at short notice and will help the instructing solicitor to cushion the blow for his/her client. While there is at least a moral duty on the barrister to do everything s/he can to keep the instructing solicitor in the picture concerning potential professional 'clashes' of cases, the instructing solicitor will recognise that sometimes a late change of representative is unavoidable. Unless somebody has been misled or there was no proper basis for referring a case, the solicitor-counsel relationship should not be harmed.

19.15   It is not easy to give anything more than general guidance about the nature of the solicitor-counsel relationship. Over and above the barrister's natural desire to establish a continuing and long-lasting working relationship with the instructing solicitor, the relationship can be enjoyable and productive.

APPENDICES

Children and Young Persons Act 1933 ss53(2)–(4) and 55

Punishment of certain grave crimes

53 (2) Subsection (3) below applies –
  (a) where a person of at least 10 but not more than 17 years is convicted on indictment of –
    (i) any offence punishable in the case of an adult with imprisonment for fourteen years or more, not being an offence the sentence for which is fixed by law, or
    (ii) an offence under section 14 (indecent assault on a woman) or section 15 (indecent assault on a man) of the Sexual Offences Act 1956;
  (b) where a young person is convicted of –
    (i) an offence under section 1 of the Road Traffic Act 1988 (causing death by dangerous driving), or
    (ii) an offence under section 3A of the Road Traffic Act 1988 (causing death by careless driving while under the influence of drink or drugs).
  (3) Where this subsection applies, then, if the court is of the opinion that none of the other methods in which the case may legally be dealt with is suitable, the court may sentence the offender to be detained for such period not exceeding the maximum term of imprisonment with which the offence is punishable in the case of an adult as may be specified in the sentence; and where such a sentence has been passed the child or young person shall, during that period, be liable to be detained in such place and on such conditions –
  (a) as the Secretary of State may direct, or
  (b) as the Secretary of State may arrange with any person.
  (4) A person detained pursuant to the directions or arrangements made by the Secretary of State under this section shall, while so detained, be deemed to be in legal custody.

Amendments

The subsections were principally substituted by Criminal Justice and Public Order Act 1994 s16. Other amendments were made by Criminal Justice Act 1948 Sch 10 Pt I, Criminal Justice Act 1961 Sch 4, Criminal Justice Act 1988 s126; Criminal Justice Act 1993 s67(2). Subsection 53(2)(a)(ii) was substituted by Crime (Sentences) Act 1997 s44.

Power to order parent or guardian to pay fine etc

55 (1) Where –

    (a) a child or young person is convicted or found guilty of any offence for the commission of which a fine or costs may be imposed or a compensation order may be made under section 35 of the Powers of Criminal Courts Act 1973; and

    (b) the court is of the opinion that the case would best be met by the imposition of a fine or costs or the making of such an order, whether with or without any other punishment,

it shall be the duty of the court to order that the fine, compensation or costs awarded be paid by the parent or guardian of the child or young person instead of by the child or young person himself, unless the court is satisfied –

    (i) that the parent or guardian cannot be found; or

    (ii) that it would be unreasonable to make an order for payment, having regard to the circumstances of the case.

(1A) Where but for this subsection –

    (a) a court would order a child or young person to pay a fine under section 15(2A) of the Children and Young Persons Act 1969 (failure to comply with requirement included in supervision order); or

    (b) a court would impose a fine on a young person under section 16(3) of the Powers of Criminal Courts Act 1973 (breach of requirements of community service order); or

    (c) a court would impose a fine on a child or young person under section 4(3) of the Criminal Justice and Public Order Act 1994 (breach of requirements of supervision under secure training order),

it shall be the duty of the court to order that the fine be paid by the parent or guardian of the child or young person instead of by the child or young person himself, unless the court is satisfied –

    (i) that the parent or guardian cannot be found; or

    (ii) that it would be unreasonable to make an order for payment, having regard to the circumstances of the case.

(1B) In the case of a young person who has attained the age of sixteen years, subsections (1) and (1A) above shall have effect as if, instead of imposing a duty, they conferred a power to make such an order as is mentioned in those subsections.

(2) An order under this section may be made against a parent or guardian who, having been required to attend, has failed to do so, but, save as aforesaid, no such order shall be made without giving the parent or guardian an opportunity of being heard.

(3) A parent or guardian may appeal to the Crown Court against an order under this section made by a magistrates' court.

(4) A parent or guardian may appeal to the Court of Appeal against an order made under this section by the Crown Court, as if he had been convicted on indictment and the order were a sentence passed on his conviction.

(5) In relation to a child or young person for whom a local authority have parental responsibility and who –

    (a) is in their care; or

(b) is provided with accommodation by them in the exercise of any functions (in particular those under the Children Act 1989) which stand referred to their social services committee under the Local Authority Social Services Act 1970,

references in this section to his parent or guardian shall be construed as references to that authority.

In this subsection 'local authority' and 'parental responsibility' have the same meanings as in the Children Act 1989.

Amendments

Subsections (1) and (2) were substituted by Criminal Justice Act 1982 s26. Subsection (1A) was inserted by Criminal Justice Act 1988 s127. Subsections (1B) and (5) were inserted by Criminal Justice Act 1991 s57(1) and (2) respectively. Subsection (1A)(c) was inserted by Criminal Justice and Public Order Act 1994 Sch 10 para 4.

Criminal Justice Act 1967 ss9 and 10

Proof by written statement

9 (1) In any criminal proceedings, other than committal proceedings, a written statement by any person shall, if such of the conditions mentioned in the next following subsection as are applicable are satisfied, be admissible as evidence to the like extent as oral evidence to the like effect by that person.

(2) The said conditions are –
  (a) the statement purports to be signed by the person who made it;
  (b) the statement contains a declaration by that person to the effect that it is true to the best of his knowledge and belief and that he made the statement knowing that, if it were tendered in evidence, he would be liable to prosecution if he wilfully stated in it anything which he knew to be false or did not believe to be true;
  (c) before the hearing at which the statement is tendered in evidence, a copy of the statement is served, by or on behalf of the party proposing to tender it, on each of the other parties to the proceedings; and
  (d) none of the other parties or their solicitors, within seven days from the service of the copy of the statement, serves a notice on the party so proposing objecting to the statement being tendered in evidence under this section:

Provided that the conditions mentioned in paragraphs (c) and (d) of this subsection shall not apply if the parties agree before or during the hearing that the statement shall be so tendered.

(3) The following provisions shall also have effect in relation to any written statement tendered in evidence under this section, that is to say –
  (a) if the statement is made by a person under the age of [eighteen], it shall give his age;
  (b) if it is made by a person who cannot read it, it shall be read to him before he signs it and shall be accompanied by a declaration by the person who so read the statement to the effect that it was so read; and
  (c) if it refers to any other document as an exhibit, the copy served on any other party to the proceedings under paragraph (c) of the last foregoing subsection shall be accompanied by a copy of that document or by such information as may be necessary in order to enable the party on whom it is served to inspect that document or a copy thereof.

(4) Notwithstanding that a written statement made by any person may be admissible as evidence by virtue of this section –

(a) the party by whom or on whose behalf a copy of the statement was served may call that person to give evidence; and

(b) the court may, of its own motion or on the application of any party to the proceedings, require that person to attend before the court and give evidence.

(5) An application under paragraph (b) of the last foregoing subsection to a court other than a magistrates' court may be made before the hearing and on any such application the powers of the court shall be exercisable [by a puisne judge of the High Court, a Circuit judge or Recorder sitting alone].

(6) So much of any statement as is admitted in evidence by virtue of this section shall, unless the court otherwise directs, be read aloud at the hearing and where the court so directs an account shall be given orally of so much of any statement as is not read aloud.

(7) Any document or object referred to as an exhibit and identified in a written statement tendered in evidence under this section shall be treated as if it had been produced as an exhibit and identified in court by the maker of the statement.

(8) A document required by this section to be served on any person may be served –

(a) by delivering it to him or to his solicitor; or

(b) by addressing it to him and leaving it at his usual or last known place of abode or place of business or by addressing it to his solicitor and leaving it at his office; or

(c) by sending it in a registered letter or by the recorded delivery service [or by first class post] addressed to him at his usual or last known place of abode or place of business or addressed to his solicitor at his office; or

(d) in the case of a body corporate, by delivering it to the secretary or clerk of the body at its registered or principal office or sending it in a registered letter or by the recorded delivery service [or by first class post] addressed to the secretary or clerk of that body at that office.

Amendments

The word in square brackets in subs(3)(a) was substituted by Criminal Procedure and Investigations Act 1996 s69. Subsection (6) and the words in square brackets in subs(5) were substituted by Courts Act 1971 s56(1) and Sch 8 Pt II para 49. The words in square brackets in subss(8)(c) and (d) were inserted by Criminal Justice and Public Order Act 1994 s168(1) and Sch 9 para 6(1).

Proof by formal admission

10 (1) Subject to the provisions of this section, any fact of which oral evidence may be given in any criminal proceedings may be admitted for the purpose of those proceedings by or on behalf of the prosecutor or defendant, and the admission by any party of any such fact under this section shall as against that party be conclusive evidence in those proceedings of the fact admitted.

(2) An admission under this section –

(a) may be made before or at the proceedings;

(b) if made otherwise than in court, shall be in writing;

   (c) if made in writing by an individual, shall purport to be signed by the person making it and, if so made by a body corporate, shall purport to be signed by a director or manager, or the secretary or clerk, or some other similar officer of the body corporate;

   (d) if made on behalf of a defendant who is an individual, shall be made by his counsel or solicitor;

   (e) if made at any stage before the trial by a defendant who is an individual, must be approved by his counsel or solicitor (whether at the time it was made or subsequently) before or at the proceedings in question.

(3) An admission under this section for the purpose of proceedings relating to any matter shall be treated as an admission for the purpose of any subsequent criminal proceedings relating to that matter (including any appeal or retrial).

(4) An admission under this section may with the leave of the court be withdrawn in the proceedings for the purpose of which it is made or any subsequent criminal proceedings relating to the same matter.

Children and Young Persons Act 1969 ss7(7), 11–13, 17, 18 and 23(1)–(5)

Alterations in treatment of young offenders etc

7 (7) Subject to the enactments requiring cases to be remitted to youth courts and to section 53(1) of the Act of 1933 [Children and Young Persons Act 1933] (which provides for detention for certain grave crimes), where a child or a young person is found guilty of any offence by or before any court, that court or the court to which his case is remitted shall have power –
[(a) repealed by Children Act 1989 Sch 15],
(b) to make a supervision order in respect of him,
[(c) repealed by Criminal Justice Act 1991 Sch 11 para 40 and Sch 13],
and, if it makes such an order as is mentioned in this subsection while another such order made by any court is in force in respect of the child or young person, shall also have power to discharge the earlier order.

Amendments

This subsection was amended by Criminal Justice Act 1982 s23, Children Act 1989 Sch 15 and Criminal Justice Act 1991 Sch 11 para 40 and Sch 13.

Supervision orders

11 Any provision of this Act authorising a court to make a supervision order in respect of any person shall be construed as authorising the court to make an order placing him under the supervision of a local authority designated by the order or of a probation officer; and in this Act 'supervision order' shall be construed accordingly and 'supervised person' and 'supervisor', in relation to a supervision order, mean respectively the person placed or to be placed under supervision by the order and the person under whose supervision he is placed or to be placed by the order.

Power to include requirements in supervision orders

12 (1) A supervision order may require the supervised person to reside with an individual named in the order who agrees to the requirement, but a requirement imposed by a supervision order in pursuance of this subsection shall be subject to any such requirement of the order as is authorised by the following provisions of this section or by section 12A, 12B or 12C below.

(2) Subject to section 19(12) of this Act, a supervision order may require the supervised person to comply with any directions given from time to time by the supervisor and requiring him to do all or any of the following things – 213

(a) to live at a place or places specified in the directions for a period or periods so specified;
(b) to present himself to a person or persons specified in the directions at a place or places and on a day or days so specified;
(c) to participate in activities specified in the directions on a day or days so specified;

but it shall be for the supervisor to decide whether and to what extent he exercises any power to give directions conferred on him by virtue of this subsection and to decide the form of any directions; and a requirement imposed by a supervision order in pursuance of this subsection shall be subject to any such requirement of the order as is authorised by section 12B(1) of this Act.

(3) The total number of days in respect of which a supervised person may be required to comply with directions given by virtue of paragraph (a), (b) or (c) of subsection (2) above in pursuance of a supervision order shall not exceed 90 or such lesser number, if any, as the order may specify for the purposes of this subsection; and for the purpose of calculating the total number of days in respect of which such directions may be given the supervisor shall be entitled to disregard any day in respect of which directions were previously given in pursuance of the order and on which the directions were not complied with.

Amendments

This section was substituted by Criminal Justice Act 1988 Sch 10 Pt I, together with the insertion of ss12A–12D.

Young offenders

12A(1) This subsection applies to any supervision order made under section 7(7) of this Act unless it requires the supervised person to comply with directions given by the supervisor under section 12(2) of this Act.

[(2) Effectively repealed by Children Act 1989 Sch 12]

(3) Subject to the following provisions of this section and to section 19(13) of this Act, a supervision order to which subsection (1) of this section applies may require a supervised person –
(a) to do anything that by virtue of section 12(2) of this Act a supervisor has power, or would but for section 19(12) of this Act have power, to direct a supervised person to do;
(b) to remain for specified periods between 6 pm and 6 am –
(i) at a place specified in the order; or
(ii) at one of several places so specified;
(c) to refrain from participating in activities specified in the order –
(i) on a specified day or days during the period for which the supervision order is in force; or
(ii) during the whole of that period or a specified portion of it.

(4) Any power to include a requirement in a supervision order which is exercisable in relation to a person by virtue of this section or the following provisions of this Act may be exercised in relation to him whether or not any other such power is exercised.

(5) The total number of days in respect of which a supervised person may be subject to requirements imposed by virtue of subsection (3)(a) or (b) above shall not exceed 90.

(6) The court may not include requirements under subsection (3) above in a supervision order unless –

    (a) it has first consulted the supervisor as to –

        (i) the offender's circumstances; and

        (ii) the feasibility of securing compliance with the requirements,

        and is satisfied, having regard to the supervisor's report, that it is feasible to secure compliance with them;

    (b) having regard to the circumstances of the case, it considers the requirements necessary for securing the good conduct of the supervised person or for preventing a repetition by him of the same offence or the commission of other offences; and

    (c) if the supervised person is under the age of sixteen, it has obtained and considered information about his family circumstances and the likely effect of the requirements on those circumstances.

(7) The court shall not include in such an order by virtue of subsection (3) above –

    (a) any requirement that would involve the co-operation of a person other than the supervisor and the supervised person unless that other person consents to its inclusion; or

    (b) any requirement requiring the supervised person to reside with a specified individual; or

    (c) any such requirement as is mentioned in section 12B (1) of this Act.

(8) The place, or one of the places, specified in a requirement under subsection (3)(b) above ('a night restriction') shall be the place where the supervised person lives.

(9) A night restriction shall not require the supervised person to remain at a place for longer than 10 hours on any one night.

(10) A night restriction shall not be imposed in respect of any day which falls outside the period of three months beginning with the date when the supervision order is made.

(11) A night restriction shall not be imposed in respect of more than 30 days in all.

(12) A supervised person who is required by a night restriction to remain at a place may leave it if he is accompanied –

    (a) by his parent or guardian;

    (b) by his supervisor; or

    (c) by some other person specified in the supervision order.

(13) A night restriction imposed in respect of a period of time beginning in the evening and ending in the morning shall be treated as imposed only in respect of the day upon which the period begins.

Amendments

This section was inserted by Criminal Justice Act 1988 Sch 10. Subsection (1) was substituted for subss(1) and (2) by Children Act 1989 Sch 12. Subsection (6)(c) was substituted by Crime (Sentences) Act 1997 s38(1).

Requirement for young offender to live in local authority accommodation

12AA(1) Where the conditions mentioned in subsection (6) of this section are satisfied, a supervision order may impose a requirement ('a residence requirement') that a child or young person shall live for a specified period in local authority accommodation.

(2) A residence requirement shall designate the local authority who are to receive the child or young person and that authority shall be the authority in whose area the child or young person resides.

(3) The court shall not impose a residence requirement without first consulting the designated authority.

(4) A residence requirement may stipulate that the child or young person shall not live with a named person.

(5) The maximum period which may be specified in a residence requirement is six months.

(6) The conditions are that –
   (a) a supervision order has previously been made in respect of the child or young person;
   (b) that order imposed –
      (i) a requirement under section 12A(3) of this Act; or
      (ii) a residence requirement;
   (c) he is found guilty of an offence which –
      (i) was committed while that order was in force;
      (ii) if it had been committed by a person over the age of twenty-one, would have been punishable with imprisonment; and
      (iii) in the opinion of the court is serious; and
   (d) the court is satisfied that the behaviour which constituted the offence was due, to a significant extent, to the circumstances in which he was living,

except that the condition in paragraph (d) of this subsection does not apply where the condition in paragraph (b)(ii) is satisfied.

[(7)–(8) Repealed.]

(9) A court shall not include a residence requirement in respect of a child or young person who is not legally represented at the relevant time in that court unless –
   (a) he has applied for legal aid for the purposes of the proceedings and the application was refused on the ground that it did not appear that his resources were such that he required assistance; or
   (b) he has been informed of his right to apply for legal aid for the purposes of the proceedings and has had the opportunity to do so, but nevertheless refused or failed to apply.

(10) In subsection (9) of this section –
   (a) 'the relevant time' means the time when the court is considering whether or not to impose the requirement; and
   (b) 'the proceedings' means –
      (i) the whole proceedings; or
      (ii) the part of the proceedings relating to the imposition of the requirement.

(11) A supervision order imposing a residence requirement may also impose any of the requirements mentioned in sections 12, 12A, 12B or 12C of this Act.

[(12) Repealed.]

Amendment

> This section was inserted by Children Act 1989 Sch 12 para 23. Subsections (7), (8) and (12) were repealed by Criminal Justice Act 1991 Sch 13.

Requirements as to mental treatment

12B(1) Where a court which proposes to make a supervision order is satisfied, on the evidence of a medical practitioner approved for the purposes of section 12 of the Mental Health Act 1983, that the mental condition of a supervised person is such as requires and may be susceptible to treatment but is not such as to warrant his detention in pursuance of a hospital order under Part III of that Act, the court may include in the supervision order a requirement that the supervised person shall, for a period specified in the order, submit to treatment of one of the following descriptions so specified, that is to say –
  (a) treatment by or under the direction of a fully registered medical practitioner specified in the order;
  (b) treatment as a non-resident patient at a place specified in the order; or
  (c) treatment as a resident patient in a hospital or mental nursing home within the meaning of the said Act of 1983, but not a special hospital within the meaning of that Act.

(2) A requirement shall not be included in a supervision order in pursuance of subsection (1) above –
  (a) in any case, unless the court is satisfied that arrangements have been or can be made for the treatment in question and, in the case of treatment as a resident patient, for the reception of the patient;
  (b) in the case of an order made or to be made in respect of a person who has attained the age of 14, unless he consents to its inclusion;

and a requirement so included shall not in any case continue in force after the person supervised becomes 18.

Amendment

> This section was inserted by Criminal Justice Act 1988 Sch 10 Pt I.

Requirements as to education

12C(1) Subject to subsection (3) below, a supervision order to which section 12A(1) of this Act applies may require a supervised person, if he is of compulsory school age, to comply, for as long as he is of that age and the order remains in force, with such arrangements for his education as may from time to time be made by his parent, being arrangements for the time being approved by the local education authority.

(2) The court shall not include such a requirement in a supervision order unless it has consulted the local education authority with regard to its proposal to include the requirement and is satisfied that in the view of the local education authority arrangements exist for the child or young person

to whom the supervision order will relate to receive efficient full-time education suitable to his age, ability and aptitude and to any special educational need he may have.

(3) Expressions used in subsection (1) above and in [the Education Act 1996] have the same meaning there as in that Act.

(4) The court may not include a requirement under subsection (1) above unless it has first consulted the supervisor as to the offender's circumstances and, having regard to the circumstances of the case, it considers the requirement necessary for securing the good conduct of the supervised person or for preventing a repetition by him of the same offence or the commission of other offences.

Amendments

This section was inserted by Criminal Justice Act 1988 Sch 10 Pt I. The words in square brackets in subs(3) were inserted by Education Act 1996 Sch 37 para 15.

Duty of court to state in certain cases that requirement is in place of custodial sentence

12D(1) Where –

(a) in pursuance of section 12A(3)(a) of this Act a court includes a requirement in a supervision order directing the supervised person to participate in specified activities; and

(b) it would have imposed a custodial sentence if it had not made a supervision order including such a requirement,

it shall state in open court –

(i) that it is making the order instead of a custodial sentence;

(ii) that it is satisfied that –

(a) the offence of which he has been convicted, or the combination of that offence and one or more offences associated with it, was so serious that only a supervision order containing such a requirement or a custodial sentence can be justified for that offence; or

(b) that offence was a violent or sexual offence and only a supervision order containing such a requirement or such a sentence would be adequate to protect the public from serious harm from him;

(iii) why it is so satisfied.

(1A) Sub-paragraphs (a) and (b) of subsection (1)(ii) above shall be construed as if they were contained in Part I of the Criminal Justice Act 1991.

(2) Where the Crown Court makes such a statement, it shall certify in the supervision order that it has made such a statement.

(3) Where a magistrates' court makes such a statement, it shall certify in the supervision order that it has made such a statement and shall cause the statement to be entered in the register.

Amendments

This section was inserted by Criminal Justice Act 1988 Sch 10 Pt I. Subsections (1)(b)(ii)(a) and (b) were substituted by Criminal Justice Act

1991 Sch 11 para 6 and subsequently amended by Criminal Justice Act 1993 s66(7). Subsection (1A) was inserted by Criminal Justice Act 1991 Sch 11 para 6.

Selection of supervisor

13 (1) A court shall not designate a local authority as the supervisor by a provision of a supervision order unless the authority agree or it appears to the court that the supervised person resides or will reside in the area of the authority.

(2) A court shall not insert in a supervision order a provision placing a child under the supervision of a probation officer unless the local authority of which the area is named or to be named in the order in pursuance of section 18(2)(a) of this Act so request and a probation officer is already exercising or has exercised, in relation to another member of the household to which the child belongs, duties imposed on probation officers by section 14, or by rules under section 25(1)(c), of the Probation Service Act 1993.

(3) Where a provision of a supervision order places a person under the supervision of a probation officer, the supervisor shall be a probation officer appointed for or assigned to the petty sessions area named in the order in pursuance of section 18(2)(a) of this Act and selected under arrangements made under section 4(1)(d) of the Probation Service Act 1993 (arrangements made by probation committee).

Amendments

This section was amended and repealed in part by Powers of Criminal Courts Act 1973 Sch 5 para 35, Criminal Law Act 1977 Schs 12 and 13, Criminal Justice Act 1982 s65(1) and Probation Service Act 1993 Sch 3 para 3.

Termination of supervision

17 A supervision order shall, unless it has previously been discharged, cease to have effect –

(a) in any case, on the expiration of the period of three years, or such shorter period as may be specified in the order, beginning with the date on which the order was originally made;

[(b)–(c) [repealed].

Amendments

Subsections (b) and (c) were repealed by Children Act 1989 Sch 15.

Supplementary provisions relating to supervision orders

18 (1) A court shall not make a supervision order unless it is satisfied that the supervised person resides or will reside in the area of a local authority; and a court shall be entitled to be satisfied that the supervised person will so reside if he is to be required to so reside by a provision to be included in the order in pursuance of section 12(1) of this Act.

(2) A supervision order –

(a) shall name the area of the local authority and the petty sessions area in which it appears to the court making the order, or to the court varying any provision included in the order in pursuance of this paragraph, that the supervised person resides or will reside; and

(b) may contain such prescribed provisions as the court aforesaid considers appropriate for facilitating the performance by the supervisor of his functions under section 14 of this Act, including any prescribed provisions for requiring visits to be made by the supervised person to the supervisor,

and in paragraph (b) of this subsection prescribed' means prescribed by rules under [section 144 of the Magistrates' Courts Act 1980].

(3) A court which makes a supervision order or an order varying or discharging supervision order shall forthwith send a copy of its order –

(a) to the supervised person and, if the supervised person is a child, to his parent or guardian, and

(b) to the supervisor and any person who has ceased to be the supervisor by virtue of the order; and

(c) to any local authority who is not entitled by virtue of the preceding paragraph to such a copy and whose area is named in the supervision order in pursuance of the preceding subsection or has ceased to be so named by virtue of the court's order; and

(d) where the supervised person is required by the order, or was required by the supervision order before it was varied or discharged, to reside with an individual or at any place, to the individual or the person in charge of that place; and

(e) where a petty sessions area named in the order or discharged order in pursuance of subsection (2) of this section is not that for which the court acts, to the clerk to the justices for the petty sessions area so named;

and, in a case falling within paragraph (e) of this subsection, shall also send to the clerk to the justices in question such documents and information relating to the case as the court considers likely to be of assistance to them.

(4) [Defrayment of supervisor's expenditure – not reproduced.]

Amendment

The words in square brackets in subs(2) were substituted by Magistrates' Courts Act 1980 Sch 7 para 82.

Remands and committals to local authority accommodation

23 (1) Where –

(a) a court remands a child or young person charged with or convicted of one or more offences or commits him for trial or sentence; and

(b) he is not released on bail,

then, unless he is declared by the court, after consultation with a probation officer or a social worker of a local authority social services department, to be a person to whom subsection (5) below applies the remand or committal shall be to local authority accommodation; and in the following provisions of this section, any reference (however expressed) to a remand shall be construed as including a reference to a committal.

(2) A court remanding a person to local authority accommodation shall designate the local authority who are to receive him; and that authority shall be –

    (a) in the case of a person who is being looked after by a local authority, that authority; and

    (b) in any other case, the local authority in whose area it appears to the court that he resides or the offence or one of the offences was committed.

(3) Where a person is remanded to local authority accommodation, it shall be lawful for any person acting on behalf of the designated authority to detain him.

(4) Where a court declares a person to be one to whom subsection (5) below applies, it shall remand him –

    (a) to a remand centre, if it has been notified that such a centre is available for the reception from the court of such persons; and

    (b) to a prison, if it has not been so notified.

(4A) A court shall not declare a person who is not legally represented in the court to be a person to whom subsection (5) below applied unless –

    (a) he applied for legal aid and the application was refused on the ground that it did not appear that his means were such that he required assistance; or

    (b) having been informed of his right to apply for legal aid and had the opportunity to do so, he refused or failed to apply.

(5) This subsection applies to a young person who is male and has attained the age of fifteen, but only if –

    (a) he is charged with or has been convicted of a violent or sexual offence, or an offence punishable in the case of an adult with imprisonment for a term of fourteen years or more; or

    (b) he has a recent history of absconding while remanded to local authority accommodation, and is charged with or has been convicted of an imprisonable offence alleged or found to have been committed while he was so remanded,

and (in either case) the court is of the opinion that only remanding him to a remand centre or prison would be adequate to protect the public from serious harm from him.

Amendment

This section is in the form substituted from 1 October 1992 for the original section by Criminal Justice Act 1991 s60(1), as amended by s62 of that Act. These amendments are intended to have force for only a defined period after which s60(1) will have full effect.

Bail Act 1976

PRELIMINARY
Meaning of 'bail in criminal proceedings'

1 (1) In this Act 'bail in criminal proceedings' means –
  (a) bail grantable in or in connection with proceedings for an offence to a person who is accused or convicted of the offence, or
  (b) bail grantable in connection with an offence to a person who is under arrest for the offence or for whose arrest for the offence a warrant (endorsed for bail) is being issued.

  (2) In this Act 'bail' means bail grantable under the law (including common law) for the time being in force.

  (3) Except as provided by section 13(3) of this Act, this section does not apply to bail in or in connection with proceedings outside England and Wales. ...

  [(4) Repealed.]

  (5) This section applies –
  (a) whether the offence was committed in England or Wales or elsewhere, and
  (b) whether it is an offence under the law of England and Wales, or of any other country or territory.

  (6) Bail in criminal proceedings shall be granted (and in particular shall be granted unconditionally or conditionally) in accordance with this Act.

Amendments
  Subsection (4) was repealed and subs(6) was amended by Criminal Justice and Public Order Act 1994 Sch 11.

Other definitions

2 (1) In this Act, unless the context otherwise requires, 'conviction' includes –
  (a) a finding of guilt,
  (b) a finding that a person is not guilty by reason of insanity,
  (c) a finding under section 30(1) of the Magistrates' Courts Act 1980 (remand for medical examination) that the person in question did the act or made the omission charged, and
  (d) a conviction of an offence for which an order is made placing the offender on probation or discharging him absolutely or conditionally, and 'convicted' shall be construed accordingly.

  (2) In this Act, unless the context otherwise requires –
  'bail hostel' and 'probation hostel' have the same meanings as in the Powers of Criminal Courts Act 1973,

'child' means a person under the age of fourteen,

'court' includes a judge of a court or a justice of the peace and, in the case of a specified court, includes a judge or (as the case may be) justice having powers to act in connection with proceedings before that court,

'Courts-Martial Appeal rules' means rules made under section 49 of the Courts-Martial (Appeals) Act 1968,

'Crown Court rules' means rules made under section 15 of the Courts Act 1971,

'magistrates' courts rules' means rules made under section 15 of the Justices of the Peace Act 1949,

'offence' includes an alleged offence,

'proceedings against a fugitive offender' means proceedings under the Extradition Act 1989 or section 2(1) or 4(3) of the Backing of Warrants (Republic of Ireland) Act 1965,

'Supreme Court rules' means rules made under section 99 of the Supreme Court of Judicature (Consolidation) Act 1925,

'surrender to custody' means, in relation to a person released on bail, surrendering himself into the custody of the court or of the constable (according to the requirements of the grant of bail) at the time and place for the time being appointed for him to do so,

'vary', in relation to bail, means imposing further conditions after bail is granted, or varying or rescinding conditions,

'young person' means a person who has attained the age of fourteen and is under the age of seventeen.

(3) Where an enactment (whenever passed) which related to bail in criminal proceedings refers to the person bailed appearing before court it is to be construed unless the context otherwise requires as referring to his surrendering himself into the custody of the court.

(4) Any reference in this Act to any other enactment is a reference thereto as amended, and includes a reference thereto as extended or applied, by or under any other enactment, including this Act.

Amendments

Subsection (1)(c) was amended by Magistrates' Courts Act 1980 Sch 7 and subs(2) by Criminal Law Act 1977 Schs 12 and 13, Criminal Justice Act 1988 Sch 15 and Extradition Act 1989 s36.

INCIDENTS OF BAIL IN CRIMINAL PROCEEDINGS
General provisions

3 (1) A person granted bail in criminal proceedings shall be under a duty to surrender to custody, and that duty is enforceable in accordance with section 6 of this Act.

(2) No recognisance for his surrender to custody shall be taken from him.

(3) Except as provided by this section –

(a) no security for his surrender to custody shall be taken from him,

(b) he shall not be required to provide a surety or sureties for his surrender to custody, and

(c) no other requirement shall be imposed on him as a condition of bail.

(4) He may be required, before release on bail, to provide a surety or sureties to secure his surrender to custody.

(5) If it appears that he is unlikely to remain in Great Britain until the time appointed for him to surrender to custody, he may be required, before release on bail, to give security for his surrender to custody.

The security may be given by him or on his behalf.

(6) He may be required to comply, before release on bail or later, with such requirements as appear to the court to be necessary to secure that –

(a) he surrenders to custody,

(b) he does not commit an offence while on bail,

(c) he does not interfere with witnesses or otherwise obstruct the course of justice whether in relation to himself or any other person,

(d) he makes himself available for the purpose of enabling inquiries or a report to be made to assist the court in dealing with him for the offence,

and, in any Act, 'the normal powers to impose conditions of bail' means the powers to impose conditions under paragraph (a), (b) or (c) above.

(6ZA) Where he is required under subsection (6) above to reside in a bail hostel or probation hostel, he may also be required to comply with the rules of the hostel.

(6A) In the case of a person accused of murder the court granting bail shall, unless it considers that satisfactory reports on his mental condition have already been obtained, impose as conditions of bail –

(a) a requirement that the accused shall undergo examination by two medical practitioners for the purpose of enabling such reports to be prepared; and

(b) a requirement that he shall for that purpose attend such an institution or place as the court directs and comply with any other directions which may be given to him for that purpose by either of those practitioners.

(6B) Of the medical practitioners referred to in subsection (6A) above at least one shall be a practitioner approved for the purposes of section 12 of the Mental Health Act 1983.

(7) If a parent or guardian of a child or young person consents to be surety for the child or young person for the purposes of this subsection, the parent or guardian may be required to secure that the child or young person complies with any requirement imposed on him by virtue of subsection (6) or (6A) above but –

(a) no requirement shall be imposed on the parent or the guardian of a young person by virtue of this subsection where it appears that the young person will attain the age of seventeen before the time to be appointed for him to surrender to custody; and

(b) the parent or guardian shall not be required to secure compliance with any requirement to which his consent does not extend and shall not, in respect of those requirements to which his consent does extend, be bound in a sum greater than £50.

(8) Where a court has granted bail in criminal proceedings that court or, where that court has committed a person on bail to the Crown Court for trial or to be sentenced or otherwise dealt with, that court or the Crown Court may on application –

(a) by or on behalf of the person to whom bail was granted, or

(b) by the prosecutor or a constable,

vary the conditions of bail or impose conditions in respect of bail which has been granted unconditionally.

(8A) Where a notice of transfer is given under a relevant transfer provision, subsection (8) above shall have effect in relation to a person in relation to whose case the notice is given as if he had been committed on bail to the Crown Court for trial.

(9) This section is subject to subsection (2) of section 30 of the Magistrates' Courts Act 1980 (conditions of bail on remand for medical examination).

(10) This section is subject, in its application to bail granted by a constable, to section 3A of this Act.

(10) In subsection (8A) above 'relevant transfer provision' means –

(a) section 4 of the Criminal Justice Act 1987, or

(b) section 53 of the Criminal Justice Act 1991.

Amendments

Subsection (6) was amended by Criminal Justice and Public Order Act 1994 s27(1). Subsection (6ZA) was inserted by Criminal Justice Act 1988 s131 and subss(6A) and (6B) by Mental Health (Amendment) Act 1982 s34. Subsection (6B) was further amended by Mental Health Act 1983 Sch 4. Subsection (8) was amended by Criminal Law Act 1977 Sch 12. Subsection (8A) was inserted by Criminal Justice Act 1987 Sch 2 and amended by Criminal Justice and Public Order Act 1994 Sch 9. Subsection (9) was amended by Magistrates' Courts Act 1980 Sch 7. The first subs(10) was inserted by Criminal Justice and Public Order Act 1994 s27(2) and the second by Sch 9 of that Act.

Conditions of bail in case of police bail

3A (1) Section 3 of this Act applies, in relation to bail granted by a custody officer under Part IV of the Police and Criminal Evidence Act 1984 in cases where the normal powers to impose conditions of bail are available to him, subject to the following modifications.

(2) Subsection (6) does not authorise the imposition of a requirement to reside in a bail hostel or any requirement under paragraph (d).

(3) Subsection (6ZA), (6A) and (6B) shall be omitted.

(4) For subsection (8), substitute the following –

'(8) Where a custody officer has granted bail in criminal proceedings he or another custody officer serving at the same police station may, at the request of the person to whom it was granted, vary the conditions of bail; and in doing so he may impose conditions or more onerous conditions.'.

(5) Where a constable grants bail to a person no conditions shall be imposed under subsections (4), (5), (6) or (7) of section 3 of this Act unless it appears to the constable that it is necessary to do so for the purpose of preventing that person from –

(a) failing to surrender to custody, or

(b) committing an offence while on bail, or

(c) interfering with witnesses or otherwise obstructing the course of justice, whether in relation to himself or any other person.

(6) Subsection (5) above also applies on any request to a custody officer under subsection (8) of section 3 of this Act to vary the conditions of bail.

Amendment

Section 3A was inserted by Criminal Justice and Public Order Act 1994 s27(3).

BAIL FOR ACCUSED PERSONS AND OTHERS
General right to bail of accused persons and others

4 (1) A person to whom this section applies shall be granted bail except as provided in Schedule 1 to this Act.

(2) This section applies to a person who is accused of an offence when –
   (a) he appears or is brought before a magistrates' court or the Crown Court in the course of or in connection with proceedings for the offence, or
   (b) he applies to a court for bail or for a variation of the conditions of bail in connection with the proceedings.

This subsection does not apply as respects proceedings on or after a person's conviction of the offence or proceedings against a fugitive offender for the offence.

(3) This section also applies to a person who, having been convicted of an offence, appears or is brought before a magistrates' court to be dealt with under Part II of Schedule 2 to the Criminal Justice Act 1991 (breach of requirement of probation, community service, combination or curfew order).

(4) This section also applies to a person who has been convicted of an offence and whose case is adjourned by the court for the purpose of enabling inquiries or a report to be made to assist the court in dealing with him for the offence.

(5) Schedule 1 to this Act also has effect as respects conditions of bail for a person to whom this section applies.

(6) In Schedule 1 to this Act 'the defendant' means a person to whom this section applies and any reference to a defendant whose case is adjourned for inquiries or a report is a reference to a person to whom this section applies by virtue of subsection (4) above.

(7) This section is subject to section 41 of the Magistrates' Courts Act 1980 (restriction of bail by magistrates' court in cases of treason).

(8) This section is subject to section 25 of the Criminal Justice and Public Order Act 1994 (exclusion of bail in cases of homicide and rape).

Amendments

Subsection (2)(b) was amended by Criminal Justice and Public Order Act 1994 Sch 10 (which also inserted subs(8)), subs(3) by Criminal Justice Act 1991 Sch 11, and subs(7) by Magistrates' Courts Act 1980 Sch 7.

SUPPLEMENTARY
Supplementary provisions about decisions on bail

5 (1) Subject to subsection (2) below, where –
   (a) a court or constable grants bail in criminal proceedings, or
   (b) a court withholds bail in criminal proceedings from a person to whom section 4 of this Act applies, or
   (c) a court, officer of a court or constable appoints a time or place or a court or officer of a court appoints a different time or place for a person granted bail in criminal proceedings to surrender to custody, or
   (d) a court or constable varies any conditions of bail or imposes conditions in respect of bail in criminal proceedings,

   that court, officer or constable shall make a record of the decision in the prescribed manner and containing the prescribed particulars and, if requested to do so by the person in relation to whom the decision was taken, shall cause him to be given a copy of the record of the decision as soon as practicable after the record is made.

   (2) Where bail in criminal proceedings is granted by endorsing a warrant of arrest for bail the constable who releases on bail the person arrested shall make the record required by subsection (1) above instead of the judge or justice who issued the warrant.

   (3) Where a magistrates' court or the Crown Court –
   (a) withholds bail in criminal proceedings, or
   (b) imposes conditions in granting bail in criminal proceedings, or
   (c) varies any conditions of bail or imposes conditions in respect of bail in criminal proceedings,

   and does so in relation to a person to whom section 4 of this Act applies, then the court shall, with a view to enabling him to consider making an application in the matter to another court, give reasons for withholding bail or for imposing or varying the conditions.

   (4) A court which is by virtue of subsection (3) above required to give reasons for its decision shall include a note of those reasons in the record of its decision and shall (except in a case where, by virtue of subsection (5) below, this need not be done) give a copy of that note to the person in relation to whom the decision was taken.

   (5) The Crown Court need not give a copy of the note of the reasons for its decision to the person in relation to whom the decision was taken where that person is represented by counsel or solicitor unless his counsel or solicitor requests the court to do so.

   (6) Where a magistrates' court withholds bail in criminal proceedings from a person who is not represented by counsel or a solicitor, the court shall –
   (a) if it is committing him for trial to the Crown Court, or if it issues a certificate under subsection (6A) below inform him that he may apply to the High Court or to the Crown Court to be granted bail;
   (b) in any other case, inform him that he may apply to the High Court for that purpose.

   (6A) Where in criminal proceedings –
   (a) a magistrates' court remands a person in custody under any of the

following provisions of the Magistrates' Courts Act 1980 –
(i) section 5 (adjournment of inquiry into offence);
(ii) section 10 (adjournment of trial);
(iii) section 18 (initial procedure on information against adult for offence triable either way); or
(iv) section 30 (remand for medical examination),
after hearing full argument on an application for bail from him; and
(b) either –
(i) it has not previously heard such argument on an application for bail from him in those proceedings; or
(ii) it has previously heard full argument from him on such an application but it is satisfied that there has been a change in his circumstances or that new considerations have been placed before it,
it shall be the duty of the court to issue a certificate in the prescribed form that they heard full argument on his application for bail before they refused the application.

(6B) Where the court issues a certificate under subsection (6A) above in a case to which paragraph (b)(ii) of that subsection applies, it shall state in the certificate the nature of the change of circumstances or the new considerations which caused it to hear a further fully argued bail application.

(6C) Where a court issues a certificate under subsection (6A) above it shall cause the person to whom it refuses bail to be given a copy of the certificate.

(7) Where a person has given security in pursuance of section 3(5) above, and a court is satisfied that he failed to surrender to custody then, unless it appears that he had reasonable cause for his failure, the court may order the forfeiture of the security.

(8) If a court orders the forfeiture of a security under subsection (7) above, the court may declare that the forfeiture extends to such amount less than the full value of the security as it thinks fit to order.

[Subsections (8A) to (9A) (inserted by Criminal Law Act 1977 Sch 12) detail procedure for taking and forfeiting a security and are not reproduced.]

(10) In this section 'prescribed' means, in relation to the decision of a court or an officer of a court, prescribed by Supreme Court rules, Courts-Martial Appeal rules, Crown Court rules or magistrates' courts rules, as the case requires or, in relation to a decision of a constable, prescribed by direction of the Secretary of State.

(11) This section is subject, in its application to bail granted by a constable, to section 5A of this Act.

Amendments

Subsection (6) was amended and subss(6A)–(6C) inserted by Criminal Justice Act 1982 s60. Subsection (11) was inserted by Criminal Justice and Public Order Act 1994 Sch 3.

Supplementary provisions in cases of police bail

5A (1) Section 5 of this Act applies, in relation to bail granted by a custody officer under Part IV of the Police and Criminal Evidence Act 1984 in cases where the normal powers to impose conditions of bail are available to him, subject to the following modifications.

(2) For subsection (3) substitute the following –
'(3) Where a custody officer, in relation to any person, –
   (a) imposes conditions in granting bail in criminal proceedings, or
   (b) varies any conditions of bail or imposes conditions in respect of bail, in criminal proceedings,
   the custody officer shall, with a view to enabling that person to consider requesting him or another custody officer, or making an application to a magistrates' court, to vary the conditions, give reasons for imposing or varying the conditions.'.

(3) For subsection (4) substitute the following –
'(4) A custody officer who is by virtue of subsection (3) above required to give reasons for his decision shall include a note of those reasons in the custody record and shall give a copy of that note to the person in relation to whom the decision was taken.'.

(4) Subsections (5) and (6) shall be omitted.

Amendments

Section 5A was inserted by Criminal Justice and Public Order Act 1994 Sch 3.

Reconsiderations of decisions granting bail

5B (1) Where a magistrates' court has granted bail in criminal proceedings in connection with an offence, or proceedings for an offence, to which this section applies or a constable has granted bail in criminal proceedings in connection with proceedings for such an offence, that court or the appropriate court in relation to the constable may, on application by the prosecutor for the decision to be reconsidered, –
(a) vary the conditions of bail,
(b) impose conditions in respect of bail which has been granted unconditionally, or
(c) withhold bail.

(2) The offences to which this section applies are offences triable on indictment and offences triable either way.

(3) No application for the reconsideration of a decision under this section shall be made unless it is based on information which was not available to the court or constable when the decision was taken.

(4) Whether or not the person to whom the application relates appears before it, the magistrates' court shall take the decision in accordance with section 4(1) (and Schedule 1) of this Act.

(5) Where the decision of the court on a reconsideration under this section is to withhold bail from the person to whom it was originally granted the court shall –
(a) if that person is before the court, remand him in custody, and
(b) if that person is not before the court, order him to surrender himself forthwith into the custody of the court.

(6) Where a person surrenders himself into the custody of the court in

compliance with an order under subsection (5) above, the court shall remand him in custody.

(7) A person who has been ordered to surrender to custody under subsection (5) above may be arrested without warrant by a constable if he fails without reasonable cause to surrender to custody in accordance with the order.

(8) A person arrested in pursuance of subsection (7) above shall be brought as soon as practicable, and in any event within 24 hours after his arrest, before a justice of the peace for the petty sessions area in which he was arrested and the justice shall remand him in custody.

In reckoning for the purposes of this subsection any period of 24 hours, no account shall be taken of Christmas Day, Good Friday or any Sunday.

(9) Magistrates' court rules shall include provision –
   (a) requiring notice of an application under this section and of the grounds for it to be given to the person affected, including notice of the powers available to the court under it;
   (b) for securing that any representations made by the person affected (whether in writing or orally) are considered by the court before making its decision; and
   (c) designating the court which is the appropriate court in relation to the decision of any constable to grant bail.

Amendments

Section 5B was inserted by Criminal Justice and Public Order Act 1994 s30.

Offence of absconding by person released on bail

6 (1) If a person who has been released on bail in criminal proceedings fails without reasonable cause to surrender to custody he shall be guilty of an offence.

(2) If a person who –
   (a) has been released on bail in criminal proceedings, and
   (b) having reasonable cause therefor, has failed to surrender to custody,

fails to surrender to custody at the appointed place as soon after the appointed time as is reasonably practicable he shall be guilty of an offence.

(3) It shall be for the accused to prove that he had reasonable cause for his failure to surrender to custody.

(4) A failure to give to a person granted bail in criminal proceedings a copy of the record of the decision shall not constitute a reasonable cause for that person's failure to surrender to custody.

(5) An offence under subsection (1) or (2) above shall be punishable either on summary conviction or as if it were a criminal contempt of court.

(6) Where a magistrates' court convicts a person of an offence under subsection (1) or (2) above the court may, if it thinks –
   (a) that the circumstances of the offence are such that greater punishment should be inflicted for that offence than the court has power to inflict, or
   (b) in a case where it commits that person for trial to the Crown Court for another offence, that it would be appropriate for him to be dealt with for the offence under subsection (1) or (2) above by the court before which

he is tried for the other offence,

commit him in custody or on bail to the Crown Court for sentence.

(7) A person who is convicted summarily of an offence under subsection (1) or (2) above and is not committed to the Crown Court for sentence shall be liable to imprisonment for a term not exceeding three months or to a fine not exceeding level 5 on the standard scale or to both and a person who is so committed for sentence or is dealt with as for such a contempt shall be liable to imprisonment for a term not exceeding 12 months or to a fine or to both.

(8) In any proceedings for an offence under subsection (1) or (2) above a document purporting to be a copy of the part of the prescribed record which relates to the time and place appointed for the person specified in the record to surrender to custody and to be duly certified to be a true copy of that part of the record shall be evidence of the time and place appointed for that person to surrender to custody.

(9) For the purposes of subsection (8) above –

(a) 'the prescribed record' means the record of the decision of the court, officer or constable made in pursuance of section 5(1) of this Act;

(b) the copy of the prescribed record is duly certified if it is certified by the appropriate officer of the court or, as the case may be, by the constable who took the decision or a constable designated for the purpose by the officer in charge of the police station from which the person to whom the record relates was released;

(c) 'the appropriate officer' of the court is –

(i) in the case of a magistrates' court, the justices' clerk or such other officer as may be authorised by him to act for the purpose;

(ii) in the case of the Crown Court, such officer as may be designated for the purpose in accordance with arrangements made by the Lord Chancellor;

(iii) in the case of the High Court, such officer as may be designated for the purpose in accordance with arrangements made by the Lord Chancellor;

(iv) in the case of the Court of Appeal, the registrar of criminal appeals or such other officer as may be authorised by him to act for the purpose;

(v) in the case of the Courts-Martial Appeal Court, the registrar or such other officer as may be authorised by him to act for the purpose.

Amendments

Section 6 was amended by Criminal Justice Act 1982 ss38 and 46.

Liability to arrest for absconding or breaking conditions of bail

7 (1) If a person who has been released on bail in criminal proceedings and is under a duty to surrender into the custody of a court fails to surrender to custody at the time appointed for him to do so the court may issue a warrant for his arrest.

(2) If a person who has been released on bail in criminal proceedings absents himself from the court at any time after he has surrendered into the custody of the court and before the court is ready to begin or to resume the hearing

of the proceedings, the court may issue a warrant for his arrest; but no warrant shall be issued under this subsection where that person is absent in accordance with leave given to him by or on behalf of the court.

(3) A person who has been released on bail in criminal proceedings and is under a duty to surrender into the custody of a court may be arrested without warrant by a constable –

   (a) if the constable has reasonable grounds for believing that that person is not likely to surrender to custody;

   (b) if the constable has reasonable grounds for believing that that person is likely to break any of the conditions of his bail or has reasonable grounds for suspecting that that person has broken any of those conditions; or

   (c) in a case where that person was released on bail with one or more surety or sureties, if a surety notifies a constable in writing that that person is unlikely to surrender to custody and that for that reason the surety wishes to be relieved of his obligations as a surety.

(4) A person arrested in pursuance of subsection (3) above –

   (a) shall, except where he was arrested within 24 hours of the time appointed for him to surrender to custody, be brought as soon as practicable and in any event within 24 hours after his arrest before a justice of the peace for the petty sessions area in which he was arrested; and

   (b) in the said excepted case shall be brought before the court at which he was to have surrendered to custody.

In reckoning for the purposes of this subsection any period of 24 hours, no account shall be taken of Christmas Day, Good Friday or any Sunday.

(5) A justice of the peace before whom a person is brought under subsection (4) above may, subject to subsection (6) below, if of the opinion that that person –

   (a) is not likely to surrender to custody, or

   (b) has broken or is likely to break any condition of his bail,

remand him in custody or commit him to custody, as the case may require, or alternatively, grant him bail subject to the same or to different conditions, but if not of that opinion shall grant him bail subject to the same conditions (if any) as were originally imposed.

(6) Where the person so brought before the justice is a child or young person and the justice does not grant him bail, subsection (5) shall have effect subject to the provisions of section 23 of the Children and Young Persons Act 1969 (remands to the care of local authorities).

Amendments

Subsection (4) was amended by Criminal Law Act 1977 Sch 12.

Bail with sureties

8 (1) This section applies where a person is granted bail in criminal proceedings on condition that he provides one or more surety or sureties for the purpose of securing that he surrenders to custody.

(2) In considering the suitability for that purpose of a proposed surety, regard

may be had (amongst other things) to –
(a) the surety's financial resources;
(b) his character and any previous convictions of his; and
(c) his proximity (whether in point of kinship, place of residence or otherwise) to the person for whom he is to be surety.

(3) Where a court grants a person bail in criminal proceedings on such a condition but is unable to release him because no surety or no suitable surety is available, the court shall fix the amount in which the surety is to be bound and subsections (4) and (5) below, or in a case where the proposed surety resides in Scotland subsection (6) below, shall apply for the purpose of enabling the recognizance of the surety to be entered into subsequently.

(4) Where this subsection applies the recognizance of the surety may be entered into before such of the following persons or descriptions of persons as the court may by order specify or, if it makes no such order, before any of the following persons, that is to say –
(a) where the decision is taken by a magistrates' court, before a justice of the peace, a justices' clerk or a police officer who either is of the rank of inspector or above or is in charge of a police station or, if magistrates' courts rules so provide, by a person of such other description as is specified in the rules;
(b) where the decision is taken by the Crown Court, before any of the persons specified in paragraph (a) above or, if Crown Court rules so provide, by a person of such other description as is specified in the rules;
(c) where the decision is taken by the High Court or the Court of Appeal, before any of the persons specified in paragraph (a) above or, if Supreme Court rules so provide, by a person of such other description as is specified in the rules;
(d) where the decision is taken by the Courts-Martial Appeal Court, before any of the persons specified in paragraph (a) above or, if Courts-Martial Appeal rules so provide, by a person of such other description as is specified in the rules;
and Supreme Court rules, Crown Court rules, Courts-Martial Appeal rules or magistrates' courts rules may also prescribe the manner in which a recognizance which is to be entered into before such a person is to be entered into and the persons by whom and the manner in which the recognizance may be enforced.

(5) Where a surety seeks to enter into his recognizance before any person in accordance with subsection (4) above but that person declines to take his recognizance because he is not satisfied of the surety's suitability, the surety may apply to –
(a) the court which fixed the amount of the recognizance in which the surety was to be bound, or
(b) a magistrates' court for the petty sessions area in which he resides,
for that court to take his recognizance and that court shall, if satisfied of his suitability, take his recognizance.

(6) Where this subsection applies, the court, if satisfied of the suitability of the proposed surety, may direct that arrangements be made for the

recognizance of the surety to be entered into in Scotland before any constable, within the meaning of the Police (Scotland) Act 1967, having charge at any police office or station in like manner as the recognizance would be entered into in England or Wales.

(7) Where, in pursuance of subsection (4) or (6) above, a recognizance is entered into otherwise than before the court that fixed the amount of the recognizance, the same consequences shall follow as if it had been entered into before that court.

MISCELLANEOUS
Offence of agreeing to indemnify sureties in criminal proceedings

9 (1) If a person agrees with another to indemnify that other against any liability which that other may incur as a surety to secure the surrender to custody of a person accused or convicted of or under arrest for an offence, he and that other person shall be guilty of an offence.

(2) An offence under subsection (1) above is committed whether the agreement is made before or after the person to be indemnified becomes a surety and whether or not he becomes a surety and whether the agreement contemplates compensation in money or in money's worth.

(3) Where a magistrates' court convicts a person of an offence under subsection (1) above the court may, if it thinks –
  (a) that the circumstances of the offence are such that greater punishment should be inflicted for that offence than the court has power to inflict, or
  (b) in a case where it commits that person for trial to the Crown Court for another offence, that it would be appropriate for him to be dealt with for the offence under subsection (1) above by the court before which he is tried for the other offence,
commit him in custody or on bail to the Crown Court for sentence.

(4) A person guilty of an offence under subsection (1) above shall be liable –
  (a) on summary conviction, to imprisonment for a term not exceeding 3 months or to a fine not exceeding the prescribed sum or to both; or
  (b) on conviction on indictment or if sentenced by the Crown Court on committal for sentence under subsection (3) above, to imprisonment for a term not exceeding 12 months or to a fine or to both.

(5) No proceedings for an offence under subsection (1) above shall be instituted except by or with the consent of the Director of Public Prosecutions.

Amendments
Subsection (4) was amended by Criminal Law Act 1977 s28.

[**10** and **11**, repealed.]
[**12** Amendments, repeals and transitional provisions, not reproduced.]
[**13** Short title, commencement, application and extent, not reproduced.]

SCHEDULE 1
PERSONS ENTITLED TO BAIL: SUPPLEMENTARY PROVISIONS
Part I – Defendants accused or convicted of imprisonable offences
Defendants to whom Part I applies

1 Where the offence or one of the offences of which the defendant is accused or convicted in the proceedings is punishable with imprisonment the following provisions of this Part of this Schedule apply.

Exceptions to right to bail

2 The defendant need not be granted bail if the court is satisfied that there are substantial grounds for believing that the defendant, if released on bail (whether subject to conditions or not) would –
   (a) fail to surrender to custody, or
   (b) commit an offence while on bail, or
   (c) interfere with witnesses or otherwise obstruct the course of justice, whether in relation to himself or any other person.

2A The defendant need not be granted bail if –
   (a) the offence is an indictable offence or an offence triable either way; and
   (b) it appears to the court that he was on bail in criminal proceedings on the date of the offence.

3 The defendant need not be granted bail if the court is satisfied that the defendant should be kept in custody for his own protection or, if he is a child or young person, for his own welfare.

4 The defendant need not be granted bail if he is in custody in pursuance of the sentence of a court or of any authority acting under any of the Services Acts.

5 The defendant need not be granted bail where the court is satisfied that it has not been practicable to obtain sufficient information for the purpose of taking the decisions required by this Part of this Schedule for want of time since the institution of the proceedings against him.

6 The defendant need not be granted bail if, having been released on bail in or in connection with the proceedings for the offence, he has been arrested in pursuance of section 7 of this Act.

Exception applicable only to defendant whose case is adjourned for inquiries or a report

7 Where his case is adjourned for inquiries or a report, the defendant need not be granted bail if it appears to the court that it would be impracticable to complete the inquiries or make the report without keeping the defendant in custody.

Restriction of conditions of bail

8 (1) Subject to subparagraph (3) below, where the defendant is granted bail, no conditions shall be imposed under subsections (4) to (7) (except subsection (6)(d)) of section 3 of this Act unless it appears to the court that it is necessary to do so for the purpose of preventing the occurrence of any of the events mentioned in paragraph 2 of this Part of this Schedule.

(1A) No condition shall be imposed under section 3(6)(d) of this Act unless it appears to be necessary to do so for the purpose of enabling inquiries or a report to be made.

(2) Subparagraphs (1) and (1A) above also apply on any application to the court to vary the conditions of bail or to impose conditions in respect of bail which has been granted unconditionally.

(3) The restriction imposed by subparagraph (1A) above shall not apply to the conditions required to be imposed under section 3(6A) of this Act or operate to override the direction in section 30(2) of the Magistrates' Courts Act 1980 to a magistrates' court to impose conditions of bail under section 3(6)(d) of this Act of the description specified in the said section 30(2) in the circumstances so specified.

Decisions under paragraph 2

9   In taking the decisions required by paragraph 2 or 2A of this Part of this Schedule, the court shall have regard to such of the following considerations as appear to it to be relevant, that is to say –
   (a) the nature and seriousness of the offence or default (and the probable method of dealing with the defendant for it),
   (b) the character, antecedents, associations and community ties of the defendant,
   (c) the defendant's record as respects the fulfilment of his obligations under previous grants of bail in criminal proceedings,
   (d) except in the case of a defendant whose case is adjourned for inquiries or a report, the strength of the evidence of his having committed the offence or having defaulted,
   as well as to any others which appear to be relevant.

9A (1) If –
   (a) the defendant is charged with an offence to which this paragraph applies; and
   (b) representations are made as to any of the matters mentioned in paragraph 2 of this Part of this Schedule; and
   (c) the court decides to grant him bail,
   the court shall state the reasons for its decision and shall cause those reasons to be included in the record of the proceedings.

(2) The offences to which this paragraph applies are –
   (a) murder;
   (b) manslaughter;
   (c) rape;
   (d) attempted murder; and
   (e) attempted rape.

Cases under section 128A of Magistrates' Courts Act 1980

9B   Where the court is considering exercising the power conferred by section 128A of the Magistrates' Courts Act 1980 (power to remand in custody for more than 8 clear days), it shall have regard to the total length of time which the accused would spend in custody if it were to exercise the power.

Part II – Defendants accused or convicted of non-imprisonable offences

Defendants to whom Part II applies

1   Where the offence or every offence of which the defendant is accused or convicted in the proceedings is one which is not punishable with imprisonment the following provisions of this Part of this Schedule apply.

Exceptions to right to bail

2   The defendant need not be granted bail if –
   (a) it appears to the court that, having been previously granted bail in criminal proceedings, he has failed to surrender to custody in accordance with his obligations under the grant of bail; and
   (b) the court believes, in view of that failure, that the defendant, if released on bail (whether subject to conditions or not) would fail to surrender to custody.

3   The defendant need not be granted bail if the court is satisfied that the defendant should be kept in custody for his own protection or, if he is a child or young person, for his own welfare

4   The defendant need not be granted bail if he is in custody in pursuance of the sentence of a court or of any authority acting under any of the Services Acts.

5   The defendant need not be granted bail if, having been released on bail in or in connection with the proceedings for the offence, he has been arrested in pursuance of section 7 of this Act.

Part IIA – Decisions where bail refused on previous hearing

1   If the court decides not to grant the defendant bail, it is the court's duty to consider, at each subsequent hearing while the defendant is a person to whom section 4 above applies and remains in custody, whether he ought to be granted bail.

2   At the first hearing after that at which the court decided not to grant the defendant bail he may support an application for bail with any argument as to fact or law that he desires (whether or not he has advanced that argument previously).

3   At subsequent hearings the court need not bear arguments as to fact or law which it has heard previously.

Part III – Interpretation

1   For the purposes of this Schedule the question whether an offence is one which is punishable with imprisonment shall be determined without regard to any enactment prohibiting or restricting the imprisonment of young offenders or first offenders.

2   References in this Schedule to previous grants of bail in criminal proceedings include references to bail granted before the coming into force of this Act; and so as respects the reference to an offence committed by a person on bail in relation to any period before the coming into force of paragraph 2A of Part I of this Schedule.

3   References in this Schedule to a defendant's being kept in custody or being

in custody include (where the defendant is a child or young person) references to his being kept or being in the care of a local authority in pursuance of a warrant of commitment under section 23(1) of the Children and Young Persons Act 1969.

4   In this Schedule –

'court', in the expression 'sentence of a court', includes a service court as defined in section 12(1) of the Visiting Forces Act 1952 and 'sentence', in that expression, shall be construed in accordance with that definition;

'default', in relation to the defendant, means the default for which he is to be dealt with under section 6 or section 16 of the Powers of Criminal Courts Act 1973;

'the Services Acts' means the Army Act 1955, the Air Force Act 1955 and the Naval Discipline Act 1957.

Amendments

In Part I: para 2A was inserted by Criminal Justice and Public Order Act 1994 s26 (which also amended para 9), para 8(1A) by Criminal Justice Act 1991 Sch 11 (which also amended paras 8(1)–(3)), and paras 9A and 9B by Criminal Justice Act 1988 ss153 and 155; para 8(3) was also amended by Magistrates' Courts Act 1980 Sch 7 and Mental Health (Amendment) Act 1982 s34. Part IIA was inserted by Criminal Justice Act 1988 s154. In Part III: para 2 was amended by Criminal Justice and Public Order Act 1994 Sch 10.

Bail (Amendment) Act 1993 s1

Prosecution right of appeal

1 (1) Where a magistrates' court grants bail to a person who is charged with or convicted of –

   (a) an offence punishable by a term of imprisonment of 5 years or more, or

   (b) an offence under section 12 (taking a conveyance without authority) or 12A (aggravated vehicle taking) of the Theft Act 1968,

   the prosecution may appeal to a judge of the Crown Court against the granting of bail.

   (2) Subsection (1) above applies only where the prosecution is conducted –

   (a) by or on behalf of the Director of Public Prosecutions; or

   (b) by a person who falls within such class or description of person as may be prescribed for the purposes of this section by order made by the Secretary of State.

   (3) Such an appeal may be made only if –

   (a) the prosecution made representations that bail should not be granted; and

   (b) the representations were made before it was granted.

   (4) In the event of the prosecution wishing to exercise the right of appeal set out in subsection (1) above, oral notice of appeal shall be given to the magistrates' court at the conclusion of the proceedings in which such bail has been granted and before the release from custody of the person concerned.

   (5) Written notice of appeal shall thereafter be served on the magistrates' court and the person concerned within two hours of the conclusion of such proceedings.

   (6) Upon receipt from the prosecution of oral notice of appeal from its decision to grant bail the magistrates' court shall remand in custody the person concerned, until the appeal is determined or otherwise disposed of.

   (7) Where the prosecution fails, within the period of two hours mentioned in subsection (5) above, to serve one or both of the notices required by that subsection, the appeal shall be deemed to have been disposed of.

   (8) The hearing of an appeal under subsection (1) above against a decision of the magistrates' court to grant bail shall be commenced within forty-eight hours, excluding weekends and any public holiday (that is to say, Christmas Day, Good Friday or a bank holiday), from the date on which oral notice of appeal is given.

(9) At the hearing of any appeal by the prosecution under this section, such appeal shall be by way of re-hearing, and the judge hearing any such appeal may remand the person concerned in custody or may grant bail subject to such conditions (if any) as he thinks fit.

(10) In relation to a child or young person (within the meaning of the Children and Young Persons Act 1969) –

   (a) the reference in subsection (1) above to an offence punishable by a term of imprisonment is to be read as a reference to an offence which would be so punishable in the case of an adult; and

   (b) the reference in subsection (6) above to remand in custody is to be read subject to the provisions of section 23 of the Act of 1969 (remands to local authority accommodation).

(11) The power to make an order under subsection (2) above shall be exercisable by statutory instrument and any instrument shall be subject to annulment in pursuance of a resolution of either House of Parliament.

Criminal Procedure and Investigations Act 1996 ss3–12 and 49

PART I – DISCLOSURE
THE MAIN PROVISIONS
Primary disclosure by prosecutor

3 (1) The prosecutor must –

    (a) disclose to the accused any prosecution material which has not previously been disclosed to the accused and which in the prosecutor's opinion might undermine the case for the prosecution against the accused, or

    (b) give to the accused a written statement that there is no material of a description mentioned in paragraph (a).

  (2) For the purposes of this section prosecution material is material –

    (a) which is in the prosecutor's possession, and came into his possession in connection with the case for the prosecution against the accused, or

    (b) which, in pursuance of a code operative under Part II, he has inspected in connection with the case for the prosecution against the accused.

  (3) Where material consists of information which has been recorded in any form the prosecutor discloses it for the purposes of this section –

    (a) by securing that a copy is made of it and that the copy is given to the accused, or

    (b) if in the prosecutor's opinion that is not practicable or not desirable, by allowing the accused to inspect it at a reasonable time and a reasonable place or by taking steps to secure that he is allowed to do so;

and a copy may be in such form as the prosecutor thinks fit and need not be in the same form as that in which the information has already been recorded.

  (4) Where material consists of information which has not been recorded the prosecutor discloses it for the purposes of this section by securing that it is recorded in such form as he thinks fit and –

    (a) by securing that a copy is made of it and that the copy is given to the accused, or

    (b) if in the prosecutor's opinion that is not practicable or not desirable, by allowing the accused to inspect it at a reasonable time and a reasonable place or by taking steps to secure that he is allowed to do so.

  (5) Where material does not consist of information the prosecutor discloses it for the purposes of this section by allowing the accused to inspect it at a reasonable time and a reasonable place or by taking steps to secure that he

is allowed to do so.

(6) Material must not be disclosed under this section to the extent that the court, on an application by the prosecutor, concludes it is not in the public interest to disclose it and orders accordingly.

(7) Material must not be disclosed under this section to the extent that –

(a) it has been intercepted in obedience to a warrant issued under section 2 of the Interception of Communications Act 1985, or

(b) it indicates that such a warrant has been issued or that material has been intercepted in obedience to such a warrant.

(8) The prosecutor must act under this section during the period which, by virtue of section 12, is the relevant period for this section.

Primary disclosure: further provisions

4 (1) This section applies where –

(a) the prosecutor acts under section 3, and

(b) before so doing he was given a document in pursuance of provision included, by virtue of section 24(3), in a code operative under Part II.

(2) In such a case the prosecutor must give the document to the accused at the same time as the prosecutor acts under section 3.

Compulsory disclosure by accused

5 (1) Subject to subsections (2) to (4), this section applies where –

(a) this Part applies by virtue of section 1(2), and

(b) the prosecutor complies with section 3 or purports to comply with it.

(2) Where this Part applies by virtue of section 1(2)(b), this section does not apply unless –

(a) a copy of the notice of transfer, and

(b) copies of the documents containing the evidence,

have been given to the accused under regulations made under section 5(9) of the Criminal Justice Act 1987.

(3) Where this Part applies by virtue of section 1(2)(c), this section does not apply unless –

(a) a copy of the notice of transfer, and

(b) copies of the documents containing the evidence,

have been given to the accused under regulations made under paragraph 4 of Schedule 6 to the Criminal Justice Act 1991.

(4) Where this Part applies by virtue of section 1(2)(e), this section does not apply unless the prosecutor has served on the accused a copy of the indictment and a copy of the set of documents containing the evidence which is the basis of the charge.

(5) Where this section applies, the accused must give a defence statement to the court and the prosecutor.

(6) For the purposes of this section a defence statement is a written statement –

(a) setting out in general terms the nature of the accused's defence,

(b) indicating the matters on which he takes issue with the prosecution, and

(c) setting out, in the case of each such matter, the reason why he takes issue with the prosecution.

(7) If the defence statement discloses an alibi the accused must give particulars of the alibi in the statement, including –

    (a) the name and address of any witness the accused believes is able to give evidence in support of the alibi, if the name and address are known to the accused when the statement is given;

    (b) any information in the accused's possession which might be of material assistance in finding any such witness, if his name or address is not known to the accused when the statement is given.

(8) For the purposes of this section evidence in support of an alibi is evidence tending to show that by reason of the presence of the accused at a particular place or in a particular area at a particular time he was not, or was unlikely to have been, at the place where the offence is alleged to have been committed at the time of its alleged commission.

(9) The accused must give a defence statement under this section during the period which, by virtue of section 12, is the relevant period for this section.

Voluntary disclosure by accused

6 (1) This section applies where –

    (a) this Part applies by virtue of section 1(1), and

    (b) the prosecutor complies with section 3 or purports to comply with it.

(2) The accused –

    (a) may give a defence statement to the prosecutor, and

    (b) if he does so, must also give such a statement to the court.

(3) Subsections (6) to (8) of section 5 apply for the purposes of this section as they apply for the purposes of that.

(4) If the accused gives a defence statement under this section he must give it during the period which, by virtue of section 12, is the relevant period for this section.

Secondary disclosure by prosecutor

7 (1) This section applies where the accused gives a defence statement under section 5 or 6.

(2) The prosecutor must –

    (a) disclose to the accused any prosecution material which has not previously been disclosed to the accused and which might be reasonably expected to assist the accused's defence as disclosed by the defence statement given under section 5 or 6, or

    (b) give to the accused a written statement that there is no material of a description mentioned in paragraph (a).

(3) For the purposes of this section prosecution material is material –

    (a) which is in the prosecutor's possession and came into his possession in connection with the case for the prosecution against the accused, or

    (b) which, in pursuance of a code operative under Part II, he has inspected in connection with the case for the prosecution against the accused.

(4) Subsections (3) to (5) of section 3 (method by which prosecutor discloses) apply for the purposes of this section as they apply for the purposes of that.

(5) Material must not be disclosed under this section to the extent that the court, on an application by the prosecutor, concludes it is not in the public

interest to disclose it and orders accordingly.

(6) Material must not be disclosed under this section to the extent that –
   (a) it has been intercepted in obedience to a warrant issued under section 2 of the Interception of Communications Act 1985, or
   (b) it indicates that such a warrant has been issued or that material has been intercepted in obedience to such a warrant.

(7) The prosecutor must act under this section during the period which, by virtue of section 12, is the relevant period for this section.

Application by accused for disclosure

8 (1) This section applies where the accused gives a defence statement under section 5 or 6 and the prosecutor complies with section 7 or purports to comply with it or fails to comply with it.

(2) If the accused has at any time reasonable cause to believe that –
   (a) there is prosecution material which might be reasonably expected to assist the accused's defence as disclosed by the defence statement given under section 5 or 6, and
   (b) the material has not been disclosed to the accused,
   the accused may apply to the court for an order requiring the prosecutor to disclose such material to the accused.

(3) For the purposes of this section prosecution material is material –
   (a) which is in the prosecutor's possession and came into his possession in connection with the case for the prosecution against the accused,
   (b) which, in pursuance of a code operative under Part II, he has inspected in connection with the case for the prosecution against the accused, or
   (c) which falls within subsection (4).

(4) Material falls within this subsection if in pursuance of a code operative under Part II the prosecutor must, if he asks for the material, be given a copy of it or be allowed to inspect it in connection with the case for the prosecution against the accused.

(5) Material must not be disclosed under this section to the extent that the court, on an application by the prosecutor, concludes it is not in the public interest to disclose it and orders accordingly.

(6) Material must not be disclosed under this section to the extent that –
   (a) it has been intercepted in obedience to a warrant issued under section 2 of the Interception of Communications Act 1985, or
   (b) it indicates that such a warrant has been issued or that material has been intercepted in obedience to such a warrant.

Continuing duty of prosecutor to disclose

9 (1) Subsection (2) applies at all times –
   (a) after the prosecutor complies with section 3 or purports to comply with it, and
   (b) before the accused is acquitted or convicted or the prosecutor decides not to proceed with the case concerned.

(2) The prosecutor must keep under review the question whether at any given time there is prosecution material which –
   (a) in his opinion might undermine the case for the prosecution against the

accused, and

(b) has not been disclosed to the accused;

and if there is such material at any time the prosecutor must disclose it to the accused as soon as is reasonably practicable.

(3) In applying subsection (2) by reference to any given time the state of affairs at that time (including the case for the prosecution as it stands at that time) must be taken into account.

(4) Subsection (5) applies at all times –

(a) after the prosecutor complies with section 7 or purports to comply with it, and

(b) before the accused is acquitted or convicted or the prosecutor decides not to proceed with the case concerned.

(5) The prosecutor must keep under review the question whether at any given time there is prosecution material which –

(a) might be reasonably expected to assist the accused's defence as disclosed by the defence statement given under section 5 or 6, and

(b) has not been disclosed to the accused;

and if there is such material at any time the prosecutor must disclose it to the accused as soon as is reasonably practicable.

(6) For the purposes of this section prosecution material is material –

(a) which is in the prosecutor's possession and came into his possession in connection with the case for the prosecution against the accused, or

(b) which, in pursuance of a code operative under Part II, he has inspected in connection with the case for the prosecution against the accused.

(7) Subsections (3) to (5) of section 3 (method by which prosecutor discloses) apply for the purposes of this section as they apply for the purposes of that.

(8) Material must not be disclosed under this section to the extent that the court, on an application by the prosecutor, concludes it is not in the public interest to disclose it and orders accordingly.

(9) Material must not be disclosed under this section to the extent that –

(a) it has been intercepted in obedience to a warrant issued under section 2 of the Interception of Communications Act 1985, or

(b) it indicates that such a warrant has been issued or that material has been intercepted in obedience to such a warrant.

Prosecutor's failure to observe time limits

10 (1) This section applies if the prosecutor –

(a) purports to act under section 3 after the end of the period which, by virtue of section 12, is the relevant period for section 3, or

(b) purports to act under section 7 after the end of the period which, by virtue of section 12, is the relevant period for section 7.

(2) Subject to subsection (3), the failure to act during the period concerned does not on its own constitute grounds for staying the proceedings for abuse of process.

(3) Subsection (2) does not prevent the failure constituting such grounds if it involves such delay by the prosecutor that the accused is denied a fair trial.

Faults in disclosure by accused

11 (1) This section applies where section 5 applies and the accused –
  (a) fails to give a defence statement under that section,
  (b) gives a defence statement under that section but does so after the end of the period which, by virtue of section 12, is the relevant period for section 5,
  (c) sets out inconsistent defences in a defence statement given under section 5,
  (d) at his trial puts forward a defence which is different from any defence set out in a defence statement given under section 5,
  (e) at his trial adduces evidence in support of an alibi without having given particulars of the alibi in a defence statement given under section 5, or
  (f) at his trial calls a witness to give evidence in support of an alibi without having complied with subsection (7)(a) or (b) of section 5 as regards the witness in giving a defence statement under that section.

  (2) This section also applies where section 6 applies, the accused gives a defence statement under that section, and the accused –
  (a) gives the statement after the end of the period which, by virtue of section 12, is the relevant period for section 6,
  (b) sets out inconsistent defences in the statement,
  (c) at his trial puts forward a defence which is different from any defence set out in the statement,
  (d) at his trial adduces evidence in support of an alibi without having given particulars of the alibi in the statement, or
  (e) at his trial calls a witness to give evidence in support of an alibi without having complied with subsection (7)(a) or (b) of section 5 (as applied by section 6) as regards the witness in giving the statement.

  (3) Where this section applies –
  (a) the court or, with the leave of the court, any other party may make such comment as appears appropriate;
  (b) the court or jury may draw such inferences as appear proper in deciding whether the accused is guilty of the offence concerned.

  (4) Where the accused puts forward a defence which is different from any defence set out in a defence statement given under section 5 or 6, in doing anything under subsection (3) or in deciding whether to do anything under it the court shall have regard –
  (a) to the extent of the difference in the defences, and
  (b) to whether there is any justification for it.

  (5) A person shall not be convicted of an offence solely on an inference drawn under subsection (3).

  (6) Any reference in this section to evidence in support of an alibi shall be construed in accordance with section 5.

Time limits

12 (1) This section has effect for the purpose of determining the relevant period for sections 3, 5, 6 and 7.

  (2) Subject to subsection (3), the relevant period is a period beginning and ending with such days as the Secretary of State prescribes by regulations for

the purposes of the section concerned.

(3) The regulations may do one or more of the following –

   (a) provide that the relevant period for any section shall if the court so orders be extended (or further extended) by so many days as the court specifies;

   (b) provide that the court may only make such an order if an application is made by a prescribed person and if any other prescribed conditions are fulfilled;

   (c) provide that an application may only be made if prescribed conditions are fulfilled;

   (d) provide that the number of days by which a period may be extended shall be entirely at the court's discretion;

   (e) provide that the number of days by which a period may be extended shall not exceed a prescribed number;

   (f) provide that there shall be no limit on the number of applications that may be made to extend a period;

   (g) provide that no more than a prescribed number of applications may be made to extend a period;

and references to the relevant period for a section shall be construed accordingly.

(4) Conditions mentioned in subsection (3) may be framed by reference to such factors as the Secretary of State thinks fit.

(5) Without prejudice to the generality of subsection (4), so far as the relevant period for section 3 or 7 is concerned –

   (a) conditions may be framed by reference to the nature or volume of the material concerned;

   (b) the nature of material may be defined by reference to the prosecutor's belief that the question of non-disclosure on grounds of public interest may arise.

(6) In subsection (3) 'prescribed' means prescribed by regulations under this section.

Commencement

Criminal Procedure and Investigations Act 1996 (Appointed Day No 3) Order 1997 SI No 682 appointed 1 April 1997 for the purposes of Part I.

PART VI – MAGISTRATES' COURTS
Either way offences: accused's intention as to plea

49 (1) The Magistrates' Courts Act 1980 shall be amended as follows.

(2) The following sections shall be inserted after section 17 (offences triable on indictment or summarily) –

'Initial procedure: accused to indicate intention as to plea

17A(1) This section shall have effect where a person who has attained the age of 18 years appears or is brought before a magistrates' court on an information charging him with an offence triable either way.

(2) Everything that the court is required to do under the following provisions of this section must be done with the accused present in court.

(3) The court shall cause the charge to be written down, if this has not already been done, and to be read to the accused.

(4) The court shall then explain to the accused in ordinary language that he may indicate whether (if the offence were to proceed to trial) he would plead guilty or not guilty, and that if he indicates that he would plead guilty –

   (a) the court must proceed as mentioned in subsection (6) below; and

   (b) he may be committed for sentence to the Crown Court under section 38 below if the court is of such opinion as is mentioned in subsection (2) of that section.

(5) The court shall then ask the accused whether (if the offence were to proceed to trial) he would plead guilty or not guilty.

(6) If the accused indicates that he would plead guilty the court shall proceed as if –

   (a) the proceedings constituted from the beginning the summary trial of the information; and

   (b) section 9(1) above was complied with and he pleaded guilty under it.

(7) If the accused indicates that he would plead not guilty section 18(1) below shall apply.

(8) If the accused in fact fails to indicate how he would plead, for the purposes of this section and section 18(1) below he shall be taken to indicate that he would plead not guilty.

(9) Subject to subsection (6) above, the following shall not for any purpose be taken to constitute the taking of a plea –

   (a) asking the accused under this section whether (if the offence were to proceed to trial) he would plead guilty or not guilty;

   (b) an indication by the accused under this section of how he would plead.

Intention as to plea: absence of accused

17B(1) This section shall have effect where –

   (a) a person who has attained the age of 18 years appears or is brought before a magistrates' court on an information charging him with an offence triable either way,

   (b) the accused is represented by a legal representative,

   (c) the court considers that by reason of the accused's disorderly conduct before the court it is not practicable for proceedings under section 17A above to be conducted in his presence, and

   (d) the court considers that it should proceed in the absence of the accused.

(2) In such a case –

   (a) the court shall cause the charge to be written down, if this has not already been done, and to be read to the representative;

   (b) the court shall ask the representative whether (if the offence were to proceed to trial) the accused would plead guilty or not guilty;

   (c) if the representative indicates that the accused would plead guilty the court shall proceed as if the proceedings constituted from the beginning the summary trial of the information, and as if section 9(1) above was complied with and the accused pleaded guilty under it;

(d) if the representative indicates that the accused would plead not guilty section 18(1) below shall apply.

(3) If the representative in fact fails to indicate how the accused would plead, for the purposes of this section and section 18(1) below he shall be taken to indicate that the accused would plead not guilty.

(4) Subject to subsection (2)(c) above, the following shall not for any purpose be taken to constitute the taking of a plea –

(a) asking the representative under this section whether (if the offence were to proceed to trial) the accused would plead guilty or not guilty;

(b) an indication by the representative under this section of how the accused would plead.

Intention as to plea: adjournment

17C   A magistrates' court proceeding under section 17A or 17B above may adjourn the proceedings at any time, and on doing so on any occasion when the accused is present may remand the accused, and shall remand him if –

(a) on the occasion on which he first appeared, or was brought, before the court to answer to the information he was in custody or, having been released on bail, surrendered to the custody of the court; or

(b) he has been remanded at any time in the course of proceedings on the information;

and where the court remands the accused, the time fixed for the resumption of proceedings shall be that at which he is required to appear or be brought before the court in pursuance of the remand or would be required to be brought before the court but for section 128(3A) below.'

(3) In section 18(1) (initial procedure) after 'either way' there shall be inserted 'and –

(a) he indicates under section 17A above that (if the offence were to proceed to trial) he would plead not guilty, or

(b) his representative indicates under section 17B above that (if the offence were to proceed to trial) he would plead not guilty.'.

(4) In section 19 (court to consider which mode of trial appears more suitable) paragraph (a) of subsection (2) (charge to be read to accused) shall be omitted.

(5) In –

(a) subsections (1A), (3A), (3C) and (3E) of section 128 (remand), and

(b) subsection (1) of section 130 (transfer of remand hearings), after '10(1)' there shall be inserted ', 17C'.

(6) This section applies where a person appears or is brought before a magistrates' court on or after the appointed day, unless he has appeared or been brought before such a court in respect of the same offence on a previous occasion falling before that day.

(7) The reference in subsection (6) to the appointed day is to such day as is appointed for the purposes of this section by the Secretary of State by order.

Commencement

Criminal Procedure and Investigations Act 1996 (appointed Day No 6) Order 1997 SI No 2199 appointed 1 October 1997 for the purposes of s49.

APPENDIX G

Crime (Sentences) Act 1997
ss1, 2, 5 and 6

PART I – MANDATORY AND MINIMUM CUSTODIAL SENTENCES

Conditions relating to mandatory and minimum custodial sentences

1 (1) This section has effect for the purposes of setting out the basis on which the court shall carry out its sentencing functions under this Part.

(2) Under section 2 below, when determining whether it would be appropriate not to impose a life sentence the court shall have regard to the circumstances relating to either of the offences or to the offender.

(3) Under sections 3 and 4 below, when determining whether it would be appropriate not to impose a custodial sentence of at least seven years under section 3(2) or, as the case may be, of at least three years under section 4(2) the court shall have regard to the specific circumstances which –
  (a) relate to any of the offences or to the offender, and
  (b) would make the prescribed custodial sentence unjust in all the circumstances.

Mandatory life sentence for second serious offence

2 (1) This section applies where –
  (a) a person is convicted of a serious offence committed after the commencement of this section; and
  (b) at the time when that offence was committed, he was 18 or over and had been convicted in any part of the United Kingdom of another serious offence.

(2) The court shall impose a life sentence, that is to say –
  (a) where the person is 21 or over, a sentence of imprisonment for life;
  (b) where he is under 21, a sentence of custody for life under section 8(2) of the Criminal Justice Act 1982 ('the 1982 Act'),

unless the court is of the opinion that there are exceptional circumstances relating to either of the offences or to the offender which justify its not doing so.

(3) Where the court does not impose a life sentence, it shall state in open court that it is of that opinion and what the exceptional circumstances are.

(4) An offence the sentence for which is imposed under subsection (2) above shall not be regarded as an offence the sentence for which is fixed by law.

(5) An offence committed in England and Wales is a serious offence for the purposes of this section if it is any of the following, namely –

254 Criminal litigation / appendix G

(a) an attempt to commit murder, a conspiracy to commit murder or an incitement to murder;

(b) an offence under section 4 of the Offences Against the Person Act 1861 (soliciting murder);

(c) manslaughter;

(d) an offence under section 18 of the Offences Against the Person Act 1861 (wounding, or causing grievous bodily harm, with intent);

(e) rape or an attempt to commit rape;

(f) an offence under section 5 of the Sexual Offences Act 1956 (intercourse with a girl under 13);

(g) an offence under section 16 (possession of a firearm with intent to injure), section 17 (use of a firearm to resist arrest) or section 18 (carrying a firearm with criminal intent) of the Firearms Act 1968; and

(h) robbery where, at some time during the commission of the offence, the offender had in his possession a firearm or imitation firearm within the meaning of that Act.

(6) An offence committed in Scotland is a serious offence for the purposes of this section if the conviction for it was obtained on indictment in the High Court of Justiciary and it is any of the following, namely –

(a) culpable homicide;

(b) attempted murder, incitement to commit murder or conspiracy to commit murder;

(c) rape or attempted rape;

(d) clandestine injury to women or an attempt to cause such injury;

(e) sodomy, or an attempt to commit sodomy, where the complainer, that is to say, the person against whom the offence was committed, did not consent;

(f) assault where the assault –
   (i) is aggravated because it was carried out to the victim's severe injury or the danger of the victim's life; or
   (ii) was carried out with an intention to rape or to ravish the victim;

(g) robbery where, at some time during the commission of the offence, the offender had in his possession a firearm or imitation firearm within the meaning of the Firearms Act 1968;

(h) an offence under section 16 (possession of a firearm with intent to injure), section 17 (use of a firearm to resist arrest) or section 18 (carrying a firearm with intent) of that Act;

(i) lewd, libidinous or indecent behaviour or practices; and

(j) an offence under section 5(1) of the Criminal Law (Consolidation) (Scotland) Act 1995 (unlawful intercourse with a girl under 13).

(7) An offence committed in Northern Ireland is a serious offence for the purposes of this section if it is any of the following, namely –

(a) an offence falling within any of paragraphs (a) to (e) of subsection (5) above;

(b) an offence under section 4 of the Criminal Law Amendment Act 1885 (intercourse with a girl under 14);

(c) an offence under Article 17 (possession of a firearm with intent to injure), Article 18(1) (use of a firearm to resist arrest) or Article 19 (carrying a firearm with criminal intent) of the Firearms (Northern Ireland) Order 1981; and

(d) robbery where, at some time during the commission of the offence, the offender had in his possession a firearm or imitation firearm within the meaning of that Order.

Appeals where previous convictions set aside

5 (1) This section applies where –

(a) a sentence has been imposed on any person under subsection (2) of section 2, 3 or 4 above; and

(b) any previous conviction of his without which that section would not have applied has been subsequently set aside on appeal.

(2) Notwithstanding anything in section 18 of the Criminal Appeal Act 1968, notice of appeal against the sentence may be given at any time within 28 days from the date on which the previous conviction was set aside.

Certificates of convictions for purposes of Part I

6 (1) Where –

(a) on any date after the commencement of this section a person is convicted in England and Wales of a serious offence, a class A drug trafficking offence or a domestic burglary; and

(b) the court by or before which he is so convicted states in open court that he has been convicted of such an offence on that date; and

(c) that court subsequently certifies that fact,

the certificate shall be evidence, for the purposes of the relevant section, that he was convicted of such an offence on that date.

(2) Where –

(a) after the commencement of this section a person is convicted in England and Wales of a class A drug trafficking offence or a domestic burglary; and

(b) the court by or before which he is so convicted states in open court that the offence was committed on a particular day or over, or at some time during, a particular period; and

(c) that court subsequently certifies that fact,

the certificate shall be evidence, for the purposes of the relevant section, that the offence was committed on that day or over, or at some time during, that period.

(3) In this section –

'serious offence, 'class A drug trafficking offence' and 'domestic burglary' have the same meanings as in sections 2, 3 and 4 respectively; and

'the relevant section', in relation to any such offence, shall be construed accordingly.

Commencement

Sections 1(1), (2) and (3) (so far as relating to s3), 2, 5 (so far as relating to sentences imposed under s2(2) or 3(2)), and 6 (so far as relating to serious offences within the meaning of s2 or class A drug trafficking offences within the meaning of s3) were brought into force on 1 October 1997 by Crime (Sentences) Act 1997 (Commencement No 2 and Transitional Provisions) Order 1997 SI No 2200.

Crime and Disorder Act 1998 ss8–9, 28–32, 58–60, 72–79

PART I – PREVENTION OF CRIME AND DISORDER
YOUTH CRIME AND DISORDER
Parenting orders

8 (1) This section applies where, in any court proceedings –

    (a) a child safety order is made in respect of a child;

    (b) an anti-social behaviour order or sex offender order is made in respect of a child or young person;

    (c) a child or young person is convicted of an offence; or

    (d) a person is convicted of an offence under section 443 (failure to comply with school attendance order) or section 444 (failure to secure regular attendance at school of registered pupil) of the Education Act 1996.

(2) Subject to subsection (3) and section 9(1) below, if in the proceedings the court is satisfied that the relevant condition is fulfilled, it may make a parenting order in respect of a person who is a parent or guardian of the child or young person or, as the case may be, the person convicted of the offence under section 443 or 444 ('the parent').

(3) A court shall not make a parenting order unless it has been notified by the Secretary of State that arrangements for implementing such orders are available in the area in which it appears to the court that the parent resides or will reside and the notice has not been withdrawn.

(4) A parenting order is an order which requires the parent –

    (a) to comply, for a period not exceeding twelve months, with such requirements as are specified in the order; and

    (b) subject to subsection (5) below, to attend, for a concurrent period not exceeding three months and not more than once in any week, such counselling or guidance sessions as may be specified in directions given by the responsible officer;

and in this subsection 'week' means a period of seven days beginning with a Sunday.

(5) A parenting order may, but need not, include such a requirement as is mentioned in subsection (4)(b) above in any case where such an order has been made in respect of the parent on a previous occasion.

(6) The relevant condition is that the parenting order would be desirable in the interests of preventing –

    (a) in a case falling within paragraph (a) or (b) of subsection (1) above, any repetition of the kind of behaviour which led to the child safety order, 257 anti-social behaviour order or sex offender order being made;

(b) in a case falling within paragraph (c) of that subsection, the commission of any further offence by the child or young person;

(c) in a case falling within paragraph (d) of that subsection, the commission of any further offence under section 443 or 444 of the Education Act 1996.

(7) The requirements that may be specified under subsection (4)(a) above are those which the court considers desirable in the interests of preventing any such repetition or, as the case may be, the commission of any such further offence.

(8) In this section and section 9 below 'responsible officer', in relation to a parenting order, means one of the following who is specified in the order, namely –

(a) a probation officer;

(b) a social worker of a local authority social services department; and

(c) a member of a youth offending team.

Parenting orders: supplemental

9 (1) Where a person under the age of 16 is convicted of an offence, the court by or before which he is so convicted –

(a) if it is satisfied that the relevant condition is fulfilled, shall make a parenting order; and

(b) if it is not so satisfied, shall state in open court that it is not and why it is not.

(2) Before making a parenting order –

(a) in a case falling within paragraph (a) of subsection (1) of section 8 above;

(b) in a case falling within paragraph (b) or (c) of that subsection, where the person concerned is under the age of 16; or

(c) in a case falling within paragraph (d) of that subsection, where the person to whom the offence related is under that age,

a court shall obtain and consider information about the person's family circumstances and the likely effect of the order on those circumstances.

(3) Before making a parenting order, a court shall explain to the parent in ordinary language –

(a) the effect of the order and of the requirements proposed to be included in it;

(b) the consequences which may follow (under subsection (7) below) if he fails to comply with any of those requirements; and

(c) that the court has power (under subsection (5) below) to review the order on the application either of the parent or of the responsible officer.

(4) Requirements specified in, and directions given under, a parenting order shall, as far as practicable, be such as to avoid –

(a) any conflict with the parent's religious beliefs; and

(b) any interference with the times, if any, at which he normally works or attends an educational establishment.

(5) If while a parenting order is in force it appears to the court which made it,

on the application of the responsible officer or the parent, that it is appropriate to make an order under this subsection, the court may make an order discharging the parenting order or varying it –

(a) by cancelling any provision included in it; or

(b) by inserting in it (either in addition to or in substitution for any of its provisions) any provision that could have been included in the order if the court had then had power to make it and were exercising the power.

(6) Where an application under subsection (5) above for the discharge of a parenting order is dismissed, no further application for its discharge shall be made under that subsection by any person except with the consent of the court which made the order.

(7) If while a parenting order is in force the parent without reasonable excuse fails to comply with any requirement included in the order, or specified in directions given by the responsible officer, he shall be liable on summary conviction to a fine not exceeding level 3 on the standard scale.

Commencement

Sections 8 and 9 were brought into force on 30 September 1998 by virtue of Crime and Disorder Act 1998 (Commencement No 2 and Transitional Provisions) Order 1998 SI No 2327.

PART II – CRIMINAL LAW
RACIALLY-AGGRAVATED OFFENCES: ENGLAND AND WALES
Meaning of 'racially aggravated'

28 (1) An offence is racially aggravated for the purposes of sections 29 to 32 below if –

(a) at the time of committing the offence, or immediately before or after doing so, the offender demonstrates towards the victim of the offence hostility based on the victim's membership (or presumed membership) of a racial group; or

(b) the offence is motivated (wholly or partly) by hostility towards members of a racial group based on their membership of that group.

(2) In subsection (1)(a) above –

'membership', in relation to a racial group, includes association with members of that group;

'presumed' means presumed by the offender.

(3) It is immaterial for the purposes of paragraph (a) or (b) of subsection (1) above whether or not the offender's hostility is also based, to any extent, on –

(a) the fact or presumption that any person or group of persons belongs to any religious group; or

(b) any other factor not mentioned in that paragraph.

(4) In this section 'racial group' means a group of persons defined by reference to race, colour, nationality (including citizenship) or ethnic or national origins.

Racially-aggravated assaults

29 (1) A person is guilty of an offence under this section if he commits –

(a) an offence under section 20 of the Offences Against the Person Act

1861 (malicious wounding or grievous bodily harm);

(b) an offence under section 47 of that Act (actual bodily harm); or

(c) common assault,

which is racially aggravated for the purposes of this section.

(2) A person guilty of an offence falling within subsection (1)(a) or (b) above shall be liable –

(a) on summary conviction, to imprisonment for a term not exceeding six months or to a fine not exceeding the statutory maximum, or to both;

(b) on conviction on indictment, to imprisonment for a term not exceeding seven years or to a fine, or to both.

(3) A person guilty of an offence falling within subsection (1)(c) above shall be liable –

(a) on summary conviction, to imprisonment for a term not exceeding six months or to a fine not exceeding the statutory maximum, or to both;

(b) on conviction on indictment, to imprisonment for a term not exceeding two years or to a fine, or to both.

Racially-aggravated criminal damage

30 (1) A person is guilty of an offence under this section if he commits an offence under section 1(1) of the Criminal Damage Act 1971 (destroying or damaging property belonging to another) which is racially aggravated for the purposes of this section.

(2) A person guilty of an offence under this section shall be liable –

(a) on summary conviction, to imprisonment for a term not exceeding six months or to a fine not exceeding the statutory maximum, or to both;

(b) on conviction on indictment, to imprisonment for a term not exceeding fourteen years or to a fine, or to both.

(3) For the purposes of this section, section 28(1)(a) above shall have effect as if the person to whom the property belongs or is treated as belonging for the purposes of that Act were the victim of the offence.

Racially-aggravated public order offences

31 (1) A person is guilty of an offence under this section if he commits –

(a) an offence under section 4 of the Public Order Act 1986 (fear or provocation of violence);

(b) an offence under section 4A of that Act (intentional harassment, alarm or distress); or

(c) an offence under section 5 of that Act (harassment, alarm or distress), which is racially aggravated for the purposes of this section.

(2) A constable may arrest without warrant anyone whom he reasonably suspects to be committing an offence falling within subsection (1)(a) or (b) above.

(3) A constable may arrest a person without warrant if –

(a) he engages in conduct which a constable reasonably suspects to constitute an offence falling within subsection (1)(c) above;

(b) he is warned by that constable to stop; and

(c) he engages in further such conduct immediately or shortly after the warning.

The conduct mentioned in paragraph (a) above and the further conduct need not be of the same nature.

(4) A person guilty of an offence falling within subsection (1)(a) or (b) above shall be liable –

   (a) on summary conviction, to imprisonment for a term not exceeding six months or to a fine not exceeding the statutory maximum, or to both;

   (b) on conviction on indictment, to imprisonment for a term not exceeding two years or to a fine, or to both.

(5) A person guilty of an offence falling within subsection (1)(c) above shall be liable on summary conviction to a fine not exceeding level 4 on the standard scale.

(6) If, on the trial on indictment of a person charged with an offence falling within subsection (1)(a) or (b) above, the jury find him not guilty of the offence charged, they may find him guilty of the basic offence mentioned in that provision.

(7) For the purposes of subsection (1)(c) above, section 28(1)(a) above shall have effect as if the person likely to be caused harassment, alarm or distress were the victim of the offence.

Racially-aggravated harassment, etc

32 (1) A person is guilty of an offence under this section if he commits –

   (a) an offence under section 2 of the Protection from Harassment Act 1997 (offence of harassment); or

   (b) an offence under section 4 of that Act (putting people in fear of violence),

   which is racially aggravated for the purposes of this section.

(2) In section 24(2) of the 1984 Act [Police and Criminal Evidence Act 1984] (arrestable offences), after paragraph (o) there shall be inserted –

   '(p) an offence falling within section 32(1)(a) of the Crime and Disorder Act 1998 (racially-aggravated harassment);'.

(3) A person guilty of an offence falling within subsection (1)(a) above shall be liable –

   (a) on summary conviction, to imprisonment for a term not exceeding six months or to a fine not exceeding the statutory maximum, or to both;

   (b) on conviction on indictment, to imprisonment for a term not exceeding two years or to a fine, or to both.

(4) A person guilty of an offence falling within subsection (1)(b) above shall be liable –

   (a) on summary conviction, to imprisonment for a term not exceeding six months or to a fine not exceeding the statutory maximum, or to both;

   (b) on conviction on indictment, to imprisonment for a term not exceeding seven years or to a fine, or to both.

(5) If, on the trial on indictment of a person charged with an offence falling within subsection (1)(a) above, the jury find him not guilty of the offence charged, they may find him guilty of the basic offence mentioned in that provision.

(6) If, on the trial on indictment of a person charged with an offence falling

within subsection (1)(b) above, the jury find him not guilty of the offence charged, they may find him guilty of an offence falling within subsection (1)(a) above.

(7) Section 5 of the Protection from Harassment Act 1997 (restraining orders) shall have effect in relation to a person convicted of an offence under this section as if the reference in subsection (1) of that section to an offence under section 2 or 4 included a reference to an offence under this section.

Commencement

Sections 28 to 32 were brought into force on 30 September 1998 by virtue of Crime and Disorder Act 1998 (Commencement No 2 and Transitional Provisions) Order 1998 SI No 2327.

PART IV – DEALING WITH OFFENDERS
SEXUAL OR VIOLENT OFFENDERS
Sentences extended for licence purposes

58 (1) This section applies where a court which proposes to impose a custodial sentence for a sexual or violent offence considers that the period (if any) for which the offender would, apart from this section, be subject to a licence would not be adequate for the purpose of preventing the commission by him of further offences and securing his rehabilitation.

(2) Subject to subsections (3) to (5) below, the court may pass on the offender an extended sentence, that is to say, a custodial sentence the term of which is equal to the aggregate of –

(a) the term of the custodial sentence that the court would have imposed if it had passed a custodial sentence otherwise than under this section ('the custodial term'); and

(b) a further period ('the extension period') for which the offender is to be subject to a licence and which is of such length as the court considers necessary for the purpose mentioned in subsection (1) above.

(3) Where the offence is a violent offence, the court shall not pass an extended sentence the custodial term of which is less than four years.

(4) The extension period shall not exceed –

(a) ten years in the case of a sexual offence; and

(b) five years in the case of a violent offence.

(5) The term of an extended sentence passed in respect of an offence shall not exceed the maximum term permitted for that offence.

(6) Subsection (2) of section 2 of the 1991 Act [Criminal Justice Act 1991] (length of custodial sentences) shall apply as if the term of an extended sentence did not include the extension period.

(7) The Secretary of State may by order amend paragraph (b) of subsection (4) above by substituting a different period, not exceeding ten years, for the period for the time being specified in that paragraph.

(8) In this section –

'licence' means a licence under Part II of the 1991 Act;

'sexual offence' and 'violent offence' have the same meanings as in Part I of that Act.

Effect of extended sentences

59 For section 44 of the 1991 Act there shall be substituted the following section –

'Extended sentences for sexual or violent offenders

44(1) This section applies to a prisoner serving an extended sentence within the meaning of section 58 of the Crime and Disorder Act 1998.

(2) Subject to the provisions of this section and section 51(2D) below, this Part, except sections 40 and 40A, shall have effect as if the term of the extended sentence did not include the extension period.

(3) Where the prisoner is released on licence under this Part, the licence shall, subject to any revocation under section 39(1) or (2) above, remain in force until the end of the extension period.

(4) Where, apart from this subsection, the prisoner would be released unconditionally –
(a) he shall be released on licence; and
(b) the licence shall, subject to any revocation under section 39(1) or (2) above, remain in force until the end of the extension period.

(5) The extension period shall be taken to begin as follows –
(a) for the purposes of subsection (3) above, on the date given by section 37(1) above;
(b) for the purposes of subsection (4) above, on the date on which, apart from that subsection, the prisoner would have been released unconditionally.

(6) Sections 33(3) and 33A(1) above and section 46 below shall not apply in relation to the prisoner.

(7) For the purposes of sections 37(5) and 39(1) and (2) above the question whether the prisoner is a long-term or short-term prisoner shall be determined by reference to the term of the extended sentence.

(8) In this section "extension period" has the same meaning as in section 58 of the Crime and Disorder Act 1998.'

Re-release of prisoners serving extended sentences

60 After section 44 of the 1991 Act [Criminal Justice Act 1991] there shall be inserted the following section –

'Re-release of prisoners serving extended sentences

44A(1) This section applies to a prisoner serving an extended sentence within the meaning of section 58 of the Crime and Disorder Act 1998 who is recalled to prison under section 39(1) or (2) above.

(2) Subject to subsection (3) below, the prisoner may require the Secretary of State to refer his case to the Board at any time.

(3) Where there has been a previous reference of the prisoner's case to the Board (whether under this section or section 39(4) above), the Secretary of State shall not be required to refer the case until after the end of the period of one year beginning with the disposal of that reference.

(4) On a reference –
(a) under this section; or
(b) under section 39(4) above,
the Board shall direct the prisoner's release if satisfied that it is no

longer necessary for the protection of the public that he should be confined (but not otherwise).

(5) If the Board gives a direction under subsection (4) above it shall be the duty of the Secretary of State to release the prisoner on licence.'

Commencement

Sections 58 to 60 were brought into force on 30 September 1998 by virtue of Crime and Disorder Act 1998 (Commencement No 2 and Transitional Provisions) Order 1998 SI No 2327.

YOUNG OFFENDERS: NON-CUSTODIAL ORDERS
Breach of requirements in supervision orders

72 (1) In subsection (3) of section 15 of the 1969 Act [Children and Young Persons Act 1969] (variation and discharge of supervision orders), for paragraphs (a) and (b) there shall be substituted the following paragraphs –

'(a) whether or not it also makes an order under subsection (1) above, may order him to pay a fine of an amount not exceeding £1,000, or make in respect of him –

(i) subject to section 16A(1) of this Act, an order under section 17 of the Criminal Justice Act 1982 (attendance centre orders); or

(ii) subject to section 16B of this Act, an order under section 12 of the Criminal Justice Act 1991 (curfew orders);

(b) if the supervision order was made by a relevant court, may discharge the order and deal with him, for the offence in respect of which the order was made, in any manner in which he could have been dealt with for that offence by the court which made the order if the order had not been made; or

(c) if the order was made by the Crown Court, may commit him in custody or release him on bail until he can be brought or appear before the Crown Court.'

(2) For subsections (4) to (6) of that section there shall be substituted the following subsections –

'(4) Where a court deals with a supervised person under subsection (3)(c) above, it shall send to the Crown Court a certificate signed by a justice of the peace giving –

(a) particulars of the supervised person's failure to comply with the requirement in question; and

(b) such other particulars of the case as may be desirable;

and a certificate purporting to be so signed shall be admissible as evidence of the failure before the Crown Court.

(5) Where –

(a) by virtue of subsection (3)(c) above the supervised person is brought or appears before the Crown Court; and

(b) it is proved to the satisfaction of the court that he has failed to comply with the requirement in question,

that court may deal with him, for the offence in respect of which the order was made, in any manner in which it could have dealt with him for that offence if it had not made the order.

(6) Where the Crown Court deals with a supervised person under subsection (5) above, it shall discharge the supervision order if it is still in force.'

(3) In subsections (7) and (8) of that section, for the words 'or (4)' there shall be substituted the words 'or (5)'.

Commencement

Section 72 was brought into force on 30 September 1998 by virtue of Crime and Disorder Act 1998 (Commencement No 2 and Transitional Provisions) Order 1998 SI No 2327.

YOUNG OFFENDERS: DETENTION AND TRAINING ORDERS
Detention and training orders

73 (1) Subject to section 53 of the 1933 Act [Children and Young Persons Act 1933], section 8 of the Criminal Justice Act 1982 ('the 1982 Act') and subsection (2) below, where –

(a) a child or young person ('the offender') is convicted of an offence which is punishable with imprisonment in the case of a person aged 21 or over; and

(b) the court is of the opinion that either or both of paragraphs (a) or (b) of subsection (2) of section 1 of the 1991 Act [Criminal Justice Act 1991] apply or the case falls within subsection (3) of that section,

the sentence that the court is to pass is a detention and training order.

(2) A court shall not make a detention and training order –

(a) in the case of an offender under the age of 15 at the time of the conviction, unless it is of the opinion that he is a persistent offender;

(b) in the case of an offender under the age of 12 at that time, unless –

(i) it is of the opinion that only a custodial sentence would be adequate to protect the public from further offending by him; and

(ii) the offence was committed on or after such date as the Secretary of State may by order appoint.

(3) A detention and training order is an order that the offender in respect of whom it is made shall be subject, for the term specified in the order, to a period of detention and training followed by a period of supervision.

(4) A detention and training order shall be a custodial sentence for the purposes of Part I of the 1991 Act; and the provisions of sections 1 to 4 of that Act shall apply accordingly.

(5) Subject to subsection (6) below, the term of a detention and training order shall be 4, 6, 8, 10, 12, 18 or 24 months.

(6) The term of a detention and training order may not exceed the maximum term of imprisonment that the Crown Court could (in the case of an offender aged 21 or over) impose for the offence.

(7) The following provisions, namely –

(a) section 1B of the 1982 Act (detention in young offender institutions: special provision for offenders under 18); and

(b) sections 1 to 4 of the 1994 Act [Criminal Justice and Public Order Act 1994] (secure training orders), which are superseded by this section and sections 74 to 78 below, shall cease to have effect.

Duties and powers of court

74 (1) On making a detention and training order in a case where subsection (2) of section 73 above applies, it shall be the duty of the court (in addition to the duty imposed by section 1(4) of the 1991 Act) to state in open court that it is of the opinion mentioned in paragraph (a) or, as the case may be, paragraphs (a) and (b)(i) of that subsection.

(2) Subject to subsection (3) below, where –
   (a) an offender is convicted of more than one offence for which he is liable to a detention and training order; or
   (b) an offender who is subject to a detention and training order is convicted of one or more further offences for which he is liable to such an order,
   the court shall have the same power to pass consecutive detention and training orders as if they were sentences of imprisonment.

(3) A court shall not make in respect of an offender a detention and training order the effect of which would be that he would be subject to detention and training orders for a term which exceeds 24 months.

(4) Where the term of the detention and training orders to which an offender would otherwise be subject exceeds 24 months, the excess shall be treated as remitted.

(5) In determining the term of a detention and training order for an offence, the court shall take account of any period for which the offender has been remanded in custody in connection with the offence, or any other offence the charge for which was founded on the same facts or evidence.

(6) The reference in subsection (5) above to an offender being remanded in custody is a reference to his being –
   (a) held in police detention;
   (b) remanded in or committed to custody by an order of a court;
   (c) remanded or committed to local authority accommodation under section 23 of the 1969 Act and placed and kept in secure accommodation; or
   (d) remanded, admitted or removed to hospital under section 35, 36, 38 or 48 of the Mental Health Act 1983.

(7) A person is in police detention for the purposes of subsection (6) above –
   (a) at any time when he is in police detention for the purposes of the 1984 Act; and
   (b) at any time when he is detained under section 14 of the Prevention of Terrorism (Temporary Provisions) Act 1989;
   and in that subsection 'secure accommodation' has the same meaning as in section 23 of the 1969 Act.

(8) For the purpose of any reference in this section or sections 75 to 78 below to the term of a detention and training order, consecutive terms of such orders and terms of such orders which are wholly or partly concurrent shall be treated as a single term if –
   (a) the orders were made on the same occasion; or
   (b) where they were made on different occasions, the offender has not been released (by virtue of subsection (2), (3), (4) or (5) of section 75 below)

at any time during the period beginning with the first and ending with the last of those occasions.

The period of detention and training

75 (1) An offender shall serve the period of detention and training under a detention and training order in such secure accommodation as may be determined by the Secretary of State or by such other person as may be authorised by him for that purpose.

(2) Subject to subsections (3) to (5) below, the period of detention and training under a detention and training order shall be one-half of the term of the order.

(3) The Secretary of State may at any time release the offender if he is satisfied that exceptional circumstances exist which justify the offender's release on compassionate grounds.

(4) The Secretary of State may release the offender –
   (a) in the case of an order for a term of 8 months or more but less than 18 months, one month before the half-way point of the term of the order; and
   (b) in the case of an order for a term of 18 months or more, one month or two months before that point.

(5) If the youth court so orders on an application made by the Secretary of State for the purpose, the Secretary of State shall release the offender –
   (a) in the case of an order for a term of 8 months or more but less than 18 months, one month after the half-way point of the term of the order; and
   (b) in the case of an order for a term of 18 months or more, one month or two months after that point.

(6) An offender detained in pursuance of a detention and training order shall be deemed to be in legal custody.

(7) In this section and sections 77 and 78 below 'secure accommodation' means –
   (a) a secure training centre;
   (b) a young offender institution;
   (c) accommodation provided by a local authority for the purpose of restricting the liberty of children and young persons;
   (d) accommodation provided for that purpose under subsection (5) of section 82 of the 1989 Act [Prevention of Terrorism (Temporary Provisions) Act 1989] (financial support by the Secretary of State); or
   (e) such other accommodation provided for the purpose of restricting liberty as the Secretary of State may direct.

The period of supervision

76 (1) The period of supervision of an offender who is subject to a detention and training order –
   (a) shall begin with the offender's release, whether at the half-way point of the term of the order or otherwise; and
   (b) subject to subsection (2) below, shall end when the term of the order ends.

(2) The Secretary of State may by order provide that the period of supervision shall end at such point during the term of a detention and training order as may be specified in the order under this subsection.

(3) During the period of supervision, the offender shall be under the supervision of –
  (a) a probation officer;
  (b) a social worker of a local authority social services department; or
  (c) a member of a youth offending team;
  and the category of person to supervise the offender shall be determined from time to time by the Secretary of State.

(4) Where the supervision is to be provided by a probation officer, the probation officer shall be an officer appointed for or assigned to the petty sessions area within which the offender resides for the time being.

(5) Where the supervision is to be provided by –
  (a) a social worker of a local authority social services department; or
  (b) a member of a youth offending team,
  the social worker or member shall be a social worker of, or a member of a youth offending team established by, the local authority within whose area the offender resides for the time being.

(6) The offender shall be given a notice from the Secretary of State specifying –
  (a) the category of person for the time being responsible for his supervision; and
  (b) any requirements with which he must for the time being comply.

(7) A notice under subsection (6) above shall be given to the offender –
  (a) before the commencement of the period of supervision; and
  (b) before any alteration in the matters specified in subsection (6)(a) or (b) above comes into effect.

Breaches of supervision requirements

77 (1) Where a detention and training order is in force in respect of an offender and it appears on information to a justice of the peace acting for a relevant petty sessions area that the offender has failed to comply with requirements under section 76(6)(b) above, the justice –
  (a) may issue a summons requiring the offender to appear at the place and time specified in the summons before a youth court acting for the area; or
  (b) if the information is in writing and on oath, may issue a warrant for the offender's arrest requiring him to be brought before such a court.

(2) For the purposes of this section a petty sessions area is a relevant petty sessions area in relation to a detention and training order if –
  (a) the order was made by a youth court acting for it; or
  (b) the offender resides in it for the time being.

(3) If it is proved to the satisfaction of the youth court before which an offender appears or is brought under this section that he has failed to comply with requirements under section 76(6)(b) above, that court may –
  (a) order the offender to be detained, in such secure accommodation as the Secretary of State may determine, for such period, not exceeding the shorter of three months or the remainder of the term of the detention and training order, as the court may specify; or
  (b) impose on the offender a fine not exceeding level 3 on the standard scale.

(4) An offender detained in pursuance of an order under subsection (3) above shall be deemed to be in legal custody; and a fine imposed under that

subsection shall be deemed, for the purposes of any enactment, to be a sum adjudged to be paid by a conviction.

Offences during currency of order

78 (1) This section applies to a person subject to a detention and training order if –
- (a) after his release and before the date on which the term of the order ends, he commits an offence punishable with imprisonment in the case of a person aged 21 or over; and
- (b) whether before or after that date, he is convicted of that offence ('the new offence').

(2) Subject to section 7(8) of the 1969 Act [Children and Young Persons Act 1969], the court by or before which a person to whom this section applies is convicted of the new offence may, whether or not it passes any other sentence on him, order him to be detained in such secure accommodation as the Secretary of State may determine for the whole or any part of the period which –
- (a) begins with the date of the court's order; and
- (b) is equal in length to the period between the date on which the new offence was committed and the date mentioned in subsection (1) above.

(3) The period for which a person to whom this section applies is ordered under subsection (2) above to be detained in secure accommodation –
- (a) shall, as the court may direct, either be served before and be followed by, or be served concurrently with, any sentence imposed for the new offence; and
- (b) in either case, shall be disregarded in determining the appropriate length of that sentence.

(4) Where the new offence is found to have been committed over a period of two or more days, or at some time during a period of two or more days, it shall be taken for the purposes of this section to have been committed on the last of those days.

(5) A person detained in pursuance of an order under subsection (2) above shall be deemed to be in legal custody.

Interaction with sentences of detention

79 (1) Where a court passes a sentence of detention in a young offender institution in the case of an offender who is subject to a detention and training order, the sentence shall take effect as follows –
- (a) if the offender has been released by virtue of subsection (2), (3), (4) or (5) of section 75 above, at the beginning of the day on which it is passed;
- (b) if not, either as mentioned in paragraph (a) above or, if the court so orders, at the time when the offender would otherwise be released by virtue of that subsection.

(2) Where a court makes a detention and training order in the case of an offender who is subject to a sentence of detention in a young offender institution, the order shall take effect as follows –
- (a) if the offender has been released under Part II of the 1991 Act [Criminal Justice Act 1991], at the beginning of the day on which it is made;
- (b) if not, either as mentioned in paragraph (a) above or, if the court so

orders, at the time when the offender would otherwise be released under that Part.

(3) Subject to subsection (4) below, where at any time an offender is subject concurrently –

(a) to a detention and training order; and

(b) to a sentence of detention in a young offender institution,

he shall be treated for the purposes of sections 75 to 78 above, section 1C of the 1982 Act [Criminal Justice Act 1982] and Part II of the 1991 Act as if he were subject only to the one of them that was imposed on the later occasion.

(4) Nothing in subsection (3) above shall require the offender to be released in respect of either the order or the sentence unless and until he is required to be released in respect of each of them.

(5) Where, by virtue of any enactment giving a court power to deal with a person in a manner in which a court on a previous occasion could have dealt with him, a detention and training order for any term is made in the case of a person who has attained the age of 18, the person shall be treated as if he had been sentenced to detention in a young offender institution for the same term.

Commencement

Sections 73 to 79 are due to be brought into force in Summer 1999 in accordance with Home Office Circular 38/1998: *Implementation of the Crime and Disorder Act 1998: England and Wales.*

Legal Aid Board Duty Solicitor Arrangements 1997 Part V

PART V – SELECTION OF DUTY SOLICITORS
Application

31 Only a current application form in a form approved by the Duty Solicitor Committee and obtained from the Board and submitted by the prospective duty solicitor to the Board shall be considered by the appropriate local committee.

Selection criteria – magistrates' courts

32 (1) The criteria for the selection of a duty solicitor to provide advice and representation at a magistrates' court shall be as follows:

(a) the applicant's office shall, in connection with a magistrates' court at which a duty solicitor is required to be in attendance under paragraph 13(1)(a), be within the area of that court or, if it is outside the area of the court, be reasonably accessible to the court for the convenience of any defendant who wishes to instruct the duty solicitor to continue to act for him or her; [Alternative arrangements apply in London details of which are available from the Legal Aid Board.]

(b) the applicant shall, in connection with a magistrates' court at which a duty solicitor is required to be in attendance under paragraph 13(1)(a), normally be in attendance at the office referred to in paragraph 32(1)(a) and that office shall be open during the majority of normal business hours;

(c) the applicant's office shall, in connection with a magistrates' court or courts not falling within paragraph 13(1)(a), be reasonably accessible to the court or courts taking into account relevant local considerations;

(d) the applicant shall hold a current practising certificate which may (in the discretion of the local committee) be conditional;

(e) the applicant shall be willing to act personally as duty solicitor and to undertake the majority of rota duties allocated to him or her;

(f) (i) the applicant, who must not be a special constable, shall regularly practise in criminal defence work;

(ii) the applicant shall have comprehensive experience of criminal defence work including advocacy in Crown or magistrates' courts throughout the previous 12 months, except in the circumstances in sub-paragraph (iii) below;

(iii) if the applicant has been in recent full-time employment as a prosecuting solicitor or in another similar position for a period of 18

271

months he or she must have had comprehensive experience of criminal defence work throughout the six months immediately prior to the application;

(iv) the experience of criminal defence work referred to in sub-paragraphs (ii) and (iii) above need not have been gained in the magistrates' court or courts in connection with which the local committee is appointed;

(v) any interval of up to 12 months, during or at the end of the periods of experience required by sub-paragraphs (ii) and (iii) above, when the applicant was absent from work because of sickness, injury, pregnancy or confinement or for other good reason may be disregarded;

(vi) if the applicant does not comply with paragraphs 32(1)(f)(i)–(v) but the local committee considers that the applicant would make a competent duty solicitor the local committee may recommend to the regional committee in exceptional circumstances that the latter exercises its power under paragraph 15(16) to waive the relevant paragraph;

(g) subject to the approval or direction of the appropriate regional committee under paragraph 15(1), the applicant shall provide advice at police stations for which the local committee is responsible as a duty solicitor and, where that sub-paragraph is in effect, the local committee shall exclude a solicitor from providing advice and representation at magistrates' courts as duty solicitor if he or she does not provide advice at police stations for which the local committee is responsible as duty solicitor;

(h) the applicant shall be prepared, if selected as a duty solicitor, to carry out his or her duties so as not to discriminate on grounds of race, gender, sexual orientation, religion or disability;

(i) any other criteria as approved by the appropriate regional committee and the Duty Solicitor Committee.

(2) In assessing an application the local committee shall be satisfied that the solicitor is competent to provide advice and representation having regard to the nature, frequency and quality of the solicitor's advocacy including:

(a) an ability to provide advice and representation to a number of defendants in a limited time without the opportunity to prepare the cases before arriving at court;

(b) an adequate knowledge of the procedure in magistrates' courts; and

(c) an adequate knowledge of the law relating to the more common offences coming before the court.

(3) The applicant shall have attended an advocacy training course appropriate to advice and representation at magistrates' courts by a duty solicitor, unless he or she has substantial experience of defence advocacy.

(4) Where the applicant:

(a) has been charged with or convicted of a criminal offence since admission, or

(b) has been the subject of any adverse findings by the Adjudication Committee of the Solicitors Complaints Bureau or by the Solicitors

Disciplinary Tribunal, or there are any hearings pending in either forum, or

(c) for other good reason

the committee considering the application has a discretion to reject the application, if it considers that to do so would be in the interests of suspects or defendants provided that it provides the applicant with written reasons for its decision.

(5) The applicant shall possess or have access to relevant up to date legal reference material.

Selection criteria – police stations

33   The criteria for the selection of a duty solicitor to provide advice at a police station shall be as follows:

(1) the criteria set out in paragraphs 32(1)(d) to (i) and 32(2), (3), (4) and (5);

(2) the applicant's home or office shall be within 45 minutes travel time of the relevant police station, [Alternative arrangements apply in London details of which are available from the Legal Aid Board.] and the applicant shall be prepared to make arrangements to be reasonably accessible to the relevant police station when on rota duty, except where adherence to these requirements would make it impracticable for a police station to be covered; in which case the relevant regional committee may agree for the requirement of 45 minutes travel time to be varied under paragraph 14(4). The applicant may, in the discretion of the committee, be required to satisfy the committee that he or she will be in a position to accept panel cases referred by the telephone service;

(3) the applicant shall have attended a course on advice at the police station unless he or she has substantial experience of that area of work;

(4) adequate experience of providing advice to persons arrested and held in custody at police stations;

(5) the applicant shall agree not to provide any money or other gifts to a suspect except items of refreshment and smoking materials for immediate consumption by the suspect;

(6) subject to the approval or direction of the appropriate regional committee under paragraph 15(1), the applicant shall provide advice and representation at magistrates' courts for which the local committee is responsible as a duty solicitor and, where that paragraph is in effect, the local committee shall exclude a solicitor from providing advice at police stations as duty solicitor if he or she does not provide advice and representation at magistrates' courts for which the local committee is responsible as a duty solicitor.

Interview

34 (1) The appropriate local committee shall interview all applicants. Interviews may be conducted by a sub-committee of the local committee. Where the applicant has been approved by another local committee the appropriate local committee is under no duty to interview him or her but may in its discretion do so. An applicant cannot be rejected by the appropriate local committee without an interview.

(2) Any local committee, or sub-committee when interviewing must include a lay member appointed under paragraph 18(2) or (8) provided that any member appointed under paragraph 18(8) is, in this case, not a member of court staff. If no such member can attend, one who is entitled to attend must agree to the interview being conducted in his or her absence.

(3) A member of the relevant regional committee from another part of the region may be included on any local committee or sub-committee when interviewing and selecting applicants.

(4) The composition of the local committee or sub-committee when interviewing applicants is otherwise subject to paragraph 21.

Approval of applications

35   If the applicant meets the criteria set out in paragraph 32 or 33 (whichever is appropriate) the appropriate local committee shall, within 60 days of the submission of the application, approve the application and give notice of such approval to the applicant.

Rejection of applications

36   If the committee decides not to allow the application it shall provide the applicant with a statement of the reasons for its decision, showing which of the criteria in paragraph 32 or 33 he or she does not meet and an explanation of why they have not been met.

Appeals to regional committee

37 (1) Where an application has been rejected under paragraph 36 the applicant may appeal to the appropriate regional committee within 28 days of the decision being notified to him or her subject to the appropriate regional committee having discretion to accept an appeal outside the period of 28 days for good reason.

(2) Where an appeal is referred back to the appropriate local committee under paragraph 15(7)(g), the local committee must approve or reject the application within 60 days.

(3) If the appropriate local committee has not approved an application within a period of 60 days from the date of its submission or from when it was referred back to it under paragraph 15(7)(g) the application shall be deemed to have been rejected and the applicant may within 28 days of the expiration of such period appeal to the appropriate regional committee subject to that committee having discretion to accept an appeal outside the period of 28 days for good reason.

Reselection

38 (1) A duty solicitor shall be subject to reselection by the appropriate local committee at least every five years.

(2) The duty solicitor shall, when subject to reselection, complete a current form approved by the Duty Solicitor Committee and obtained from the Board and shall return it to the Board within the time scale specified thereon failing which the duty solicitor will be deemed not to be seeking reselection.

(3) If the committee is satisfied that the duty solicitor meets the criteria set out

in paragraph 39(1) and/or (2) (whichever is appropriate) and, paragraph 40, it shall reselect him or her and give him or her notice of such reselection. If it is not satisfied that he or she meets such criteria, the committee shall give him or her a statement of any representations received under paragraph 41 and shall invite him or her to an interview. Acceptance of the invitation to an interview must be submitted within 21 days of the committee having invited the duty solicitor to the interview. If having interviewed the duty solicitor the committee decides not to reselect the duty solicitor it shall provide him or her with a statement of the reasons for its decision.

(4) Reselection shall take place, in respect of all duty solicitors admitted during a particular year, to take effect on December 31 of the fifth following year.

Reselection criteria – magistrates' courts and police stations

39 (1) The criteria for the reselection of duty solicitors providing advice and representation at magistrates' courts shall be:
  (a) continued ability to satisfy the criteria in paragraph 32;
  (b) regularity of personal attendance at court as duty solicitor; and
  (c) compliance with these Arrangements and instructions to duty solicitors made under paragraph 27(7)(a).

(2) The criteria for the reselection of duty solicitors providing advice at police stations shall be:
  (a) continued ability to satisfy the criteria in paragraph 33(1), (2), (4) and (5);
  (b) the availability of the duty solicitor to receive telephone calls concerning requests for advice from suspects at police stations, and willingness to accept calls when a panel duty solicitor;
  (c) the attendance of the duty solicitor at police stations in the circumstances set out in paragraph 54;
  (d) the appropriate use of duty solicitors' representatives at police stations.

Reselection criteria – continuing training

40 Any duty solicitor wishing to be reselected whether providing advice and representation at a magistrates' court or advice at a police station or both must have undertaken a minimum of six hours tuition during the previous five years on a course or courses relevant to advice and representation at magistrates' courts or advice at police stations or both.

Representations about performance

41 The appropriate local committee shall, when considering reselection, take into account any representations received as to the performance of the duty solicitor or duty solicitor's representative, provided that where any such representations are received the duty solicitor, or appropriate duty solicitor where a representative is involved, shall be provided with a written statement of them and shall have an opportunity in any representations he or she may make under paragraphs 38 or 48 to respond.

Changes in circumstances – duty to report

42 A duty solicitor, or, in the case of a duty solicitor's representative, the appropriate duty solicitor, shall immediately notify the appropriate local committee in any of the following circumstances:

(a) if his or her practising address changes or if his or her home address changes if the home address was relevant for selection under paragraph 33(2);

(b) if he or she or a representative is unable to comply with the criteria set out in paragraphs 32, 33, 39, or 40 where duty solicitors are concerned, or 45 in the case of representatives;

(c) on resignation giving one month's notice;

(d) if he or she or a representative of him or her is incapable of carrying out his or her duties for more than 28 days;

(e) if he or she or a representative of him or her is charged with or convicted of a criminal offence;

(f) if (where appropriate) a hearing by the Adjudication Committee of the Solicitors Complaints Bureau or by the Solicitors Disciplinary Tribunal is pending in respect of him or her; or

(g) where the Adjudication Committee of the Solicitors Complaints Bureau or the Solicitors Disciplinary Tribunal has made an adverse finding in respect of him or her or a representative of him or her.

Changes in rota

43 A duty solicitor may arrange for another duty solicitor to take his or her place on a rota provided that:

(i) the telephone service is notified in connection with the provision of advice at police stations,

(ii) the court is notified in connection with the provision of advice and representation

and, in either case, if the local committee so request, the local administrator is notified of any such rota change.

Application & Statement of Means for Legal Aid in Criminal and Care Proceedings Magistrates'/Crown Court (including Youth Court)

Application for Legal Aid in Criminal Proceedings
Magistrates' or Crown Court

Form 1
Reg 11 & 18
(also known as
Crown Court Form 5131)

I apply for Legal Aid –

For the purpose of proceedings before the _____ Crown/Magistrates'/Youth Court*

1. Personal details: *(Please use BLOCK letters and BLACK ink)*

a) Surname _____   e) Date of birth _____

b) Forenames _____

c) Permanent address _____

d) Present address
   (if different from above) _____

2. Case Details:

a) Describe briefly what it is you
   are accused of doing,
   e.g. "stealing £50 from my
   employer," "kicking a door
   causing £50 damage." _____

b) The following other person(s)
   is/are charged in this case. _____

c) Give reasons why you and the
   other persons charged in this
   case, if any, should not be
   represented by the same
   solicitor. _____

3. Court Proceedings: *(Complete section a or b whichever applies) *Cross out whichever does not apply*

a) I am due to appear before
   the _____ Magistrates'/Youth Court*
   on _____ 19 __ at __ am/pm

or

b) I appeared before
   the _____ Magistrates'/Youth Court*
   on _____ 19 __ at __ am/pm

and
(tick whichever applies)

☐ my case has been transferred to the Crown Court for trial

☐ I was convicted and committed for sentence to the Crown Court

☐ I was convicted and/or sentenced and I wish to appeal against the _____ conviction and/or sentence*

A1

4. Outstanding Matters:

If there are any other
outstanding criminal charges
or cases against you, give details
including the court where you
are due to appear (only those
cases that are not yet concluded)

5. Your Financial Position: *(Tick the box which applies)*

a) ☐ I receive Income-based Jobseeker's Allowance, Income Support, Family Credit or Disability Working Allowance, and I attach documentary evidence that I am receiving such a benefit *(e.g. order book).*

(You may also tick this box if your spouse or partner receives any of these benefits, and you are living together)

Give:

i)   The address of the Social Security or Jobcentre office dealing with the benefit

ii) National Insurance number of person receiving benefit

iii) Type of benefit

If you do not produce documentary evidence that you are receiving benefit, the court will assume that you are not receiving benefit and you will also have to complete a Form 5 (statement of means). If you cannot produce evidence you should give your reasons below.

b) ☐ I have already given a statement of my means to the   Court and in a previous application for legal aid in this case there has been no change in my financial position. *(A new statement is required if there has been any change)*

c) ☐ I attach a statement of my means in these proceedings *(details of your income and expenditure)*

d) ☐ I am under 16 and I attach a statement of my parents means. If you are unable to provide a statement of their means, give their name and address.

6. Legal Representation:

Note

a) If you do not give the name and address of a solicitor the court will select a solicitor for you.
b) You must tell the solicitor that you have named him, unless he has helped you complete this form.
c) If you have been charged together with another person or persons, the court may assign a solicitor other than the solicitor of your choice.

a) The solicitor I wish to
act for me is

b) Give the firm's name
and address (if known)

A2

7. Reasons for wanting Legal Aid:

- To avoid the possibility of your application being delayed or legal aid being refused because the court does not have enough information about the case, you must complete the rest of the form.
- When deciding whether to grant legal aid, the court will need to know the reasons why it is in the interest of justice for you to be represented.
- If you need help in completing this form, and especially if you have previous convictions, you should see a solicitor. He may be able to advise you free of charge or at a reduced fee.

Note: If you plead **NOT GUILTY** neither the information in this form nor that in your statement of means will be made available to the members of the court trying your case unless you are convicted or you consent. If you are acquitted, only the financial information you have given in your statement of means will be given to the court

Tick any boxes which apply and give brief details or reasons in the space provided

	Details	Reasons for grant or refusal *(for court use only)*
a) It is likely that I will lose my liberty *(You should consider seeing a solicitor before answering this question)* ☐		
b) I am subject to a: suspended or partly suspended prison sentence ☐ conditional discharge ☐ probation order ☐ supervision order ☐ deferment of sentence ☐ community service order ☐ care order ☐ combination order ☐ *Give details as far as you are able, including the nature of the offence and when the order was made.*		
c) It is likely that I will lose my livelihood ☐		
d) It is likely that I will suffer serious damage to my reputation ☐		
e) A substantial question of law is involved ☐ *(You will need the help of a solicitor to answer this question)*		

(Please give authorities to be quoted with law reports references)

A3

	Details	Reasons for grant or refusal *(for court use only)*
f) I shall be unable to understand the court proceedings or state my own case because: i) My understanding of English is inadequate ☐ ii) I suffer from a disability *(Give full details)* ☐		
g) Witnesses have to be traced and/or interviewed on my behalf *(State circumstances)* ☐		
h) The case involves expert cross examination of a prosecution witness *(Give brief details)* ☐		
i) It is in someone's else's interest that I am represented ☐		
j) Any other reasons *(Give full particulars)* ☐		

8. Declaration:

If you knowingly make a statement which is false, or knowingly withhold information, you may be prosecuted. If convicted, you may be sent to prison for up to three months or be fined or both *(Section 39 (1) Legal Aid Act 1988)*. After your application has been considered by the court, you may be asked to give further information or to clarify information or to provide further proof of the information you have given.

If you stop receiving Income-based Jobseeker's Allowance, Income Support, Family Credit, Disability Working Allowance or if your financial position changes in any way after you have submitted this form, you must tell the court. This is a requirement of the Legal Aid regulations. I understand that, if I do not produce all the information which the court needs, it may make such enquiries of the Benefits Agency as it considers necessary and I authorise it so to do. I consent to the disclosure of information to confirm that I am in receipt of benefit.

I understand that the court may order me to make a contribution to the costs of Legal Aid, or to pay the whole costs if it considers that I can afford to do so and, if I am under 16, make a similar order with respect to my parents.

Signed: **Dated:**

A4

For Court use only

Any additional factors considered when determining the application, including any information given orally.

Decision on the interest of justice test

I have considered all available details of all the charges and it is/is not* in the interests of justice that representation be granted because:

Signed [_____] Proper Officer

Dated [_____]

Statement of Means
by Applicant or Appropriate Contributor
for Legal Aid purposes

Form 5
Regulation 23
(also known as
Crown Court Form 5132)

To apply for criminal legal aid you must complete this form unless you can prove that you are in receipt of Income-based Jobseeker's Allowance, Income Support, Family Credit or Disability Working Allowance and have provided documentary evidence that you receive one of those benefits when you completed Form 1. *(See Section 5 of Form 1 headed* **Your Financial Position).**

If you are not yet sixteen, then your mother or father may also be asked to complete one. If you have applied for legal aid for a child of yours who is aged sixteen or over **you** do not need to fill in this form. **Your child** should complete it, giving details of his or her **own income.**

To avoid delay in your application being considered please complete the form as fully and carefully as possible and provide the information and documentary evidence the form requires. If you cannot provide the documentary evidence you must explain why at Section 5.

1 Personal Details   (please use BLOCK letters)

1. Surname   Mr ☐   Mrs ☐   Miss ☐   Ms ☐

2. Forenames

3. Date of birth

4. Home address

5. Marital status   Single ☐   Single and living together ☐   Widow(er) ☐
   (please tick one box)
                           Married ☐   Married but separated ☐   Divorced ☐

6. Are you claiming legal aid for a dependent child who is not yet sixteen? YES ☐
   If Yes, give the following details about the child

   Surname   NO ☐   (go to section 2)

   Forenames

   Date of birth

   Home address
   (if different
   from yours)

   Your relationship to the child (eg. father)

1

2 Financial Details – Part A : Income

In this section you are asked to give details of the money you receive. If you are living with your spouse or partner then you must provide details of the income of your spouse or partner as well. The details will be used to work out whether you have to pay a contribution towards legal aid and if so how much. The assessment is based on weekly income so your answers must show the amount you get *each week*. If any of the sections do not apply, write NONE in the space.

Work	Employer's name and address	Amount received Your Income	Income of Spouse or Partner	Official use
Enter gross earnings *per week* (before tax and insurance), including overtime, commission or bonuses. You must attach documentary evidence of the pay you have received over the past 13 weeks. Three monthly or 13 weekly pay slips would be the best evidence.		£	£	
If you are self-employed write SELF-EMPLOYED. Show your gross earnings and attach the most recent accounts, showing gross income.		£	£	
Part time work Enter gross earnings *per week* (before tax and insurance) from any part time job not included above and attach documentary evidence.		£	£	
State Benefits Enter *weekly amounts* eg. from unemployment benefit, child benefit, etc. Say which benefit(s) you get in the space provided. You should produce evidence of the benefit payment (eg. order book).	Types of benefit	£ £ £	£ £ £	
Money from property Enter *weekly amounts* (before any deductions) of money from sub-letting a house or rooms and attach documentary evidence.		£	£	
Any other income Please give details *and weekly* amounts and attach documentary evidence.		£	£	

Important: If the information you have given above is going to change soon, please give details of the changes in Section 4 of this form.

2 Financial details – Part B : Capital and Savings

Please give details of all your capital and savings. If you are living with your spouse or partner you must also give details of their capital and savings.

Property. *Note: In the questions which follow the value of the equity means the sum which you would receive from the sale of the property after paying the mortgage or other loan on it.*

1 – Main Dwelling

Do you or your spouse/partner own the house or property which you treat as your main dwelling? If so please provide the following information. *(Tick appropriate box)*

	You	Spouse or Partner	
	Yes ☐ No ☐	Yes ☐ No ☐	Official Use
i) What is the value of the equity* in your main dwelling?	£	£	
ii) What is your main dwelling worth now, that is, what is its market value?	£	£	
iii) What is the mortgage on your main dwelling?	£	£	

2 – Other houses or Property

Do you or your spouse/partner own a house or property other than the house or property which you treat as your main dwelling? If so, please provide the following information. *(Tick appropriate box)*

	You	Spouse or Partner
	Yes ☐ No ☐	Yes ☐ No ☐
i) What is the value of the equity* in the house(s)/other property?	£	£
ii) What are the house(s)/other property worth now, that is, what are their market values?	£	£
iii) What are the mortgages on the house(s)/other property?	£	£

	You	Spouse or Partner
Savings Give details of where your savings are, and the amounts. Include money in any bank, building society, National Savings Certificates, cash, stocks and shares or any other investments. You should produce pass books etc.	£	£
Articles of value Give details of any articles of value that you own (eg. jewellery, furs, paintings) with their approximate value. You may be asked to produce valuation certificates.	£	£

3 Allowances and Deductions

1. Enter Tax and National Insurance Contributions deducted from your earnings *per week.*

You		Spouse or Partner	
Tax	☐	Tax	☐
N.I.	☐	N.I.	☐

2. Enter the NUMBER of dependants who are living with you. If you are claiming legal aid for a child, please include that child. *N.B. Dependants are the people you and your spouse or partner look after financially.*

Spouse or Partner ☐	Children under 19 ☐	Date of birth for each child ☐	Children and other relatives 19 and over ☐

Other relatives under 19 ☐	Date of birth for each relative ☐	Others (please say who) ☐

3 Allowances and Deductions (continued)

3. If you pay maintenance to any dependant who does **NOT** live with you, please give details of the amounts you, or your spouse or partner, pay.

Age(s) of dependant(s)

Your relationship to the dependant

Amount per week

You should supply copies of agreements or court orders

4. Give the amounts of Council Tax which you and your spouse or partner pay.

(a) The amount of Council Tax paid. You must provide evidence of this (eg. the demand from the local authority).

£ ☐ a week ☐ a month ☐ a year

(b) Is Council Tax benefit received?

☐ YES ☐ NO

(please say how much)

£ ☐ a week ☐ a month ☐ a year

5. Give the following details of housing expenses of you and your spouse/partner. If you own more than one house only give details for the house in which you live. If you are paying the expenses of a dependent who is not living with you, enter the details in the spaces on the right. You should produce rent books, evidence of mortgage instalments, and evidence of water and sewerage charges. It is in your interests to provide evidence of any other expenses claimed and you may be required to provide this.

Rent	£ /week	Amount for dependant(s)	£ /week
Mortgage Payment	£ /week		£ /week
Ground Rent	£ /week		£ /week
Service charge	£ /week		£ /week
Water and sewerage charges	£ /week		£ /week
Board and lodging	£ /week		£ /week
Bed and Breakfast	£ /week		£ /week

	You	Your spouse or partner
6. How much does it cost you and your spouse or partner **each week** to travel to and from work?	£	£
7. Give details of any other expenses which you think the court should know about. You may include any payments on court orders, and contributions to approved pension schemes, but not: money for food, clothing or heating. You should produce documentary evidence of the payments.	£	£

4 Further Information

1 Have you directly or indirectly transferred any resources (such as sums of money, stocks or shares, the equity value in your home or any other valuable items) to another person since you became aware that these proceedings would be brought? If so, please give details.

2 Has another person been paying your legal fees and expenses in respect of these or other proceedings before you applied for legal aid? If so, please give details.

3 Are the resources of another person available to you eg. is another person providing you with free accommodation or paying your bills? If so, please give details.

4 Please give any other financial information that you think that the court should have when deciding upon your application for legal aid. You should also include any future changes in circumstances that might alter your position.

5 If you have not produced documentary evidence of all income/benefits that you receive and each allowance you have claimed, you must explain why you cannot do so.

6 Declaration

If you knowingly make a statement which is false, or knowingly withhold information, you may be prosecuted. If convicted, you may be sent to prison for up to three months, or be fined, or both, *(section 39(1) Legal Aid Act 1988)*.
After your application has been considered by the court, you may be asked to give further information or to clarify information or to provide further proof of the information that you have given.
If your financial position changes in any way after you have submitted this form, you must tell the court. This is a requirement of the Legal Aid Regulations.

I declare that to the best of my knowledge and belief, I have given a complete and correct statement of my income, savings and capital (and that of my spouse or partner)*(and that of my child).**
I authorise the court to make such enquiries of the Benefits Agency as it considers necessary and I consent to the disclosure of information to confirm that I am in receipt of benefit.

Signed

Date

* Delete if you are single or if you are not living with your spouse or partner
** Delete if legal aid is not sought for your child

5

Guidance on Criminal Legal Aid

(issued jointly by the Lord Chancellor's Department, Legal Aid Board and Justices' Clerks' Society)

Criticisms of the Present System

Uncertainty over whether legal aid in criminal cases was being granted in the magistrates' courts in accordance with the requirements of the Legal Aid Act 1988 and regulations thereunder resulted in the Comptroller and Auditor-General being unable to approve the Lord Chancellor's Department's Legal Aid Account in 1990/91, 1991/92 and 1992/93. That uncertainty has increased following the findings of the research report [R Young, T Moloney and A Sanders, *In the Interests of Justice? The Determination of Criminal Legal Aid Applications by Magistrates' Courts in England and Wales*, Legal Aid Board, September 1992].

The report was commissioned by the Legal Aid Board. Its findings were:

(a) differences between courts in granting legal aid are attributable to the approaches of individual clerks;

(b) grants are more likely to be made according to court clerks' perception of the seriousness of the case, rather than according to the statutory criteria;

(c) applications for legal aid are often of poor quality, and the information provided to courts is frequently inadequate.

Consequently, the Lord Chancellor has directed that guidance be issued to remind justices' clerks of the requirements of the Legal Aid Act 1988 and to promote greater consistency of approach to the consideration of criminal legal aid applications generally.

The Law

(a) Justices' clerks and other granting authorities are reminded that there is no authority to grant legal aid other than in accordance with the Legal Aid Act 1988. They are further reminded that the discretion granted to them under that Act should be exercised reasonably; that is, in a way which takes into account the relevant factors and does not take into account any that are irrelevant. Relevant factors here include, but are not limited to, the 'interests of justice criteria' discussed from paragraph 7 onwards. The Lord Chancellor will shortly lay before Parliament regulations directing granting authorities to record the specific reasons why they consider that particular applications do or do not meet the criteria under which they have been made. This will apply to applications determined by magistrates, by justices' clerks or by Area Committees of the Legal Aid Board.

(b) Section 21(5) of the Legal Aid Act 1988 provides that legal aid shall not be granted unless the applicant's financial resources are such as to require assistance in meeting the costs of legal representation. Section 21(2) provides that, subject to means, representation may be granted where it is desirable in the interests of justice. Regulation 11(3) of the Legal Aid in Criminal and Care Proceedings (General) Regulations 1989 requires that a legal aid order shall not be made until the court or the justices' clerk has considered the applicant's statement of means, unless the applicant is incapable of furnishing such a statement on account of his physical or mental condition. Guidance on the financial test is contained in the Justices' Clerks Accounting Manual, and in the Circular issued every March to those courts with responsibility for the grant of legal aid. Copies of that Circular are available from the Lord Chancellor's Department on request.

(c) The factors set out in section 22(2) have no application in those instances where statute provides that legal aid *shall* be granted to a person whose means are such that he cannot meet the likely cost of representation. These provisions are:

'(3) Subject to subsection (5) below, representation must be granted –

    (a) where a person is committed for trial on a charge of murder, for his trial;

    (b) where the prosecutor appeals or applies for leave to appeal to the House of Lords, for the proceedings on the appeal;

    (c) where a person charged with an offence before a magistrates' court –

        (i) is brought before the court in pursuance of a remand in custody when he may be again remanded or committed in custody, and

        (ii) is not, but wishes to be, legally represented before the court (not having been legally represented when he was so remanded),

    for so much of the proceedings as relates to the grant of bail, and

    (d) where a person:

        (i) is to be sentenced or otherwise dealt with for an offence by a magistrates' court or the Crown Court, and

        (ii) is to be kept in custody to enable enquiries or a report to be made to assist the court,

    for the proceedings on sentencing or otherwise dealing with him.'

(d) Moreover, there are statutory restrictions on a court passing certain sentences on a person who is not legally represented, unless either he applies for legal aid and the application is refused on the ground that it does not appear his means are such that he requires assistance; or he refuses or fails to apply for legal aid. Accordingly, an applicant whose means are insufficient to meet the cost of legal representation *shall* be granted legal aid before the court passes or makes any of the following sentences or orders:

    (i) A sentence of imprisonment on a person who has not been previously sentenced to imprisonment by a court in any part of the UK (Powers of Criminal Courts Act 1973 s21(1));

    (ii) A sentence of detention in a young offender institution under the Criminal Justice Act 1982 s1A (Criminal Justices Act 1982 s3);

    (iii) A sentence of custody for life under the Criminal Justice Act 1982 s8(2) (Criminal Justice Act 1982 s3);

(iv) An order for detention under the Children and Young Persons Act 1933 s53(2) (Criminal Justice Act 1982 s3).

Exercise of Discretion

(a) This guidance is intended to assist those determining applications for the grant of criminal legal aid in the interpretation of the limits of their discretion. It is issued for guidance only. It does not affect the right and responsibility of granting authorities to exercise their discretion in every case in deciding whether the criteria in section 22 of the Legal Aid Act 1988 have been met.

(b) Section 21(7) of the Legal Aid Act 1988 provides that 'where a doubt arises whether representation under this Part should be granted to any person, the doubt shall be resolved in that person's favour'.

Insufficient Information

(a) If it is not possible to make a proper determination because insufficient information has been provided on the application form, or some detail needs clarification, it is suggested that this does not constitute a 'doubt' for the purposes of section 21(7). In such circumstances, further detail should be requested from the applicant or the applicant's solicitor. Section 21(7) should only come into play if, once all the appropriate information has been provided, a genuine doubt remains as to whether a grant of legal aid should be made.

(b) The granting authority is entitled to sufficient information to enable it to reach a properly informed decision on the grant of legal aid, and is entitled to ask for, and receive, such information. If an application does not contain sufficient information, further details should be sought. When seeking further information, the granting authority may declare to the applicant that the application will not be considered for grant until such time as the information is received and that it would be prudent for him to await a final decision before incurring any further costs.

Legal Aid Applications – General Considerations

(a) Every application for legal aid must be considered on its merits and must be determined in accordance with the provision of Part V of the Legal Aid Act 1988.

(b) The specific criterion or other interests of justice consideration which is relied upon must be identified clearly in the application form.

(c) The decision must always be based on the information contained in the form of application for legal aid, together with any other oral or written information provided by or on behalf of the applicant, particulars of the offence(s) alleged as set out in the information(s) before the court, and any other relevant particulars which may be properly taken into account as a result of statements made in open court during the course of the proceedings against the applicant. If the decision to grant or refuse legal aid is influenced by information provided orally, then *the relevant information provided should be clearly recorded on the application*.

(d) In respect of offences triable either-way, the approach to the grant of legal aid should be the same whether the offence is to be tried in the Crown Court or the magistrates' court; accordingly, for example, an accused charged with an offence triable either-way, who does not merit legal aid for summary, trial, should not automatically be granted legal aid simply because he elects to be tried at the Crown Court.

(c) It is suggested that the need for a Newton hearing (ie, a dispute on the facts following a plea of guilty) may justify a grant of legal aid if, for example, witnesses need to be traced by a legal representative or expert cross-examination is necessary. This may also apply for other disputes of fact and/or law arising after a guilty plea.

The Interests of Justice Criteria – Detailed Considerations

(a) The factors set out in section 22 of the Legal Aid Act 1988 apply to proceedings by way of a trial by or before a magistrates' court or the Crown Court or on an appeal to the Crown Court against conviction.

(b) Section 22(2) specifies five factors which must be taken into account when a competent authority is determining whether it is in the interests of justice that representation be granted.

(c) In some cases the interaction of two or more of the factors may dictate that legal aid should be granted when neither by itself would have sufficed. For example, whereas a minor question of law could normally be dealt with under the Green Form Scheme, or a person's knowledge of English may be adequate rather than good, those two factors in combination could merit a grant of legal aid. Where such interaction is used this should clearly be noted on the application form.

(d) The five factors (considered below) are not exhaustive:

Section 22(2) states that 'The factors to be taken into account ... shall include the following ...'. In *R v Liverpool City Magistrates ex p McGhee* it was stated that '... these magistrates were plainly wrong in regarding the factors statutorily identified [in section 22(2)(a)–(e)] as being exhaustive and there may be, according to the circumstances of a particular case, other than the identified factors which have to be taken into consideration in deciding whether or not the justice of the case requires that legal aid should be granted.'

(e) While some applications may rely on all or several of the factors, an application which relies on only one must be given equal consideration. It also follows from *McGhee* that reliance on none of the statutory factors is not necessarily fatal. When a non-statutory factor is held to have founded or supported the grant of legal aid this should be clearly specified on the application form.

(f) For example, where the behaviour of a defendant is so disruptive as to distract the court from the exercise of its judicial function, that alone could justify a grant of legal aid if the presence of a lawyer would mitigate the distraction – if only, as a last resort, enabling the court to continue the hearing in the absence of the defendant but in the presence of his legal representative. It is further suggested that behaviour which affects the court's administrative performance is outside the scope of section 22 and cannot, therefore, be the basis for a grant of legal aid.

Section 22(2)(a) – the offence is such that if proved it is likely that the court would impose a sentence which would deprive the accused of his liberty or lead to loss of his livelihood or serious damage to his reputation

(a) *Likelihood of deprivation of liberty*

(i) The person considering the application must be provided with sufficient information to enable him to be satisfied that, in the event of a conviction, the accused's liberty would be at risk. Accordingly, information about the seriousness and circumstances of the offence alleged should be taken into account, including details of any aggravating circumstances which, in the event of the accused being convicted, might expose him to a more severe sentence than would normally be the case. Details relating to previous convictions should also be supplied for the purposes of determining seriousness. Regard should also be had to the gravity of the offence. Where any aggravating factors influence the decision on the grant of legal aid, these should be clearly recorded.

(ii) It is recommended that reference in appropriate cases be made to 'The Magistrates' Association Sentencing Guidelines' issued on 20 September 1993, which provide examples of 'seriousness indictors' (aggravating factors and mitigating factors) for various types of offence.

(iii) The onus is on the applicant to state why such a sentence is likely.

(iv) Legal aid should normally be granted where there is a real and practical (as opposed to theoretical) risk of imprisonment or other form of deprivation of liberty. For example an offender of previous good character, charged with possessing a small quantity of cannabis, would have difficulty in establishing that he was likely to lose his liberty because, although the offence is punishable with three months' imprisonment on summary conviction, it would be most unusual for any court to pass a custodial sentence for such an offence.

(v) For the purpose of determining whether the accused is likely to lose his liberty etc, regard should be had to the sentencing approaches of courts generally and, in particular, to the sentencing approach of the court before which the accused is appearing,

(vi) The likelihood of conviction should not be taken into account; the grant of legal aid should not be based on the merits of the defence; conviction should always be assumed.

(vii) 'Deprivation of liberty' includes any sentence of imprisonment, whether immediate or suspended; detention in a young offender institution; custody for life; detention under section 53(2) of the Children and Young Persons Act 1933; hospital and guardianship orders.

(viii) As noted above, section 22(2)(a) refers specifically to the likelihood of deprivation of liberty and it has been a matter of some debate whether community sentences are capable of falling within that category. This debate has now been settled by the judgment in *R v Liverpool City Magistrates ex p McGhee*. In giving judgment, Rose LJ said that '... I am not persuaded ... that the risk of a community service order amount(s) to a risk of deprivation of liberty within the meaning of that section' [section

22(2)(a)]. In concurring, Waller J said '... I am also clear that the words in section 22(2)(a) 'The offence is such that if proved it is likely that the court would impose a sentence which would deprive the accused of his liberty', do not include a community service order'. The judgement went on to state that the possibility of a community service order being made might be a factor to be considered when considering whether or not to grant legal aid, and Rose LJ made plain that this should not be taken to imply that legal aid should be granted if community service was likely. It was, however, a factor other than the listed factors which could be taken into account in particular cases.

(ix) Legal aid should normally be granted:
   (a) upon a committal to the Crown Court for sentence (*R v Serghiou* [1966] 3 All ER 637);
   (b) where the court is considering making a recommendation for deportation (*R v Edgehill* [1963] 1 All ER 181);
   (c) where the court is considering making a hospital order (*R v King's Lynn Justices ex p Fysh* [1964] Crim LR 143).

(x) A grant of legal aid for mitigation only might be appropriate, for example, when the court's assessment of the gravity of the case is substantially altered by factors which come to light after conviction. Courts should also bear in mind the statutory restrictions on imposing certain sentences as referred to at paragraph 3(d) of these notes.

(b) Loss of livelihood

(i) It follows from the provisions of the Act that the granting authority should consider how likely it is that loss of livelihood will result from a sentence imposed by the court on conviction. It is suggested that legal aid should only be granted where there is a real risk of loss of livelihood.

(ii) The applicant must explain why he believes that it is likely that he will lose his livelihood. In some cases this will be obvious, eg a bank clerk accused of an offence of dishonesty; in others it may be obscure, eg a teacher convicted of indecency with a child is likely to lose his livelihood, but a coach driver convicted of a similar offence might not appear so vulnerable until he explains to the court that he drives school buses. The likely loss of livelihood should be a direct consequence of the conviction or the sentence.

(iii) It is suggested that loss of livelihood would normally refer to current livelihood. Therefore, someone who is not currently employed would be less likely to meet this criterion, although other criteria under section 22 may be met, such as 'serious damage to reputation' (eg see paragraph 8(c)(v) below).

(iv) Assertions that disqualification from driving will result in a loss of livelihood should be examined critically. There can seldom be justification to grant legal aid to resist a mandatory driving disqualification alone arising from a drink/driving charge unless a cogent argument as to special reasons can be put forward. Though a grant could be justified in exceptional circumstances (for example if the applicant could show that the disqualification would result in a real risk of dismissal), legal aid would not usually be justified where the accused sought to avoid a 'totting-up' disqualification, having acquired twelve or more penalty points.

(c) Serious damage to reputation

(i) In many cases, conviction will damage the accused's reputation. However, section 22 refers to *serious* damage. It is considered that this would relate to those cases in which the offence, or the offender's circumstances, are such that the disgrace of conviction, or consequent damage to the applicant's standing, would greatly exceed the direct effect of the penalty which might be imposed. 'Reputation' for these purposes is a question of good character, including honesty and trustworthiness. Social class and position must not be taken into account. The loss of reputation consequent on a conviction for dishonesty is absolute and not relevant to the amount.

(ii) As a general rule, offences of varying degrees of seriousness attract different levels of damage to reputation. The Act refers to *serious* damage as justifying the grant of legal aid.

(iii) An effective plea in mitigation for any charge may lessen the severity of the sentence and thereby lessen the seriousness of the damage to reputation. An applicant who either has a previous conviction for a *like* offence or a conviction for a more serious offence can be assumed to have lost reputation and the criterion will not apply. However, the fact that a person has previous convictions should not preclude consideration of legal aid under this head. For example, it may be that someone with the previous conviction for a minor assault might still suffer serious damage to reputation if convicted of an offence of dishonesty or a sexual offence.

(iv) In deciding upon the seriousness of the damage to reputation, it is suggested that special factors about the accused, for example religious background, might aggravate the damage to reputation caused by a conviction which may not have the same effect on another person.

(v) Consideration should be given to whether an accused who is undertaking vocational or professional training might suffer damage to reputation so serious that there is a risk that future livelihood might be lost.

Section 22(2)(b) – The determination of the case may involve consideration of a substantial question of law

(i) Legal aid should only be granted under this criterion if a question of law is raised which the applicant cannot be expected to deal with unaided and is a substantial question and is relevant to the applicant's case. It should be noted that this criterion may also apply when legal aid is being considered for an appeal against conviction.

If the applicant intends to plead guilty, the likelihood of substantial questions of law arising must generally be remote, though there may be exceptions, such as some 'special reasons' (such as laced drinks) in drink/driving cases. There may also be some instances in which sentencing considerations could give rise to a substantial question of law.

(ii) The defence solicitor should specify the point of law on the application form. Quite often issues coming before the courts involve mixed questions of fact and law but again, in such circumstances, to justify grant of legal aid the question of law must be a *substantial* one.

(iii) Except in circumstances where the applicant faces serious or complex charges, legal aid should not generally be granted solely for the purpose of obtaining advice as to the appropriate plea, since this can rarely be described as a substantial question of law. Preliminary advice as to plea can usually be provided satisfactorily by advice from the duty solicitor or from any solicitor under the green form scheme.

Section 22(2)(c) – The accused may be unable to understand the proceedings or to state his own case because of his inadequate knowledge of English, mental illness or other mental or physical disability

(a) Inadequate knowledge of English

(i) Legal aid should not be granted unless the applicant's knowledge is sufficiently poor to prevent him from following the proceedings or conducting his case. It is suggested that the fact that the services of an interpreter are available is not a sufficient ground for refusing legal aid under this criterion.

(ii) The accused's difficulties of comprehension may differ with the complexity of the case; he may be able to manage in a very straightforward case but may be unable to do so in a more complex one. Courts should, therefore, consider carefully whether the stated impediment to understanding is likely to be operative in the particular case.

iii) Generally, it is the ability to understand spoken English which is important. It should be borne in mind that, while the language of the courts is often technical, it is the responsibility of those working in the courts to use plain English. A lack of fluent literacy will not, in most cases, impair the accused's ability to prepare and present his case. Relevant factors could include the degree of literacy, the complexity of the case and the extent of reading required.

(b) Mental or physical disability

(i) Legal aid should be granted if the applicant is unable to follow the proceedings or properly conduct his case by reason of substantial physical disability, for example deafness or blindness, or by reason of mental disorder, mental impairment or subnormality.

(ii) Courts may think it appropriate to request a medical report or certificate, especially in cases where it is claimed that the applicant is suffering from a form of mental illness that is likely to worsen significantly due to a court hearing and, as a consequence, is unlikely to be able to represent himself properly.

Section 22(2)(d) – the nature of the defence is such as to involve the tracing and interviewing of witnesses or expert cross-examination of a witness for the prosecution

(a) Trace and interview witnesses

(i) Details of the witnesses, and why there is a necessity for representation to trace and/or interview them, should be included in the application. If details of witnesses are not included, consideration of the legal aid application should be deferred until the applicant has provided the court with sufficient information to make a determination.

(b) Expert cross-examination of a prosecution witness

(i) In cases where the applicant requires legal aid for the benefit of expert cross-examination of prosecution witnesses, he should be expected to explain why this is necessary.

(ii) It should be noted that section 22(2)(d) refers to expert cross-examination of a witness and *not* only to cross-examination of an expert witness. Giving judgement in *R v Liverpool City Magistrates ex p McGhee*, Rose LJ said 'These justices ... were clearly under the misapprehension ... that because expert witnesses were not to be called, the factor identified in part of section 22(2)(d) was not satisfied. That, in itself, as it seems to me, is sufficient to flaw the approach of these justices'.

Thus, legal aid should be granted under this heading when there is a need for professional cross examination of a witness. This may very likely be the case when the evidence is provided by an expert, since an accused person would rarely be capable, for example, of cross-examining a medical or handwriting expert. it may also apply in other cases, such as those where shades of emphasis in the evidence can make an action appear more sinister than it was in fact. But in considering applications under this heading, the emphasis should be clearly on the nature of the evidence, rather than on the status of the person providing the evidence.

Section 22(2)(e) – it is in the interests of someone other than the accused that the accused be represented

(i) It should be borne in mind when considering legal aid under this heading that section 34A of the Criminal Justice Act 1988 provides that a defendant charged with certain offences specified in section 32(2) of that Act shall not cross-examine in person any child witness who is an alleged victim or alleged witness to the commission of the offence.

(ii) It is suggested that legal aid should also be considered when, for example, the accused is charged with a sexual offence where it is desirable that the complainant should be spared the great strain of being cross-examined by a person whom they believe has committed a sexual offence against them.

(iii) This principle may also apply where the alleged victim or witness of, for example, an offence against the person or a burglary is very young or elderly, when cross-examination by the accused might put them under undue strain.

APPENDIX L

National Mode of Trial Guidelines (1995)

The purpose of these guidelines is to help magistrates decide whether or not to commit 'either way' offences for trial in the Crown Court. Their object is to provide guidance not direction. They are not intended to impinge upon a magistrate's duty to consider each case individually and on its own particular facts.

These guidelines apply to all defendants aged 18 and above.

General mode of trial considerations

Section 19 of the Magistrates' Courts Act 1980 requires magistrates to have regard to the following matters in deciding whether an offence is more suitable for summary trial or trial on indictment: (1) the nature of the case; (2) whether the circumstances make the offence one of a serious character; (3) whether the punishment which a magistrates' court would have power to inflict for it would be adequate; (4) any other circumstances which appear to the court to make it more suitable for the offence to be tried in one way rather than the other; (5) any representations made by the prosecution or the defence.

Certain general observations can be made: (a) the court should never make its decision on the grounds of convenience or expedition; (b) the court should assume for the purpose of deciding mode of trial that the prosecution version of the facts is correct; (c) the fact that the offences are alleged to be specimens is a relevant consideration; the fact that the defendant will be asking for other offences to be taken into consideration, if convicted, is not; (d) where cases involve complex questions of fact or difficult questions of law, the court should consider [transfer] for trial; (e) where two or more defendants are jointly charged with an offence each has an individual right to elect his mode of trial; (f) in general, except where otherwise stated, either-way offences should be tried summarily unless the court considers that the particular case has one or more of the features set out in the following pages *and* that its sentencing powers are insufficient; (g) the court should also consider its powers to commit an offender for sentence, under section 38 of the Magistrates' Courts Act 1980, as amended by section 25 of the Criminal Justice Act 1991, if information emerges during the course of the hearing which leads them to conclude that the offence is so serious, or the offender such a risk to the public, that their powers to sentence him are inadequate. This amendment means that committal for sentence is no longer determined by reference to the character or antecedents of the defendant.

Features relevant to the individual offences

Note: Where reference is made in these guidelines to property or damage of 'high value' it means a figure equal to at least twice the amount of the limit (currently £5,000) imposed by stature on a magistrates' court when making a compensation order.

[**Note:** Each of the guidelines in respect of the individual offences set out below (except those relating to drugs offences) are prefaced by a reminder in the following terms 'Cases should be tried summarily unless the court considers that one or more of the following features is present in the case *and* that its sentencing powers are insufficient. Magistrates should take account of their powers under section 25 of the Criminal Justice Act 1991 to commit for *sentence*'.]

Burglary

1   *Dwelling-house*
(1) Entry in the daytime when the occupier (or another) is present.
(2) Entry at night of a house which is normally occupied, whether or not the occupier (or another) is present.
(3) The offence is alleged to be one of a series of similar offences.
(4) When soiling, ransacking, damage or vandalism occurs.
(5) The offence has professional hallmarks.
(6) The unrecovered property is of high value [see above for definition of 'high value'].

Note: Attention is drawn to para 28(c) of Schedule 1 to the Magistrates' Courts Act 1980, by which offences of burglary in a dwelling *cannot* be tried summarily if any person in the dwelling was subjected to violence or the threat of violence.

2   *Non-dwellings*
(1) Entry of a pharmacy or doctor's surgery.
(2) Fear is caused or violence is done to anyone lawfully on the premises (eg night-watchman; security guard).
(3) The offence has professional hallmarks.
(4) Vandalism on a substantial scale.
(5) The unrecovered property is of high value [see above for definition of 'high value'].

Theft and fraud

(1) Breach of trust by a person in a position of substantial authority, or in whom a high degree of trust is placed.
(2) Theft or fraud which has been committed or disguised in a sophisticated manner.
(3) Theft or fraud committed by an organised gang.
(4) The victim is particularly vulnerable to theft or fraud (eg the elderly or infirm).
(5) The unrecovered property is of high value [see above for definition of 'high value'].

Handling
(1) Dishonest handling of stolen property by a receiver who has commissioned the theft.
(2) The offence has professional hallmarks.
(3) The property is of high value [see above for definition of 'high value'].

Social security frauds
(1) Organised fraud on a large scale.
(2) The frauds are substantial and carried out over a long period of time.

Violence (sections 20 and 47 of the Offences Against the Person Act 1861)
(1) The use of a weapon of a kind likely to cause serious injury.
(2) A weapon is used and serious injury is caused.
(3) More than minor injury is caused by kicking, head-butting or similar forms of assault.
(4) Serious violence is caused to those whose work has to be done in contact with the public or who are likely to face violence in the course of their work.
(5) Violence to vulnerable people (eg the elderly and infirm).
(6) The offence has clear racial motivation.
Note: The same considerations apply to cases of domestic violence.

Public Order Act offences
1   Cases of violent disorder should generally be committed for trial.
2   Affray.
(1) Organised violence or use of weapons.
(2) Significant injury or substantial damage.
(3) The offence has clear racial motivation.
(4) An attack upon police officers, prison officers, ambulancemen, firemen and the like.

Violence to and neglect of children
(1) Substantial injury.
(2) Repeated violence or serious neglect, even if the physical harm is slight.
(3) Sadistic violence (eg deliberate burning or scalding).

Indecent assault
(1) Substantial disparity in age between victim and defendant, and the assault is more than trivial.
(2) Violence or threats of violence.
(3) Relationship of trust or responsibility between defendant and victim.
(4) Several similar offences, and the assaults are more than trivial.
(5) The victim is particularly vulnerable.
(6) Serious nature of the assault.

Unlawful sexual intercourse
(1) Wide disparity of age.
(2) Breach of position of trust.
(3) The victim is particularly vulnerable.

Note: Unlawful sexual intercourse with a girl under 13 is triable only on indictment.

Drugs

1   *Class A*

(a) Supply; possession with intent to supply: these cases should be committed for trial.

(b) Possession: should be committed for trial unless the amount is consistent only with personal use.

2   *Class B*

(a) Supply; possession with intent to supply: should be committed for trial unless there is only small scale supply for no payment.

(b) Possession: should be committed for trial when the quantity is substantial and not consistent only with personal use.

Dangerous driving

(1) Alcohol or drugs contributing to dangerousness.

(2) Grossly excessive speed.

(3) Racing.

(4) Prolonged course of dangerous driving.

(5) Degree of injury or damage sustained.

(6) Other related offences.

Criminal damage

(1) Deliberate fire-raising.

(2) Committed by a group.

(3) Damage of a high value [see above for definition of 'high value'].

(4) The offence has clear racial motivation.

Note: Offences set out in Schedule 2 to the Magistrates' Courts Act 1980 (which includes offences of criminal damage which do not amount to arson) *must* be tried summarily if the value of the property damaged or destroyed is £5,000 or less.

List of grave crimes

Detention under Children and Young Persons Act 1933 s53(2) is available for the following offences:

- Aggravated burglary (Theft Act 1968 s10 – life)
- Arson (Criminal Damage Act 1971 s1 – life)
- Assault with intent to rob (Theft Act 1968 s8 – life)
- Attempting to strangle with intent to endanger life (Offences Against the Person Act 1861 s21 – life)
- Blackmail (Theft Act 1968 s21 – 14 years)
- Buggery with a person under the age of 16 or with an animal (Sexual Offences Act 1956 s12 – life)
- Burglary of dwelling (Theft Act 1968 s9 – 14 years) (**Note**: does not include non-dwelling burglaries)
- Causing death by dangerous driving (Road Traffic Act 1988 s1 – 10 years) (**Note**: applies only to offenders who have attained the age of 14 by the date of conviction)
- Causing death by careless driving while under the influence of alcohol or drugs (Road Traffic Act 1988 s3 – 10 years) (**Note**: applies only to offenders who have attained the age of 14 by the date of conviction)
- Causing explosion likely to endanger life (Explosive Substances Act 1883 s2 – life)
- Demanding money with menaces (Theft Act 1968 s21 – 14 years)
- Destroying property with intent to endanger life (Criminal Damage Act 1971 s1 – life)
- Drugs:
- production (Misuse of Drugs Act 1971 s4(2): class A – life; class B – 14 years)
- supplying/offering to supply/being concerned in the supply (Misuse of Drugs Act 1971 s4(3): class A – life; class B – 14 years)
- possession with intent to supply (Misuse of Drugs Act 1971 s5(3): class A – life; class B – 14 years)
- cultivation of cannabis (Misuse of Drugs Act 1971 s6(2) – 14 years)
- False imprisonment (common law)

⬛ Firearms:

- possession with intent to endanger life (Firearms Act 1968 s16 – life)
- using a firearm with intent to resist arrest (Firearms Act 1968 s17(1) – life)
- possession of a firearm during the commission of a scheduled offence (Firearms Act 1968 s17(2) – 14 years)
- possession with intent to commit an indictable offence or to resist arrest (Firearms Act 1968 s18 – 14 years)

⬛ GBH with intent (Offences Against the Person Act 1861 s18 – life)

⬛ Handling stolen goods (Theft Act 1968 s22 – 14 years)

⬛ Incest by man with girl under the age of 13 (Sexual Offences Act 1956 s10 – life)

⬛ Indecent assault upon a female (Sexual Offences Act 1956 s15 – 10 years) (grave crime by virtue of Criminal Justice Act 1991 s64)

⬛ Infanticide (Infanticide Act 1938 s1 – life)

⬛ Kidnapping (common law)

⬛ Manslaughter (Offences Against the Person Act 1981 s5 – life)

⬛ Rape (Sexual Offences Act 1956 s1 – life)

⬛ Robbery (Theft Act 1968 s8 – life)

⬛ Throwing corrosive liquid with intent to endanger life (Offences Against the Person Act 1861 s29 – life)

⬛ Unlawful sexual intercourse with a girl under the age of 13 (Sexual Offences Act 1956 s5 – life)

⬛ Wounding with intent (Offences Against the Person Act 1861 s18 – life)

Practice Direction (Court of Appeal: Criminal Division) (Custodial Sentences: Explanations) 1998

[1998] 1 WLR 278; (1998) *Times* 24 January, CA

The practical effect of custodial sentences imposed by the courts is almost entirely governed by statutory provisions. Those statutory provisions, changed by Parliament from time to time, are not widely understood by the general public.

It is desirable that when sentence was passed the practical effect of the sentence should be understood by the defendant, any victim and any member of the public who is present in court or reads a full report of the proceedings.

In future, whenever a custodial sentence is imposed on an offender, the court should explain the practical effect of the sentence in addition to complying with existing statutory requirements. This will be no more than an explanation: the sentence will be that pronounced by the court.

Sentencers should give the explanation in terms of their own choosing, taking care to ensure that the explanation is clear and accurate. No form of words is prescribed. Annexed to this Practice Direction are short statements which may, adapted as necessary, be of value as models.

These statements are based on the statutory provisions in force on January 1, 1998 and will of course require modification if those provisions are materially amended.

Sentencers will continue to give such explanation as they judge necessary of ancillary orders relating to matters such as disqualification, compensation, confiscation, costs and so on.

Forms of words

Forms of words are provided for use where the offender will be: (1) a short term prisoner not subject to licence; (2) a short term prisoner subject to licence; (3) a long term prisoner, (4) subject to a discretionary sentence of life imprisonment.

Sentencers will bear in mind that where an offender is sentenced to terms which are consecutive, or wholly or partly concurrent, they are to be treated as a single term: section 51(2) of the Criminal Justice Act 1991.

1 Total term less than 12 months

'The sentence is [...] months. You will serve half that sentence in prison/a young offender institution. After that time the rest of your sentence will be suspended and you will be released. Your release will not bring this sentence to an end.

'If after your release and before the end of the period covered by the sentence you commit any further offence, you may be ordered to return to custody to serve the balance of the original sentence outstanding at the date of the further offence, as well as being punished for that new offence.

'Any time you have spent on remand in custody in connection with the offence[s] for which you are now being sentenced will count as part of the sentence to be served, unless it has already been counted.'

2 Total term of 12 months and less than 4 years

'The sentence is [...] [months/years]. You will serve half that sentence in a prison/a young offender institution. After that time the rest of your sentence will be suspended and you will be released. Your release will not bring this sentence to an end.

'If after your release and before the end of the period covered by the sentence you commit any further offence you may be ordered to return to custody to serve the balance of the original sentence outstanding at the date of the further offence, as well as being punished for that new offence.

'Any time you have spent on remand in custody in connection with the offence[s] for which you are now being sentenced will count as part of the sentence to be served, unless it has already been counted.

'After your release you will also be subject to supervision on licence until the end of three-quarters of the total sentence.'

[If an order has been made under section 44 of the Criminal Justice Act 1991: 'After your release you will also be subject to supervision on licence for the remainder of the sentence.']

'If you fail to comply with any of the requirements of your licence then again you may be brought before a court which will have power to suspend your licence and order your return to custody.'

3 Total term of 4 years or more

'The sentence is [...] [years/months]. Your case will not be considered by the Parole Board until you have served at least half that period in custody. Unless the Parole Board recommends earlier release, you will not be released until you have served two-thirds of that sentence. Your release will not bring the sentence to an end.

'Instead, the remainder will be suspended. If after your release and before the end of the period covered by the sentence you commit any further offence you may be ordered to return to custody to serve the balance of the original sentence outstanding at the date of the new offence, as well as being punished for that new offence.

'Any time you have spent in custody on remand in connection with the offence[s] for which you are now being sentenced will count as part of the sentence to be served, unless it has already been counted.

'After your release you will also be subject to supervision on licence until the end of three-quarters of the total sentence.'

[If an order has been made under section 44 of the Criminal Justice Act 1991: 'After your release you will also be subject to supervision on licence for the remainder of the sentence.'

'You will be liable to be recalled to prison if your licence is revoked, either on the recommendation of the Parole Board, or, if it is thought expedient in the public interest, by the secretary of state.'

4 Discretionary life sentence

'The sentence of the court is life imprisonment/custody for life/detention for life under section 53(2), (3) of the Children and Young Persons Act 1933. For the purposes of section 28 of the Crime (Sentences) Act 1997 the court specifies a period of [x] years. That means that your case will not be considered by the Parole Board until you have served at least [x] years in custody.

'After that time the Parole Board will be entitled to consider your release. When it is satisfied that you need no longer be confined in custody for the protection of the public it will be able to direct your release. Until it is so satisfied you will remain in custody.

'If you are released, it will be on terms that you are subject to a licence for the rest of your life and liable to be recalled to prison at any time if your licence is revoked, either on the recommendation of the Parole Board, or, if it is thought expedient in the public interest, by the secretary of state.'

Index

Crown Court *continued*
  committal for sentence 7.14–7.16
  committal proceedings 7.1, 7.3,
    7.11–7.12
  cross-examination 12.2,
    12.11–12.14, 12.19, 12.25
  custodial sentences 15.5–15.13
  cut-throat defence 12.18
  defence case 12.17–12.22
  defence statements 12.24
  defendant, calling the 12.19–12.21
  evidence 12.3, 12.10, 12.26, 12.35
  judges 12.31, 12.33–12.37
  judicial review 17.28
  juries 12.5–12.7, 12.38–12.40
  legal aid 2.24, 18.1–18.11
  mode of trial 5.3–5.6, 5.9–5.14,
    5.17–5.20, 5.22
  no case to answer 12.15–12.16
  opening speeches 12.8
  plea and directions hearings 11.1
  pleas 12.4
    change of 12.46–12.47
  preliminary matters 12.5
  preparation 12.2–12.3
  proof of evidence 12.2
  prosecution case 12.8–12.16
  right to silence 12.19–12.21, 12.34
  sentences 15.5–15.13, 16.2
  summing up 12.33–12.37
  sureties 3.22
  taxation 18.1–18.11
  trials 12.1–12.47
  verdicts 12.41–12.45
  witnesses 12.2, 12.9–12.10, 12.14,
    12.22–12.25, 12.29
  youth court 5.23
  young people 15.5–15.13
Crown Prosecution Service
  bail, liaison on 3.11
  duty solicitors 1.8–1.9
  information 1.8–1.9
  judicial review 17.28
Custodial sentences 5.25, 13.1,
    13.5–13.7, 15.3–15.13, 16.2,
    16.8–16.9
Custody records 8.18
Cut-throat defence 12.18

Defence statements 9.1–9.14
  advantages 9.11–9.12
  alibis 9.10
  adverse inferences 9.7
  briefs 8.14
  contents 9.9–9.10
  counsel 9.14
  coverage 9.13
  Crown Court 12.24
  disclosure 9.1–9.2, 9.4, 9.7–9.8,
    9.11–9.13
  drafting 9.14
  failure to serve 9.3
  plea and directions hearings 11.7
  proof of evidence 4.6
  service 9.1
    failure 9.3
    time limits 9.4–9.8, 11.7
  solicitors 9.14
  summary trials 6.10
  time limits 9.4–9.8, 11.7, 19.5, 19.7
    extension 9.5–9.7
Defendants. *See also* Mentally-
    disordered defendants, Previous
    convictions
  addiction 4.11
  age 14.24–14.25
  antecedents 14.15
  bail 3.8
  calling the 12.19–12.21
  character 12.18, 12.22
  co-operation 14.21–14.23
  Crown Court trials 12.19–12.21
  duty solicitors 1.11
  information needed from 1.11, 3.8
  medical history 4.9
  multi-defendant cases 2.10
  personal factors 14.26–14.28
  remorse/contrition 4.14
  right to silence 12.19–12.21, 12.34
  statements 8.14, 9.1–9.14
  version of events 4.5–4.6
  witnesses, as 6.22
Deferred sentences 13.4
Deportation orders 13.29
Deprivation orders 13.28
Detention and training orders 15.13,
    16.9

LAG Legal Action Group

Supporting the work of criminal practitioners working in the legal aid and advice sectors

Legal Action magazine

The only monthly magazine published specifically for legal aid practitioners and the advice sector, providing news and comment, topical features and law, practice and procedure.

1998/99 annual subscription: £73
Concessionary rates available for students and trainees – call the LAG office for details

Books

LAG's catalogue includes a range of criminal titles:

Defending Suspects at Police Stations (3rd edition)
Ed Cape with Jawaid Luqmani
March 1999   0 905099 84 2   c£35

Defending Young People
Mark Ashford and Alex Chard
1997   0 905099 76 1   £28

Police Powers (3rd edition)
Howard Levenson, Fiona Fairweather and Ed Cape
1996   0 905099 62 1   £35

Police Misconduct: Legal Remedies (3rd edition)
John Harrison and Stephen Cragg
1996   0 905099 62 1   £28

Advocacy in the Magistrates' Court
John Mackenzie
1994   0 905099 51 6   £18

Community Care Law Reports

The first and only law reports devoted entirely to community care issues. Compiled by an expert team and published quarterly, each issue contains:

- editorial review
- community care law update
- law reports
- cumulative index
- full tables

Training

LAG's training programme features topical courses for criminal practitioners at all levels of experience.

Conferences

LAG runs major conferences to examine issues at the cutting-edge of legal services policy and to inform practitioners of their implications.

Membership

LAG campaigns for equal access to justice through improvements in the law and the administration of justice. If you support our aims, join us!

For further information about any of Legal Action Group's activities please contact:

Legal Action Group
242 Pentonville Road
London
N1 9UN
DX 130400 London (Pentonville Road)
Telephone: 0171 833 2931
Fax: 0171 837 6094
e-mail: lag@lag.org.uk